Prosocial Guidance for the Preschool Child

Prosocial Guidance for the Preschool Child

Janice J. Beaty

Merrill,
an imprint of Prentice Hall
Upper Saddle River, New Jersey   Columbus, Ohio

Library of Congress Cataloging-in-Publication Data

Beaty, Janice J.
  Prosocial guidance for the preschool child / Janice J. Beaty.
    p. cm.
  Includes bibliographical references and index.
  ISBN 0-13-633512-8
    1. Behavior modification. 2. Eduation, Preschool—United States. 3. Helping behavior—
United States. 4. Socialization—United States.   I. Title.
    LB1060.2.B42   1999
  372.139'33DC21   98-6519
                                                                        CIP

Cover photo: © FPG International
Editor: Ann Castel Davis
Production Editor: Sheryl Glicker Langner
Design Coordinator: Diane C. Lorenzo
Text Designer: STELLARViSIONs
Cover Designer: Susan Unger
Production Manager: Laura Messerly
Electronic Text Management: Marilyn Wilson Phelps, Karen L. Bretz, Tracey B. Ward
Director of Marketing: Kevin Flanagan
Marketing Manager: Suzanne Stanton
Marketing Coordinator: Krista Groshong

This book was set in Zapf Humanist and Souvenir ITC by Prentice Hall and was printed and
bound by R. R. Donnelley & Sons Company. The cover was printed by Phoenix Color Corp.

© 1999 by Prentice-Hall, Inc.
Simon & Schuster/A Viacom Company
Upper Saddle River, New Jersey 07458

Photo credits: All photos by Janice J. Beaty

Printed in the United States of America

10 9 8 7 6 5 4 3 2 1

ISBN: 0-13-633512-8

Prentice-Hall International (UK) Limited, *London*
Prentice-Hall of Australia Pty. Limited, *Sydney*
Prentice-Hall of Canada, Inc., *Toronto*
Prentice-Hall Hispanoamericana, S. A., *Mexico*
Prentice-Hall of India Private Limited, *New Delhi*
Prentice-Hall of Japan, Inc., *Tokyo*
Simon & Schuster Asia Pte. Ltd., *Singapore*
Editora Prentice-Hall do Brasil, Ltda., *Rio de Janeiro*

To Linda Pratt
An Outstanding Teacher-Educator
And a Friend

Preface

Prosocial guidance is a new approach to behavior management in the preschool classroom that integrates prosocial behavior with positive guidance techniques in order for children to learn to get along together. The focus is on positive rather than inappropriate behaviors. Teachers and student teachers learn to create a prosocial physical environment in the classroom, to anticipate and prevent inappropriate behavior from happening, and to help children manage their own behavior. Children learn self-esteem, empathy, self-control, friendliness, generosity, cooperation, helpfulness, and respect.

Inappropriate behavior tends to fade away when the focus is positive like this. When conflicts do occur, teachers learn to treat them as learning opportunities for children, practicing a new highly successful conflict-conversion technique. Teachers also learn to model appropriate behavior, to coach children in what to say and do, to redirect children into calming activities when they become disruptive, and to help them develop positive communication skills.

A *Child Prosocial Behavior Checklist* helps teachers and parents alike learn where a child stands in the development of these important skills. A *Teacher Prosocial Guidance Checklist* gives teachers an opportunity to evaluate themselves and to learn the strategies necessary for implementing this new approach. When teachers focus on children's positive rather than inappropriate behaviors, everyone benefits. Children who feel good about themselves start treating others more prosocially. Teachers who reinforce this behavior are themselves reinforced by the happy classroom atmosphere that emerges. And children who need special help are rewarded with a genuine appreciation for their strengths by everyone.

ACKNOWLEDGMENTS

My special thanks goes to Ann Gilchrist, director of the Foster Grandparent program of the Central Missouri Human Development Corporation for sharing her ideas, reading the manuscript, working with me in training Head Start teachers, and helping put into practice the "other-esteem conflict conversion" technique; to the teachers and staffs of Park Avenue Head Start and Fay Street Head Start in Columbia, Missouri, and Mexico Missouri Head Start, especially Jackie Craig and Janice Jones; to the parents from these Head Start programs for allowing their children to be photographed for this book; to Carolyn Dorrell, director of the Early Childhood Professional Develop-

ment Network in Columbia, South Carolina, for ideas gained from her programs; to libraries at the University of Missouri, Columbia, and Elmira College, Elmira, New York; to the Holiday Inn Holidome at Columbia, Missouri; and to my editor, Ann Davis, for her inspiring ideas and continued support.

I would like to thank the following reviewers for their helpful insights and suggestions: Lori Beasley, University of Central Oklahoma; Susan H. Christian, Patrick Henry Community College (VA); Susan Culpepper, University of Montevallo; Karen L. Peterson, Washington State University at Vancouver; and Marie Plemons, University of Houston, Victoria.

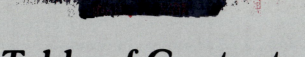

Table of Contents

7 ▢ Using Positive Reinforcement to Help Children Learn Prosocial Behaviors   106

THREE   Specific Strategies to Promote Prosocial Behavior

8 ▢ Promoting Children's Self-Esteem   126

9   Using Other-Esteem Conflict Conversion   142

10   Promoting Positive Communication among Children and Adults   164

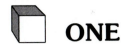 **ONE**

Prosocial Guidance

CHAPTER 1

What Is Prosocial Guidance?

Young children's behavior in the preschool classroom has always been the focus of great concern for teachers, assistants, student teachers, and parents. Is she able to get along with the other children? Can he share his favorite toys with someone else? How do you get her to pick up the materials she has scattered? What do you do if he loses his temper? What happens if a child is rejected by others? How do you handle a child who kicks or bites?

In a classroom with 15 to 25 exuberant youngsters, the excitement of numerous activities occurring at the same time and the countless materials waiting to be explored can result in engrossing experiences for most children, but not for all. Some children may grab toys away from others, refuse to share their own materials, force their way into group play, or use aggressive words or actions to get what they want. How do you manage children who get out of hand like this? Is "manage" really what you want to do?

Much of our earlier attention was directed to the aftereffects of children's behavior. We took action after something inappropriate had happened. That action was often punitive—a time-out chair for someone, a scolding for someone else. We called it "discipline." It frequently stopped the unwanted behavior but did little to prevent it from happening again. Many children learned to behave out of fear that the teacher would punish, scold, or ridicule them. But others didn't seem to care and wouldn't change their ways no matter what. More and more today we are finding that such discipline has lost its effectiveness for many teachers and children. We are learning that it was never that effective for helping children learn positive behavior in the first place.

Now we know there is a better way to bring about appropriate behavior among preschoolers that can be accepted by everyone. Rather than focusing on misbehaviors and negative results, the new approach concentrates on positive actions. It is a type of guidance that develops self-esteem, self-control, empathy, and cooperation among youngsters. We call it *prosocial guidance*, and we have proof that it works.

PROSOCIAL GUIDANCE

Prosocial guidance is a type of guidance that helps children develop prosocial behaviors (e.g., self-esteem, empathy, self-control, friendliness, generosity, cooperation, helpfulness, respect) to get along with others, to overcome conflicts, and to work and play peacefully in the preschool classroom. It gives children a basic start in developing positive attitudes and behaviors that will last a lifetime.

You as a teacher or caregiver of young children can learn how to create a prosocial environment in your classroom so that children can actually learn to control their own behavior. You can learn how to set limits, when and how to intervene in children's conflicts, and how to convert problem situations to positive outcomes. Finally, you can learn how to serve as a prosocial behavior model yourself, leading the way to your children's similar development.

Prosocial behavior, in other words, can be *taught* to children just as science, art, music, and premath skills are taught. Learning to share materials with other children without a fuss, to wait for a turn, to abide by classroom limits, to recognize other children's feelings, to control one's own feelings, and to make friends with other children are capacities that can be learned through special stories, dramatic play, physical activities, art and music, block building, science exploration, and every curriculum area of the classroom. Children who act in an out-of-bounds manner can learn self-control, self-esteem, and empathy through positive activities that do not embarrass them or put them down.

The chapters to follow offer ideas and applications of this new approach to guidance. Chapter 2 describes how children develop prosocial behaviors and how you can determine where each child stands in this development. Chapter 3 discusses teachers' own development of prosocial behavior, how teachers can model this behavior, and also mirror their children's emotions.

Part II, "Providing Prosocial Guidance," devotes four chapters to helping teachers and caregivers learn how to set up a prosocial physical environment and how to apply prevention, intervention, and reinforcement techniques to assist children in developing prosocial skills.

Part III, "Specific Strategies to Promote Prosocial Behavior," contains four chapters that discuss how to promote children's self-esteem, how to use a new conflict conversion technique to resolve children's interpersonal disputes, how to promote positive communication among children and adults, and, finally, how to involve families in providing prosocial guidance for their children.

NEW BRAIN RESEARCH

New findings about infants' and young children's brain development are opening our eyes to the importance of early adult-child interactions and a stimulating environment. New brain-imaging technologies that allow neuroscientists to study how the brain develops and what factors influence its growth are coming up with surprising results.

It is the electrical activity of brain cells (neurons) that is most important. Even before birth these cells fire electrical charges that carve mental circuits into patterns in the brain, actually changing the physical structure of the brain. You could say that the brain is wiring itself for use. Immediately after birth, an explosion of learning occurs caused by these same electrical processes, according to neurobiologist Carla Shatz (Nash, 1997, p. 50).

Experiencing Sensory Stimulation

But what happens next is up to the people and the environment surrounding the infant. The brain changes dramatically as trillions more connections (synapses) than it can possibly use are produced, laying out circuits for vision, movement, language, and the functions necessary for life itself. This time the neural activity is no longer spontaneous but driven by the sensory experiences the child encounters in the environment. As Nash (1997) notes:

Among the first circuits the brain constructs are those that govern the emotions. Beginning around two months of age, the distress and contentment experienced by newborns start to evolve into more complex feelings: joy and sadness, envy and empathy, pride and shame. (p. 53)

This is the time for loving adults to provide the infant with positive emotional stimulation. Responding promptly to demands for feeding and changing, holding and comforting, talking in soothing tones, playing games with fingers and toes, providing cuddly toys, singing nursery songs: such activities stimulate the formation of brain circuitry that produces positive emotions. But neglecting a baby "can produce brain-wave patterns that dampen happy feelings" (Nash, 1997, p. 53), whereas outright abuse produces abnormal stress responses.

Connecting with Caring Adults

As the infant develops into toddlerhood and early childhood, stimulating interactions with people and materials continue to make a tremendous difference in brain development.

A child's environment has enormous impact on how the circuits of the brain will be laid. . . . Positive interactions with caring adults stimulate a child's brain profoundly, causing synapses to grow and existing connections to be strengthened. (Newberger, 1997, p. 5)

Throughout the early years, these brain connections are strengthened each time the child is stimulated to see, to touch, to talk about, to listen to, and to think about the objects and people nearby. Caring adults are most important. Children need to connect with adults who cherish them, who watch what they are trying to accomplish and congratulate them when they succeed or encourage them to try it another way when they don't. They need adults who will listen to what they have to say and respond with pleasure to their utterances. They need adults who model good behavior, who set sensible limits on children's behavior and will enforce them consistently but not harshly.

Pleasurable experiences are also important. Young children respond best to things they enjoy: happy words, funny movements, exciting stories, peppy songs, toys they can manipulate, activities where they are featured, laughter, and love.

Repetition is important. Young children's brain connections are strengthened by positive experiences that are repeated over and over: reading a favorite story, playing with a beloved animal or doll, eating a yummy meal, receiving a hug or kiss, hearing their names happily spoken aloud. All of these experiences cause electrical activity in the brain, helping fine-tune the brain's circuitry that controls growth, thinking, and feeling.

Eliminating Excess Synapses

By age 10 or sometimes earlier, another dramatic change occurs. The brain begins a process of eliminating excess synapses—those connections between the brain cells that are seldom or never used. For children who have been deprived of a stimulating

*Children need to connect with
adults who cherish them.*

environment during their early years, their brains suffer. "Children who don't play much or are rarely touched develop brains 20% to 30% smaller than normal for their age" (Nash, 1997, p. 51).

So we see there is an important time frame for all of this brain development to occur. If young children do not experience an environment that awakens all of their senses, if they are not cared for by adults who talk to them, who show them love and affection, and who encourage them to explore and learn, their brains will lose those connections that have not been used or strengthened. By age 10, the wiring of the brain is nearly complete, and other excess synapses are eliminated if they are not used.

Experiencing a Quality Environment

This new knowledge of brain development makes the importance of quality early childhood programs more obvious than ever. As Nash (1997) notes, "It is becoming increasingly clear that well-designed preschool programs can help many children overcome glaring deficits in their home environment" (p. 52).

It is the early years that count most, when the brain is still flexible and its growth more easily influenced by the people and activities around it. No longer do scientists believe that a baby enters the world genetically preprogrammed to develop according to its inheritance alone, nor do they believe that environment alone controls the baby's growth. Nature and nurture work together in an intricate dance to create the new human being.

What is most important for us to understand is the power of the environment (including the people in it) to remodel the brain during the early years. Preschool programs can make a difference if they recognize that brain growth and learning result not only from *cognitive* activities but also from *emotional* development, the basis for the prosocial behavior to be discussed in this text.

NEW RESEARCH ON EMOTIONS

For too long child development specialists have ignored the emotions and the origins of emotional development. Even Jean Piaget, a Swiss psychologist whose studies of child development have greatly influenced early childhood educators, regarded intelligence as independent of emotions. But now all must take a second look at astounding new research that tells us more about children's brain development and what causes youngsters to act the way they do than anyone could have foreseen.

Psychologists had long believed that cognition developed separately from emotions; that emotions had nothing whatsoever to do with the development of thinking skills. Now they are finding that "emotions, not cognitive stimulation, serve as the mind's primary architect" (Greenspan, 1997, p. 1).

In his important book *The Growth of the Mind and the Endangered Origins of Intelligence*, Stanley I. Greenspan (1997) describes the surprising results of his research and that of others. Their findings show "unexpected common origins for the mind's highest capacities: intelligence, morality, and sense of self" (p. 1). That common origin is the emotions. Certain subtle *emotional exchanges* are necessary at each stage of the mind's early growth. When these do not occur, a child's intellectual, moral, and social development are endangered.

Emotional Exchanges with Infants

Neurological research and clinical work with infants show that emotions guide social skills and relationships, serve as the basis of empathy and self-esteem, and "play a specific, critical role in how intelligence develops" (Greenspan, 1997, p. 7). Early experiences actually influence the structure of the brain. For example, brain-imaging studies show that brain cells are recruited for particular functions such as seeing and hearing. But for neurons to make specific connections, they must be activated through experiences that stimulate hormonal changes.

What should these experiences be? Not the playing with toys, fitting pegs into holes, or finding beads under cups, but the *emotional exchanges with their caregivers*, as babies and young children play with materials. These are the key ingredients (Greenspan & Meisels, 1994, pp. 1–8). Playfulness, laughter, and the showing of love and affection can actually change the brain!

Neuroscientists have found that a soothing touch, for instance, causes the brain to release growth hormones. On the other hand, emotional stress such as being hit or yelled at can release a steroid hormone, cortisol, high levels of which can cause the death of brain cells and a reduction in connections between cells in areas of the brain important in learning and memory (Newberger, 1997, p. 5).

Emotional Cues

It all starts in infancy as babies begin to explore their environment of sights, sounds, touches, tastes, and smells of the people and things around them. Their whole body is involved as voluntary muscles create smiles, frowns, coos, or cries in response to these encounters. Each sensory perception the infant experiences forms part of a dual code: its physical properties (e.g., big or loud or rough) and its emotional qualities (e.g., soothing or jarring or tense). The involuntary muscles also play a part as the heart, lungs, and stomach make their own responses to these experiences. (Greenspan, 1997, p. 21).

As infants encounter these sensory impressions over and over, such experiences become increasingly tied to feelings. Eventually the young child is able to carry with her from one situation to another her own set of emotional cues. When she is confronted by new circumstances that produce familiar feelings, she will behave as these feelings have taught her to do. As Greenspan (1997) notes, "How a child behaves around a teacher depends on how the teacher makes her feel" (p. 24).

Early treatment of youngsters is the key. Those who have received a warm and caring upbringing have developed the emotions to make them feel good about themselves and therefore toward others. On the other hand, children who are emotionally deprived early in life may display not only a poor self-esteem but also negative feelings against others.

LEVELS OF THE MIND

How does a newborn baby deal with the flood of incoming sensory data to become a child whose mind can translate feelings and experiences into wishes and thoughts?

Table 1-1 Levels of the mind

Note: This table includes information from Greenspan (1997, pp. 42–88).

1. *Making sense of sensations*

   The infant gains control over her body and inner sensations; takes action on things outside herself.

2. *Establishing relationships*

   The infant exchanges sensations between herself and her caregivers. This exchange creates the capacity to feel empathy and love.

3. *Developing intentionality*

   During the first year, the infant-caregiver exchange of expressions and gestures gives rise to wishes and desires on the part of the infant, resulting in purposeful behavior (e.g., two-way intentional communication).

4. *Discriminating among basic emotions*

   Between 12 and 18 months, the child learns to distinguish facial expressions and body postures; can discriminate among basic emotions and deal with them in social interactions.

5. *Developing images, ideas, symbols*

   During the second or third year, the child creates inner pictures of her world, true symbolic expression; deals not only with behavior but ideas.

6. *Developing emotional thinking*

   The child links ideas to emotions even before she has mastered whole sentences; develops ability to relate present acts to the future, thus making consequences rather than fear the basis for controllng impulses.

Greenspan (1997) describes six developmental stages he calls "levels of the mind" that must be achieved.

These developmental levels represent deep structures of the mind that must be firmly in place during the child's first 3 years for later mental development to occur. Even language depends on this structure to acquire purpose and function. If infants and young children fail to achieve these levels, not only their mental development but also their emotional and social interactions may remain unconnected.

CHILD BEHAVIOR IN THE PRESCHOOL CLASSROOM

With this new research in mind, we realize that young children come into the preschool classroom with their brains already wired according to the treatment they have received during their first 3 years of life. Their behavior reflects the way they have been treated at home, at a babysitter's, or in an infant-toddler program. Some may display a happy exuberance in their interactions with the children and materials around them; some, a shyness or withdrawal from encounters with their peers. Other children may stake their claim to space, materials, or control over their classmates in no uncertain terms; still others may strike out against the world with aggressive words and actions.

How do you deal with such diverse behaviors by so many children? Are they overwhelming to you or an exciting challenge? Do you welcome "well-behaved" children and shake your head in exasperation over children who "always cause trouble"? Are you someone who is exhilarated by children's challenging behavior, or do you find yourself more often than not calling out for help? "What can I do about Sondra's constant snatching of other children's toys?" or "How can I keep Rinaldo from pushing or hitting anyone who comes near him?" "Nothing I do seems to work!"

Welcome to the world of *prosocial guidance*. This text invites you to participate in a unique form of positive interaction with children that truly helps them develop appropriate behavior. It does not involve punishment, harsh words, or time-out chairs. It does involve (a) your arranging of the classroom to help children become self-directed, (b) your modeling of the behavior you want children to employ, (c) your anticipating children's inappropriate behavior to channel it in a different direction, and (d) especially your assisting children to recognize each other's feelings to convert conflicts to positive resolutions.

To accomplish these goals, you must learn more about:

1. interpersonal conflict itself and its role in children's development,
2. each child and how she or he deals with interpersonal conflicts,
3. yourself and how you feel about the individual children in your group, and
4. specific strategies for promoting prosocial behavior.

THE ROLE OF CONFLICT IN THE CLASSROOM

Conflicts occur in the preschool classroom every day. Josh takes the truck Andrew was playing with and won't give it back. Charlene grabs the egg beater Sue was using in the water table. Tony knocks down Matthew's block building "on purpose." Brianna comes crying to you because the other children won't let her play with them in the house corner.

Whenever young children play together, they eventually become involved in conflicts. Teachers and teacher assistants face such disruptions daily. Student teachers must learn to deal with them from the start. Is this the way it should be? Isn't a preschool classroom supposed to be a more peaceful place?

Not necessarily. The truth of the matter lies in the fact that children ages 3 through 5 are only at the beginning stage of learning to get along with others. Some have never interacted with more children than those in their immediate families. Others seem to take over whenever they play with anyone. A few are not inclined to play at all. As a teacher you need to remember that most preschoolers are without the experience necessary to cope with so many equally unseasoned peers.

Conflicts as Learning Opportunities

This is as it should be. *Nothing is wrong with interpersonal conflict among young children.* Whenever it occurs, it presents an important *opportunity* for everyone to learn how to behave. As Crosser (1992) notes:

> Conflict is a natural part of living and working together in groups. It is good that conflicts arise in the early childhood classroom because it is only through facing conflicts that children can learn the skills necessary to resolve real-life problems. (p. 28)

Conflicts are truly learning opportunities, not only for the children involved but also for the adults in the classroom. Everyone benefits by learning how prosocial behavior can resolve difficult situations.

Too often in the past we have treated conflict as a negative occurrence that should be banished from the classroom and those involved punished for causing it. Now we know that interpersonal conflicts between young children serve a useful purpose: they create learning opportunities for youngsters to experience the power of empathy and other prosocial behaviors. They provide teachers with insights about children's levels of prosocial development and their capabilities of resolving disputes on their own.

It is a new and important way of looking at things. *When we treat conflict as something necessary for teaching youngsters prosocial skills, and not something bad for which children need to be disciplined, we open a whole new world of possibilities.* How can children learn to get along with one another unless they come face to face with real-life problems in an unbiased environment?

Child-Sensitive Environment

The key is an *unbiased* environment. The classroom must be child-sensitive. Children need to feel safe, happy, and secure in the knowledge that everyone is treated fairly and never harshly. The preschool classroom is the perfect setting for such encounters because the youngsters can learn to deal with them more objectively than in the emotionally charged home setting that many children face.

The teacher or assistants can serve as mediators who treat both sides of any conflict fairly—even those involving children who are completely out of control. Then conflictees come out feeling good about themselves, having learned new ways to resolve interpersonal problems without suffering put-downs or punishments. Other child onlookers also gain a great deal by seeing how prosocial guidance has resolved the dispute for their peers in a positive manner.

Onlookers receive other benefits. Not only do they become more inclined to try prosocial actions themselves in future conflicts of their own, but also they treat all the conflictees with more respect than if someone had been punished. In the past a child who "caused trouble" and "had to be disciplined" was often an outcast in the eyes of his peers: someone to be avoided and not played with, someone to be kept out of other children's activities because he was "bad." This frequently caused the outcast child to resort to even more disruptive behavior—a self-fulfilling prophecy and vicious cycle all around.

It is important for teachers to know that their intervention in even one conflict situation resulting in prosocial outcomes can be a learning experience for the entire class. Teachers who have used the strategies described in the chapters to follow report an impressive decline in conflicts because prosocial lessons seem to sink in for the entire group.

CONFLICTS MOST OFTEN ENCOUNTERED

Possession Disputes

What kinds of conflicts can one expect to encounter in a preschool classroom? *Possession disputes* are most common, comprising 90%–100% of the conflicts in some programs (Hay, 1984, p. 14). One child wants a toy or material that another child is using and tries to take it. The other child refuses to give it up, resulting in a "materials possession dispute." As Hay (1984) notes, "It is evident that one common source of conflict in early childhood, as in adult society, is struggle for the possession of tangible resources; in children's groups, these usually consist of toys and other play materials" (p. 14).

Such conflicts are usually settled without adult intervention, as they should be. They are generally brief, lasting only a few minutes or even a few seconds. Only when one child hits another or forcefully takes another's toy, causing crying or yelling, need an adult intervene.

Why should possession disputes be so common in preschool programs when the classroom is so full of a rich supply of blocks, books, dress-up clothes, toy cars, trucks and people, kitchen utensils, sand and water toys, puzzles, counting and sorting materials, dolls, puppets, and so on? Because young children are still at the egocentric stage of their development so that they regard *all* of the toys and materials as theirs alone. Most 3- to 5-year-olds have not yet learned to consider another child's point of view. Empathizing, sharing, and taking turns are prosocial behaviors they have yet to learn. Possession disputes like this can help teach them.

Group-Entry Disputes

Another type of conflict often caused by a youngster's same lack of social skills is the *group-entry dispute.* A child tries to enter a group of children already at play but is rejected. He may give up, or run to the teacher, or try to force his own way into the group through aggression. Ramsey (1991) tells why access struggles like this are common:

> Interactions in preschool classrooms are short, so children are constantly having to gain entry into new groups. This process is made more difficult because children who are already engaged with each other tend to protect their interactive space and reject newcomers. (p. 27)

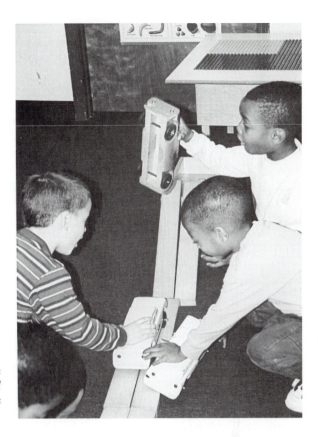

*Possession disputes over toys
or space are usually settled
without adult intervention, as
they should be.*

Such conflicts, however, are perfect learning opportunities for teachers and children to practice the prosocial guidance techniques described in the chapters to follow.

Other Types of Conflict

Other aggressive behaviors such as pushing, hitting, or fighting may result from *personality clashes* because one child is jealous of another, or *power struggles* because one child wants to control an activity, or even *superhero dramatic play* in which children pretending to be the superheroes they see on television get carried away with their aggressive actions. All of these conflict situations can become learning opportunities for both children and teachers.

Chapter 2 discusses in more detail why children behave the way they do and how teachers can determine where each child stands in the development of his or her prosocial skills for learning to get along with others.

This important topic has far-reaching implications. As I mention in *Converting Conflicts in Preschool*:

Children who learn how to convert conflicts in early childhood have the tools to convert adulthood conflicts as well. Adults armed with such tools will then be able to convert and defuse interpersonal, intercommunity, and even international conflicts. (Beaty, 1995, p. 2)

It all starts in early childhood. How the child's brain is wired to perceive the world around it depends on the emotional experiences it encounters. You can make these experiences positive ones for the youngsters you work with. The prosocial guidance techniques you use can help children learn to deal positively with conflict. Then like a pebble dropped into a pond, this conversion of conflict to positive feelings in one child can spread to the entire classroom. As these children mature, their practice of getting along with others can develop into a tidal wave of getting along with families, neighbors, communities, and even nations. It can start with you.

REFERENCES

Beaty, J. J. (1995). *Converting conflicts in preschool.* Fort Worth, TX: Harcourt Brace.

Crosser, S. (1992). Managing the early childhood classroom. *Young Children, 47*(2), 23–29.

Greenspan, S. I. (1997). *The growth of the mind and the endangered origins of intelligence.* Reading, MA: Addison-Wesley.

Greenspan, S. I., and Meisels, S. (1994). Toward a new vision for the developmental assessment of infants and young children. *Zero to Three: Bulletin of the National Center for Clinical Infant Programs, 14*(6), 1–8.

Hay, D. F. (1984). Social conflict in early childhood. *Annals of Child Development, 1,* 1–44.

Nash, J. M. (1997). Fertile minds. *Time, 149*(5), 48–56.

Newberger, J. J. (1997). New brain development research: A wonderful window of opportunity to build public support for early childhood education! *Young Children, 52*(4), 4–9.

Ramsey, P. G. (1991). *Making friends in preschool: Promoting peer relationships in early childhood.* New York: Teachers College Press.

SUGGESTED READINGS

Beaty, J. J. (1998). *Observing development of the young child* (4th ed.). Upper Saddle River, NJ: Merrill/Prentice Hall.

Begley, S. (1997). How to build a baby's brain: Your child. Special Edition, *Newsweek,* Spring/Summer, pp. 28–32.

Gartrell, D. (1994). *A guidance approach to discipline.* Albany, NY: Delmar.

Honig, A. S., & Wittmer, D. S. (1996). Helping children become more prosocial: Ideas for classrooms, families, schools, and communities. *Young Children, 51*(2), 62–75.

LeDoux, J. (1996). *The emotional brain: The mysterious underpinnings of emotional life.* New York: Simon & Schuster.

Sylwester, R. (1995). *Celebration of neurons: An educator's guide to the human brain.* Alexandria, VA: Association for Supervision and Curriculum Development.

Williams, N. F. (1997). Brain development in young children. *Children Our Concern, 22*(1), 26–27.

VIDEOTAPES

Educational Productions. (Producer). *Hand-in-hand: The child who is rejected* (no. 7). (Available from Educational Productions, 7412 S.W. Beaverton Hillsdale Hwy., Suite 210, Portland, OR 97225)

GMMB&A. (Producer). (1997). *I am your child: The first years last forever.* (Available from GMMB&A, 1010 Wisconsin Ave. N.W., Suite 800, Washington, DC 20007)

Magna Systems. (Producer). (1993). *Moral development.* (Available from Magna Systems, 95 W. County Line Rd., Barrington, IL 60010)

National Association for the Education of Young Children. (Producer). *Discipline: Appropriate guidance of young children.* (Available from NAEYC, 1509 16th St. N.W., Washington, DC 20036-1426)

LEARNING ACTIVITIES

1. What is *prosocial guidance,* and how does it differ from traditional *discipline?* Give examples of each that you have used (or observed being used) with children. What were the results?

2. Describe various prosocial behaviors you have observed being demonstrated by children in a preschool classroom. How did others (children and teachers) around them respond to their actions?

3. How does a stimulating environment promote an infant's or young child's brain development, according to new brain research? Give examples of activities or materials in your preschool that could promote this brain development.

4. How do the emotional experiences of young children affect their intellectual development in a positive as well as a negative manner? Give examples of experiences in your preschool that could affect children either way.

5. Observe the children in your preschool, making note of any possession disputes that you see. Record what the dispute was about, who started it, how long it lasted, how it was resolved, and whether the teacher became involved.

Children and Prosocial Behavior

Prosocial behavior refers to "voluntary actions that are intended to help or benefit another individual or group of individuals" (Eisenberg & Mussen, 1989, p. 3). Among preschool children that means being friendly toward another child, giving or sharing a toy, helping someone complete a task, waiting for a turn, treating materials with respect, showing concern for others, complying with behavior limits set by the teacher, using words rather than actions to express strong feelings, picking up toys or blocks when asked, taking on a classroom chore, and allowing another child to join your play.

Such behaviors would surely make the preschool classroom a delightful place to be, you must admit. But can every young child age 3 through 5 demonstrate such behaviors? Doesn't it take more maturity for most preschoolers to act in this fashion? Not necessarily. Many children have already learned much of this conduct at home. Others seem to absorb it almost effortlessly once they have entered preschool. They easily follow the teacher's lead or the responsible actions of other children.

Some children, however, do not seem to know how to get along in a group. They tend to strike out rather than reach out. Hostility, not friendliness, is their response to those around them. We must be careful not to label any of these children according to their behavior. They are neither "good" nor "bad" but instead "young learners" who have come to the preschool to develop their abilities and learn appropriate behavior.

Socialization—that is, learning to get along with others—is an important goal for all children in every preschool program. Whether or not children have learned any of the prosocial behaviors previously, now is the time for them to do so. They can reinforce what they already know or add new practices to their repertoire of behaviors necessary for getting along in the world around them.

Prosocial guidance, because it is positive in nature, can help children feel good about themselves, which in turn is reflected in their more considerate behavior toward others. Rather than negative discipline that sets limits against inappropriate actions and then punishes children who break the rules, prosocial guidance focuses on what is positive about children. It looks for children's strengths and helps them see themselves as worthwhile individuals. It helps children develop control over their own behavior by setting acceptable limits and enforcing them with compassionate, not harsh, firmness. It helps youngsters learn to anticipate their own responses so they can eventually participate in the limit-setting process themselves.

Children who are treated with respect ultimately respond with respect. Children who are given responsibilities come to act in a responsible manner. In other words, the way we treat children is reflected back to us in the youngsters' behavior.

> The more cherished a child is, the less likely he or she is to bully others or to be rejected by other children. The more nurturing parents and caregivers are—the more positive affections and responsive empathic care they provide—the more positively children will relate in social interactions with teachers, caring adults, and peers and in cooperating with classroom learning goals as well. (Honig & Wittmer, 1996, pp. 69–70)

DEVELOPING PROSOCIAL BEHAVIOR

Although all children have the potential for acquiring prosocial skills, the behavior itself must be learned. This sort of learning is a complex and often subtle process full of unforeseen twists and turns that continue over long periods time. But formal teaching is seldom a part of it. Young children learn how to behave by behaving: through trial and error, by watching what others do in certain situations, by experiencing the reactions of others to their own actions, and by following the examples of their parents, teachers, siblings, and peers.

Some children even at this early age seem to have a strong predisposition toward behaving prosocially, while other children show little concern for the people around them and display few prosocial behaviors. Has something occurred in the home environment, you may wonder, to cause such differences? Can the differences be due to a strict upbringing on the part of parents or caregivers? Are prosocial behaviors more evident in children whose parents have been lenient? Or are they more closely tied to a child's personality?

Nancy Eisenberg and Paul H. Mussen in their book *The Roots of Prosocial Behavior in Children* (1989) have examined much of the research exploring how prosocial behavior develops in young children. They have looked at research examining biological factors, culture, age, gender, social status, personality characteristics, family influences, and outside influences in the development of prosocial behavior. More recent research has examined brain growth, emotions, and the roots of morality. As a clearer picture emerges of the early development of prosocial behavior in children, we can begin to understand how preschool programs can contribute to this growth.

Biological Factors

Brain Development

Although the number of neurons (brain cells) a child possesses initially is genetically determined, this is merely a framework for the trillions more neurons and synapses (connections) that are produced by the brain after birth. It is then that environmental factors click in. If parents interact positively with the infant, these synapses will be strengthened. If caregivers abuse or neglect the infant, synapses decrease and the infant's brain becomes wired for functions such as anxiety, impulsivity, and fight or flight (Newberger, 1997, pp. 4–7). "A child raised in a stressful, unpredictable, violent environment will develop a brain that is specifically adapted for a violent, hostile world" (Williams, 1997, p. 27).

Temperament

Some researchers also believe that a child's temperament is based on his genetic inheritance. Whether he is shy and inhibited or bold and gregarious arises from his genes, they declare. Others, like Greenspan, feel that a child's initial responses derive not only from inheritance but also from a "complex interplay of multiple factors," some mental, some emotional, some physical, and some environmental (Greenspan, 1997, pp. 138–139).

Age

Does a child's age make a difference in her prosocial behavior toward others? Age or biological maturity is a factor often considered by child development researchers. Surprisingly, all of the studies in the last decade show that even children as young as 1 and 2 years old share objects and help other people. They note that many young children help their parents, often without being asked, and also spontaneously assist strangers in performing tasks (Eisenberg & Mussen, 1989, p. 56).

Children as young as a year old respond to distress in others and by a year and a half often attempt to comfort others in distress. Some studies show that caregiving like this seemed to increase with age, but not greatly. Obviously, not every child shows prosocial responses, but as children mature and encounter socializing experiences over time, they learn to respond with empathy.

Gender

Do girls behave more prosocially toward others than boys? Although we realize there are many differences in personality and social characteristics between girls and boys, the majority of studies have not found consistent gender differences in responding prosocially to others. This seems surprising when we consider the common gender-role stereotype that girls are more helpful, caring, and nurturing than boys. The main differences found were in the kinds of prosocial acts among men and women. Men performed more rescuing types of helping acts such as changing a tire, while women gave psychological assistance in helping friends (Eisenberg & Mussen, pp. 58–59).

How girls and boys are raised seems more important than their gender. In families and societies where boys are expected to be as helpful and caring as girls, they tend to be so. Thus, as teachers of preschool children, we must be careful not to let gender stereotyping color our perceptions of what to expect from boys versus girls. All children can learn to be helpful, friendly, cooperative, generous, respectful, and caring of others.

Biological factors that help determine a child's proclivity toward prosocial behavior thus include the brain cells he is born with, the brain cells and synapses that form after his birth, the hormones that stimulate or suppress growth of brain cells and their connections, and the infant's physiological traits such as sensitivity to sound or touch. However, from the very beginning of life a child's genetic inheritance (nature) works together with factors from his environment (nurture) to develop the infant into the preschool child you will come to know.

The long-debated controversy over which is more important in a child's development, nature or nurture, should not even exist, according to Greenspan (1997). "A child's constitutional makeup interacts with his emotional experience in a reciprocal manner so complex that there is no point in debating which factor contributes more" (pp. 133–134). The real question is, How does the environment interact with the biological makeup to create the individual child?

Environmental Factors

A youngster's environment consists of many factors, some more important than others as an influence on her development. Her culture, her family, her social and economic status, as well as outside influences such as school, church, neighborhood, the media, and peers all play important roles. These factors interact with one another and the child's biological inheritance in helping develop her emotions, cognition, health, and personality, as well as her proclivity toward prosocial behavior.

Culture

Most cultures, for example, teach their members to have some kind of concern for one another. But certain cultures value cooperation and working together much more highly than others. Communal cultures such as Hispanic, Native American, Asian, and Pacific peoples are more likely to raise children who respond to the needs of the group more than those of the individual. Mainstream American culture, on the other hand, treats the individual as more important than the group.

Thus, children from these cultures may learn to behave toward others in very different ways. In communal cultures cooperation rather than competition, and sharing with others rather than accumulating for yourself, are important features. Mainstream American children, however, often learn to compete very early in life as they struggle for their rights against those around them, often with support from adult caregivers.

Children in communal cultures, on the other hand, frequently learn an entirely different set of behaviors because the youngest children are cared for by the next oldest child. Thus, an infant or toddler may gain her most important lesson—cooperation rather than competition—from a 4-year-old caretaker. In addition, the 4-year-old also learns caring and responsibility in a most direct fashion when she must carry it out.

Eisenberg and Mussen (1989) came to the following tentative conclusions from their study about the effects of culture on children's prosocial development:

> Children apparently are likely to develop high levels of prosocial behavior if they are raised in cultures characterized by:
>
> 1. parental and peer stress on consideration for others, sharing, and orientation toward the group;
> 2. a simple social organization and/or a traditional rural setting;
> 3. assignment to women of important economic functions;
> 4. living in an extended family; and
> 5. early assignment of tasks and responsibility to children. (p. 53)

Family

Although the family has tremendous influence on a child's behavior, neither the family's socioeconomic status nor its size appear to have any consistent effect on children's prosocial behavior. While some studies show that growing up in a large family may promote generosity, others find that family size and sharing are unrelated (Eisenberg & Mussen, 1989, pp. 59–60).

But because the family is a child's principal agent of learning and socialization during the early years, we need to consider how its influence does affect children's prosocial behavior. We know that some families directly instruct their children on how to behave, praise them when they do things right, and punish them when they do things wrong. Whether children actually learn prosocial behavior in this manner is questionable. Although praise may stimulate children to act in a certain way, fear of punishment has more bearing on what not to do rather than on positive actions.

We do know that prosocial behavior can emerge naturally in children without any prompting. As Eisenberg and Mussen (1989) point out:

> But many of the child's prosocial actions and motivations are the products of more subtle processes, such as imitation or identification; these responses appear to emerge spontaneously, without direct training or reward—usually without anyone intending to "teach" and without the child intending to learn. (p. 66)

The effects of modeling and imitation are powerful stimulants to children's actions. Children whose parents model prosocial behavior within the family and without usually display at least some of this behavior themselves. The closer a child identifies with a particular parent, the more she is likely to act in a similar manner. As Eisenberg and Mussen (1989) note, "Many authorities believe that children's prosocial inclinations are governed primarily by the quality of their relationships with their parents, by their child-rearing practices, and by broad features of the family environment" (p. 77).

Abusive parenting has a negative effect, as we have already noted. Harsh and abusive treatment during the early years seems to inhibit the development of a child's prosocial behavior. This is often seen in a child care facility when another youngster shows some kind of distress. Others may rush to a crying child's side, showing concern and even sadness. But not children known to be abused at home: they rarely show empathy for others in distress. How is it in your preschool?

What about strict but nonabusive parents, you may wonder? If the parents are strict but also warm, loving, responsive, and supportive, their children tend to be socially responsible. On the other hand, parents who are permissive but lax in disciplining and rewarding their children may have children who display little prosocial behavior themselves. So it is not strictness or permissiveness alone that determines children's prosocial inclinations. Eisenberg and Mussen (1989) conclude by saying, "These results clearly indicate that development of children's prosocial behavior tendencies is regulated by *patterns* of parent behavior, rather than single dimensions like warmth or control" (p. 81).

ASSESSING CHILDREN'S PROSOCIAL BEHAVIOR IN THE CLASSROOM

What prosocial behaviors should you expect from children 3 to 5 years of age who come to your classroom from such diverse families, cultures, and child-rearing prac-

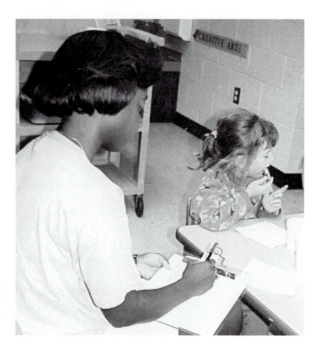

The most effective way to learn how preschool children behave is to step back from your duties as teacher and become an observer.

tices? The answer is obvious. Children's behavior will be as different as the children themselves. Some will happily search out new friends to play with. Some will sulk in a corner. Others will cooperate with the teacher's suggestions. But many may not even listen. A few may share their toys with another child. But many will resist giving up any play material and may even try to take someone else's. Some will pick up toys without being asked. Others will run and hide when the teacher announces cleanup time.

Congratulations! You have hit the jackpot once again: a wonderful new mix of children just waiting for you to get to know them and to give your best to help them develop cognitively, emotionally, physically, creatively, and, of course, prosocially. How will you do it?

Observing Prosocial Behaviors

The most effective way to learn to know preschool children in the classroom is to step back from your duties as teacher and become an observer. Although you may also talk with children, work with them, and play with them, your closeness may interfere with their natural interactions with others. That interaction is what you need to find out about: how they relate to others, how they get along with others, and how they deal with others in stressful situations. Child observation is the key. As Seefeldt (1990) notes:

Young children reveal themselves through their behaviors. Unlike older children and adults, the young are incapable of hiding their feelings, ideas, or emotions with socially approved behaviors, so observing them often yields accurate information. (p. 313)

Name_____   Age_____

1. *Self-Esteem: Feeling Good about Self*

_____Smiles, seems happy much of time

_____Is not afraid of people or things

_____Stands up for own rights

2. *Self-Control: Developing Control over Own Behavior*

_____Abides by established limits most of the time

_____Uses classroom self-regulating devices

_____Expresses strong feelings in words rather than actions

3. *Other-Esteem: Feeling Good about Other Children*

_____Gets along with other children

_____Shows concern for another child in distress

_____Can tell how another child feels

4. *Friendliness: Making Friends among Other Children*

_____Seeks other children to play with

_____Makes friends with other children

_____Plays with others in congenial manner

5. *Generosity: Giving and Sharing Things with Others*

_____Shares toys and materials with other children

_____Takes turns without a fuss

_____Gives something (a toy, a turn) to another child

6. *Cooperation: Doing Things with Others*

_____Engages in cooperative play in group activity

_____Allows others to enter ongoing play without a struggle

_____Complies with adult requests

7. *Helpfulness: Doing Things for the Common Good*

_____Picks up and puts away toys and materials

_____Helps another do a task

_____Takes on classroom chores willingly

8. *Respect: Treating People and Materials Considerately*

_____Uses toys/materials in constructive manner

_____Treats other people's materials with respect

_____Listens and responds to adults with consideration

Figure 2-1   Child Prosocial Behavior Checklist

Note: The publisher grants permission to reproduce this checklist for evaluation and record keeping.

To assist you in learning where a child stands in her prosocial development, a *Child Prosocial Behavior Checklist* has been developed containing eight behavioral components for your observation (see Figure 2-1). Each component includes three positive statements of representative behavior. Although other prosocial behaviors might be observable under each component, the three included in this checklist are important starting points in your assessment of the children and your helping them learn to get along with others in the classroom.

The statements look for positive rather than negative behaviors because that is the focus of this text: to help children learn appropriate behaviors. Prosocial guidance calls for this positive approach in helping children learn how to behave. Looking for inappropriate behaviors often gives teachers a biased view of a child and may color their responses to the child's actions.

How, then, do you record inappropriate actions on this checklist, you may wonder? If a child refuses to share a toy, for example, the observer simply leaves the statement blank under item 5, "Generosity: _____Shares toys and materials with other children." An unchecked statement is not negative. It simply means that you have not seen the child exhibiting the behavior. Through several observations, you and the staff may determine that learning to share is indeed a "need" for this child; thus, your activities with her can focus on sharing.

The checklist begins with three components relating to the child's feelings about himself, his behavior, and his feelings about others. Five important prosocial behaviors follow. Let's look at each component.

■ Self-Esteem: Feeling Good About Self

For children to feel good about others, to work and play in harmony with them, children need to feel good about themselves. *Self-esteem* thus refers to a child's sense of self-worth, which she develops over time through interactions with the people and things around her. It includes her own view of herself and what she thinks about her looks, her actions, her abilities, and how other people treat her. You do not need X-ray vision to tell how she may feel. Certain child's behaviors are keys to her self-esteem.

Take smiles, for instance. Children's emotions tend to be written on their faces. A smile indicates the feeling of happiness or joy. Although children surely smile at pleasant events outside themselves, those who do not feel good about themselves inside smile less often or not at all. Finding smiling faces during your observations is one indication that the youngsters feel good about themselves.

As you observe individual children, you can also note which ones seem excited when new people appear or new activities or materials are introduced and which ones seem more timid or insecure. Another indication of self-esteem concerns taking a stand when challenged by other children regarding activities or space, or simply not allowing themselves to be pushed around.

Self-regulating devices are tags, signs, hooks, necklaces, or tickets that give children access to one of the classroom learning centers.

■ Self-Control: Developing Control over Own Behavior

Children who feel good about themselves are usually the ones who follow directions and try to abide by established limits. These limits should be simple and understandable to the children, not a long list of do's and don'ts that make little sense. Most teachers help the children keep three limits in mind: they must not hurt themselves (e.g., follow safety rules), hurt other children, or damage materials. In any case, staff members will step in to enforce these limits in a firm but matter-of-fact way. But as children develop control over their own behavior, they soon find it possible to keep within these limits on their own. Your observations will tell you who these children are.

Self-regulating devices are tags, signs, hooks, necklaces, or tickets that give children access to one of the classroom learning centers. Each classroom has its own system for giving children independent choices during the free-play or work-play period. Left on their own, youngsters may crowd into a block center meant for no more than six builders or surround a water play table meant for four. Teachers who want children to make their own independent choices provide a means for children to see how many players each center can support and how they can choose to enter the centers.

At first you may not check the item "Expresses strong feelings in words rather than actions" for many children. Upset or angry young children often lash out at others. Teachers need to help them learn to control themselves by putting their feelings in words: "Tell him how you feel, Anthony. Don't hit him." Eventually the children who have caught on to this technique will be telling others what to do: "Tell her—don't hit her."

■ Other-Esteem: Feeling Good About Other Children

You will find that no matter how self-centered your preschoolers are, many have good feelings about their peers. Interacting peacefully with the other children and showing concern for a child in distress are sure signs of their empathy. The youngster may come to the side of a child who has been hurt or try to help the child. Some children may even report to the teacher that another child is sick.

In cases of interpersonal conflict between two children, you may be asking each how the other child feels. Children as young as 3 and even 2 years old are aware of how others feel. Their principal difficulty may be verbalizing these emotions. You can help by having a child look at another child's face and then asking whether his face tells you how he feels. Your observations and interactions with the youngsters can help you decide whether to check off this item.

■ Friendliness: Making Friends Among Other Children

Friendliness may be the easiest checklist component for you to recognize and check off. Many children seek out others to play with, and some even choose a particular friend for their activities. Most friendships among preschoolers are fleeting at best, which is the way it should be. But some friendships seem more like those of older children who will only participate in activities that the other child does. It is not helpful to make a fuss over such friendships, to say aloud in front of others, "Oh, there's Angela with Kendra again. They do everything together. Angela won't even look at a book unless Kendra does."

Friendship is, of course, a personal choice that needs to be honored. You would hope that all children will have the chance to interact with all the others. Exclusive friendships are difficult to maintain at this age and need not be encouraged. As you check off this item, keep in mind how to involve children with others who do not seem to play with anyone and how to expand the friendships of those who only play with each other.

■ Generosity: Giving and Sharing Things with Others

As pointed out in Chapter 1, most preschool conflicts involve squabbles over toys and equipment. We understand that such behavior is normal for children of this age. Children who refuse to share a toy or fight over a turn are not being bad. They are being egocentric. This self-centeredness is part of their natural inheritance as human beings, designed to help them as infants survive in their early years. Now it is time for them to broaden their spectrum to include those around them. No longer can they regard everything that happens from their own point of view. No longer can they consider the toys and equipment in the classroom as theirs alone.

But *generosity* is a learned prosocial behavior. It is up to you and the classroom staff to discover through your observations which children have learned how to share and take turns and which ones need help learning this behavior. You will have plenty of assistance in your endeavors as other children point out to the so-called "selfish" child that the toys are for everyone and he has to share and take turns.

Giving something to another child is an indication that a youngster has taken yet another step up the prosocial learning ladder. This action must, of course, be spontaneous for it to count as prosocial. Complying with a teacher's request or demand to give someone their toy is not the same.

■ Cooperation: Doing Things with Others

Cooperative play is the highest level of preschool children's social play as categorized by Mildred Parten in 1932. Her six behavior categories are still considered valid descriptions of children's social skill levels:

1. *Unoccupied behavior:* The child does not participate in the play around him. He stays in one spot, follows the teacher or wanders around.
2. *Onlooker behavior:* The child spends much time watching what other children are doing and may even talk to them, but he does not join or interact with them physically.
3. *Solitary independent play:* The child engages in play activities, but he plays on his own and not with others or with their toys or materials.
4. *Parallel play:* The child plays independently, but he plays next to other children and often uses their toys or materials.
5. *Associative play:* The child plays with other children using the same materials and even talking with them, but he acts on his own and does not subordinate his interests to those of the group.
6. *Cooperative play:* The child plays in a group that has organized itself to do a particular thing, and whose members have taken on different roles. (pp. 248–251)

These levels of social play are closely related to the age, maturity, and experience of the children. You will no doubt witness all six levels of play from time to time within your group of preschoolers. You may also see the youngest and least mature children progress from unoccupied and onlooker behavior, right through solitary play to parallel play, as they become acclimated to the children and materials around them.

Children learn from one another, and those who have been holding back may eventually come to participate in the intriguing cooperative play going on in the dramatic play center where everyone spontaneously chooses roles and acts out pretend episodes together. If you see them pretending to be mother or father or big brother or sister with the others, you can check off this cooperative play item.

Allowing someone to enter an ongoing play group is often more difficult for a child than joining one herself. Once play has started, the players may try to protect their space and activity by keeping others out. It is not up to you to force the issue. Children should be in charge of their play as long as it does not get out of hand.

Group-entry struggles are learning experiences that children need to resolve on the their own whenever possible.

The final cooperation item, "complies with adult requests," is one most preschoolers are familiar with. Adults at home expect their youngsters to do what they are asked, and most children's positive responses carry over into the classroom. Children who refuse adult requests may be using this behavior as an attention-getting ploy. Your observations will make you aware of children's cooperation with both their peers and the classroom adults.

■ Helpfulness: Doing Things for the Common Good

At least once or twice a day teachers call for cleanup of toys, blocks, and other materials that children have taken off the shelves and scattered around the learning centers during the work and play periods. Children soon learn they are responsible to help pick up in the area where they have been playing. Most are agreeable and join in without a problem. Some begin cleanup rather half-heartedly and then drift away. A few escape to another area altogether and try to avoid doing any picking up at all. Your observations will help you recognize who does what during this important transition time.

Most children seem more willing to help another child do a task than they are to pick up toys. Some children recognize right away that Curtis cannot move the large box across the room by himself and join in without being asked. Friends often work together to complete a difficult job. When teachers need help to complete a task, most children volunteer willingly.

Children also enjoy the responsibility of classroom chores if they are presented as interesting and important tasks. A sign-up chart or hookboard with name tags tells who is responsible for watering the plants, feeding the fish, giving water to the guinea pig, setting the lunch tables, getting out cots for nap, and performing other daily tasks. When teams of two children together choose a chore, completing the work is more like a game than a job. Your observations can help you determine what children demonstrate helpfulness in the classroom.

■ Respect: Treating People and Materials Considerately

One of the limits stressed by most teachers is for children to treat their play materials with respect and not damage them. Most children stay within such limits much of the time. Some, however, express their exuberance in the way they use materials: pounding crayons on their papers, sweeping blocks off shelves in crashing heaps, or tossing dress-up clothes on the floor and walking on them. A few children express their aggressive feelings through materials by throwing them, knocking them over, or banging them against things. Your observations will help you determine who uses toys in constructive ways and who does not.

Egocentric children often do not recognize the products of others as something they must not damage. They are more concerned with themselves and their products than those of others. This is the normal state of affairs for many preschool children.

They have not yet learned to recognize that other children have the same rights and feelings as they do. Block buildings, paintings, play-dough constructions, completed puzzles, and toy figure villages are creations important to their makers. In the bustle of group activities they can easily be damaged if others are not aware and concerned about their peers' products. Respect for other's rights, property, and creations is a prosocial act that children need to learn if they do not possess such awareness.

Listening is also an act of respect. Some children have learned from previous experiences to tune out adults. Now it is important for them to listen to the adults in the classroom and make appropriate responses. Your observations will help you determine who is able to act in this manner and in all of the prosocial behaviors on the checklist.

USING OBSERVATIONAL DATA

As you gather observational data to determine the prosocial behaviors being demonstrated by the children, be sure that more than one classroom staff member participates in observing and recording on the Child Prosocial Behavior Checklist for each child. Everyone sees children from different perspectives, so it is important to include as much information as possible for each child being observed. Doing the observations over time also helps accumulate a more complete impression of each youngster.

Interpreting this checklist information and applying it in the classroom are the next important steps in observing and recording. But before you begin, you need to understand that children ages 3 through 5 cannot be expected to demonstrate all of the behaviors. In fact, they may not exhibit many of them at all when they first enter the classroom. They are at the very beginning stages of learning to get along with others. For many children this may be their first group experience outside the home. Thus you must be especially careful not to label children based on the checklist results.

Children with many blanks on the checklist are not "bad." Children with most of the items checked off are not "good." Such labels are inappropriate judgments on the part of early childhood professionals. Instead, all of the children are worthy human beings in the process of developing their social skills. Some are further advanced than others in those skills. Your observations and recordings will show you this. This information can then point the way to curriculum planning for individuals and the total group.

Planning for the Group

Your first use of the data should be directed toward group planning. What do all of these completed checklists show you about your group? To collate the results, divide a paper into eight columns labeled for each of the eight components: Self-Esteem, Self-Control, Other-Esteem, Friendliness, Generosity, Cooperation, Helpfulness, and Respect. Go through each checklist, ignoring the child's name but recording a tally mark for each of the items checked under each component. This will give you an overall look at prosocial behaviors in your classroom.

What were your results? Did you find that many children demonstrated self-esteem, friendliness, cooperation, and helpfulness? Although every group is different, for many classes these are particular behaviors often observed at the beginning of the year. As you review components with fewer checkmarks, you can begin to develop overall plans for the group. Self-control, for instance, may be an area where many children need more experience and help. Chapter 6, "Using Positive Intervention to Help Children Manage Their Own Behavior," gives helpful suggestions for improving children's self-control. Other-esteem is another area children may not display. Ideas and activities from Chapter 9, "Using Other-Esteem Conflict Conversion," can be incorporated into your plans for the class.

Planning for the Individual

Prosocial behavior is only one of the aspects of child development you need to learn about in an individual. Cognitive, emotional, language, physical, and creative development are also important. As you observe and record children's behavior and accomplishments in all of these areas, you will be able to include individual plans for a child within your overall group plans.

For example, if one or more children seem to have trouble sharing materials, you may want to read them a children's picture book on sharing such as *Just Not the Same* (Lacoe, 1992) or plan a sharing activity for them with a new toy you bring in.

An individual child's Prosocial Behavior Checklist can be used with other observational data to plan individual activities based on the child's strengths and areas needing improvement. As the year progresses, new observations can be recorded on the same checklist in a different color ink, and new activities for the child can be included in group plans. If several children have the same prosocial behavior needs, set up a small-group activity and encourage those children to participate in it.

You don't need to point out to a child that she needs help learning to cooperate. This, after all, is a put-down. Be sure your activities are positive in nature and appropriate for all the children. Those with special needs can be encouraged in a sensitive manner to join in with the others, without mentioning their areas needing strengthening.

The chapters to follow describe numerous ideas and activities for helping children develop the prosocial behaviors they were born with. Your knowledge of your children's particular behaviors gives you the basis for planning an exciting curriculum and guiding youngsters toward success in learning to get along with others.

REFERENCES

Eisenberg, N., & Mussen, P. H. (1989). *The roots of prosocial behavior in children.* New York: Cambridge University Press.

Greenspan, S. I. (1997). *The growth of the mind and the endangered origins of intelligence.* Reading, MA: Addison-Wesley.

Honig, A. S., & Wittmer, D. S. (1996). Helping children become more prosocial: Ideas for classrooms, families, schools, and communities. *Young Children, 51*(2), 62–75.

Lacoe, A. (1992). *Just not the same.* Boston: Houghton Mifflin.

Newberger, J. J. (1997). New brain development research: A wonderful window of opportunity to build public support for early childhood education! *Young Children, 52*(4), 4–9.

Parten, M. B. (1932). Social participation among preschool children. *Journal of Abnormal and Social Psychology, 27,* 243–369.

Seefeldt, C. (1990). Assessing young children. In C. Seefeldt (Ed.), *Continuing issues in early childhood education* (pp. 311–330). Upper Saddle River, NJ: Merrill/Prentice Hall.

Williams, N. F. (1997). Brain development in young children. *Children Our Concern, 22*(1), 26–27.

SUGGESTED READINGS

Beaty, J. J. (1998). *Observing development of the young child* (4th ed.). Upper Saddle River, NJ: Merrill/Prentice Hall.

Damon, W. (1988). *The moral child: Nurturing children's natural moral growth.* New York: Free Press.

Edwards, C. P. (1986). *Promoting social and moral development in young children.* New York: Teachers College Press.

Eisenberg, N. (1992). *The caring child.* Cambridge, MA: Harvard University Press.

Hatch, J. A. (1994). Observing and understanding children's social interactions: An impression management perspective. *Dimensions of Early Childhood, 23*(1), 21–25.

Lawhon, T. (1997). Encouraging friendships among children. *Childhood Education, 73*(4), 228–231.

Wittmer, D. S., & Honig, A. S. (1994). Encouraging positive social development in young children. *Young Children, 49*(5), 4–12.

VIDEOTAPES

Early Childhood Professional Development Network, with J. J. Beaty. (Producers). (1997). *Take a closer look: A field guide to child observation.* (Available from ECPDN, P.O. Box 5574, Columbia, SC 29205-5574)

LEARNING ACTIVITIES

1. Make a record of prosocial behaviors you have witnessed among the preschool children you work with. Could any of these behaviors have been influenced by biological factors in the child's life? On what reasoning do you base your reply?

2. Describe the cultures of the children who display prosocial behavior in your program. What cultural influences could have affected these children's actions?

3. Use the Child Prosocial Behavior Checklist to observe and record information about two different children in your group. Make more than one observation.

4. Interpret the checklist results for each of the two children. What correlation do you see between their levels of social play and their prosocial behavior?

5. Based on the checklist results of these two children, what plans might you make for the group and for these two individuals to help them improve their prosocial behavior?

CHAPTER 3

Teachers and Prosocial Guidance

PROSOCIAL BEHAVIOR OF TEACHERS

Sometimes we forget that the way we treat children becomes the way they behave toward others. If we want children to be friendly, generous, cooperative, helpful, and respectful, then we as teachers must behave toward them in this way. Current research agrees:

> There is consistent evidence that how teachers interact with children matters to their development. Teachers who are sensitive to children's needs and who engage, encourage, and verbally communicate with them appear to be nurturing more optimal cognitive, language, and socioemotional development. (Kontos & Wilcox-Herzog, 1997, p. 11)

How, then, should you go about behaving that will send positive messages to the children in your program? Using the Child Prosocial Behavior Checklist as an outline, try applying each of its eight components to yourself.

Self-Esteem

How do you feel about yourself? It is important that you consider this first component seriously. Are you happy with yourself? Do you show it to the children by smiling and acting in a pleasant or enthusiastic manner? If you do not feel good about yourself as a person, then you may have an especially difficult time treating the children positively. You may not be able to sustain good relationships with all the youngsters over time, especially those with "challenging" behavior.

Try looking at yourself in a mirror and spending some moments considering what you think about yourself as a person and as a preschool teacher. Jot down some of your qualities that you think are the most positive. Did you include any of the following?

My Positive Qualities
I love working with young children.
I do not get upset easily.
I have a sense of humor.
I have a lot of patience.

You should feel good about yourself if these qualities are part of your makeup. It is important that you do possess some of these traits. But somehow a list like this may not be enough to make you feel better. Deep down you may have a nagging feeling of not being worthy, of not having a very strong positive self-concept. The reasons for these feelings may have come from being put down by other people in your life, from your temperament, or even from your own early childhood experiences.

Before you can give freely of yourself in the very demanding job of teaching preschool children on a daily basis, you need to find a way to reverse or eliminate these feelings. Some early childhood teachers, assistants, and student teachers have helped turn around their unfavorable feelings by making a second list of qualities they would like to possess but think they don't. Then they try working on the items one at a time to improve themselves and change their outlook. Would any of the following items be found on your second list?

Qualities I Would Like to Possess
    Better looks
    Better control over my temper
    Confidence that I am doing my job correctly
    Ability to handle out-of-control children more confidently

Don't make your list too long or difficult. Four items like this is a good start. You can work on one or more at a time until you accomplish it. Yes, you can even change your looks more easily than you suspected. Change your hair style or hair color to something you've always wanted. Dress in a more comfortable, pleasing manner—a different, more cheerful color or a new style. Children will soon pick up on these differences and be complimenting you.

To gain confidence about doing your job correctly, try making a self-assessment using a checklist. The Teacher Prosocial Guidance Checklist at the end of this chapter can help you determine how you are carrying out this type of guidance with the chil-

You understand what self-control means for a child. But how does it apply to a teacher? Can you remain calm when things get out of control for a child?

Talk softly, wait patiently, whisper something humorous until both of you feel better.

dren. Even if you cannot check all of the items, it will give you new ideas to put into practice and help you realize how much you are already accomplishing.

How to help out-of-control children get in control is a main focus of this book. Keep reading and trying out the learning activities at the ends of the chapters. Because there is no "best way" to work with every child who has lost control, you may need to experiment with some of the suggestions given to see what works best for you and the child in a particular situation.

Self-Control

Next on the checklist comes self-control. You understand what that means for young children, but how does it apply to a teacher, you may wonder? Do you ever get angry in the classroom? What do you do then? Talk loudly? Talk harshly? Scold a child? These are signs you are not in control.

Think about "controlling your temper," as mentioned in the qualities list. Try to analyze what sets it off. If you can pinpoint the trigger, you can often prevent an emotional outburst by changing the conditions that cause it. Do you lose your temper more often when you are tired? Then get more rest.

Keep your classroom role more low-key when you are feeling tired. Then things may not bother you as much. If the noise in the classroom gets too much for you to bear, you might try putting up some colorful sound-absorbing hangings; putting down fluffy carpets to soak up more sound; turning off the tape recorder. Then have everyone sit down right where they are and think of something quiet. Shhhhh! Go around to each one and have them whisper it to you. Whisper some funny things yourself, or read a humorous book like *A Porcupine Named Fluffy* (Lester, 1986). Are you feeling better yet? The children are!

Other-Esteem

How do you feel about each of the children in your program? Positive feelings should prevail. If you find yourself feeling negative about a child who continually "misbehaves," look for good things about him or her. Write down something that you like about everyone. Then tell them about it. You can always find something to compliment a child about. One teacher made a point of showering compliments on "behaviorally challenging" children right from the beginning of school, even if all she could find to say was "I love the way you're *breathing*" (McCloskey, 1996, p. 15). Such positive attention made a real difference in their behavior.

Do you esteem children from a different racial, cultural, or economic background from your own? Such feelings come across to children quite readily. They quickly pick up facial expressions, body language, and being included or ignored. How often do you speak to children from a different background or choose them to participate in an activity? Do you listen to what they have to tell you or turn your attention to someone more like yourself? Nonverbal cues like these tell children what you think of them. Ramsey (1987) tells about prejudice being subtle as well as overt:

> Prejudice clearly is associated with explicit and dramatic racism; yet it also is present when we disparage another person's taste in dress, food, or music or when we dismiss children as "unlikable" because they have a different cultural style of interaction or a background of neglect that makes it hard for us to relate to them. (p. 41)

One effective way to get to know the children better is to have a brief conversation with each child every day. Talk about something you like about what you see them doing, something they are wearing, the way they are smiling or acting. Listen to what they have to say in return. Keep a list of children handy but inconspicuous, and check it off as you progress around the class during the day as children are busy in learning centers, on the playground, at lunch, or getting ready for nap. Then you won't miss anyone.

Take a photo of each child and display it in a prominent place in the classroom. Make duplicate photos for children to paste in a journal or scrapbook they are compiling about themselves. Spend time every week to look at the book with every child. Listen to what they have to tell you about themselves, and respond with enthusiasm.

Such activities help you develop esteem for every child in the program, as they too feel your affection for them.

Friendliness

Conversing with each child every day is an excellent way to show your friendliness toward everyone. Greeting each child as he or she arrives in the morning and saying "See you tomorrow" when they leave at the end of the day also convey this message. Showing enthusiasm for the children's activities and participating briefly yourself as children work and play together are other friendly gestures. But staff members must be careful not to pick out one child as their special friend.

The other youngsters are soon aware of this situation and may wonder why the teacher chose to befriend that child and not them. By lavishing affection on a particular child, the teacher is using a subtle form of manipulation—perhaps without even knowing it—to win the child's affection. Creating a teacher's pet always involves the problem of the unspoken messages you are delivering to the other children: (1) that they are not as good as the chosen one; (2) that if they act like the chosen child, the teacher may choose them, too; (3) that when this does not happen, they feel even worse about themselves. It is best to act friendly toward all the children, but be careful about developing special friendships.

Generosity

How much of your time do you give or share with the children? As a preschool teacher, you might feel that most of your time is devoted to them. This is not necessarily the case. Research about how frequently preschool teachers interact with children shows just the opposite. Although teachers were often close to children in university preschool classrooms, one study showed that teachers interacted with the nearby children only 18% of the time (Kontos & Wilcox-Herzog, 1997, p.4). A *Life in Preschool* study by Layzer, Goodson, and Moss (1993) showed that 31% of the children in Head Start, child care, and preschool classrooms received no individual attention during the researchers' observations, and in 12% of those classrooms more than half of the children received no individual attention at all.

What draws teachers to give time to certain children? Kontos and Wilcox-Herzog (1997) speculate that

> teachers interact more frequently with children who seek adult contact, whose behavior requires frequent intervention, who spend more time in activities that require adult assistance, and who are personally more appealing to the individual teacher. (p. 5)

Positive teacher interactions such as reading a book, giving a hug, tying a shoe, giving a compliment, or posing a question about a child's activity helped youngsters in their social, cognitive, and language development. "Preschool children in center-based care were more competent in their peer interactions when they had more frequent responsive involvement with their teachers" (Kontos & Wilcox-Herzog, 1997,

p. 11). These significant findings make prosocial guidance by teachers more important than ever in promoting children's growth and development.

What do teachers do when they are not giving their attention to individual children, you may wonder? Setting up activities, observing children, talking with other staff members, or working with a small group or the total class are common activities they engage in. But it is their positive interactions with individuals that make the difference in children's behavior. As Kontos and Wilcox-Herzog (1997) conclude, "when teachers are attentive and encouraging to children, children exhibit less stress" (p. 11).

Thus, *generosity* in teacher behavior means giving of yourself and your time to individuals. It is not as easy as it sounds when you consider how many more children there are than teachers in a classroom. Yet having more than one adult staff member makes it possible for one of the teachers to spend time with individuals while the other(s) works with the group. Keep a list of the children on top of a room divider and check off each one you or another staff member spend individual time with. If you miss any, be sure to interact with them the next day.

Do you recognize a pattern in which children are interacted with most and least? If this is the case, all of the staff members can make it a point to balance their interactions. Then be alert to changes in the children, the classroom atmosphere, and yourselves after you have begun this practice. Are things going more smoothly for everyone? Do you feel better about your teaching?

Cooperation

How can a classroom teacher cooperate with a child, you may wonder? One way is to comply with a child's request if it is appropriate. Some children, of course, spend more time than necessary trying to get the teacher to do something for them that is better done by themselves. If this is the case, you can help them get started: for instance, putting on a jacket, zipping it up, or tying their shoes. If such children continue asking for favors day after day, it may be a sign they desperately need adult attention. Indulge them when you can. But also tell them when you need to respond to the other children. Ask them what they would like to do by themselves, and help them get started. Pairing them with a partner also helps.

A child will often approach a teacher to read a book. This is a request that should be honored if at all possible. Reading to individuals has long been considered one of the most important influences on children's success in learning to read. Make a note of who asks you to read to them. Be sure you comply whenever possible. For individuals who never ask, you or another staff member should offer to read to those children, too.

When children ask you to join their dramatic play or block building, try to cooperate at least for a while. Your presence as a player gives a whole new flavor to the experience, making the children feel that you recognize them and their activities as important enough to take time with them. But be sure you interact as a follower of the children and not as a director of the play. When the time is right, you can extract yourself by thanking the children for letting you join them but adding that now you have your own work to do.

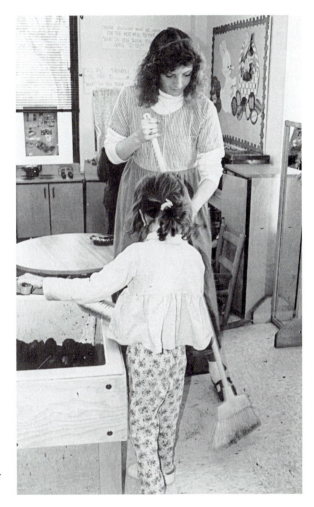

Cleanup goes so much faster
when the teacher joins in.

Helpfulness

We expect children to help us whenever we ask them, but how does this prosocial behavior apply to teachers? Look around the classroom and you will see instances where children may need your help. For example, is the block center completely covered with all the blocks from the shelves during cleanup time? Give the cleaners a helping hand. It may be too much to expect them to accomplish the cleanup alone. Help them organize block pickup into a game, perhaps using a large block as a bulldozer to push the other blocks over to the shelves. Or treat the shelves as hungry animals that need to be fed. You can join in the feeding by stacking blocks on the shelves yourself. Cleanup goes so much faster when the teacher joins in. Go around the room to the various learning centers just to get the cleanup started. You can make it fun and not a chore.

When children are struggling to make something work, be careful about helping unless they ask for it. Preschoolers need to do as much as they can on their own, trying out new skills and solving their own problems. Use your judgment about individuals and their needs before joining in. Some puzzle makers, for example, will stay with the puzzle forever, it seems, until they find a way to complete it. Others give up almost before they get started. You can help such a child by sitting next to her and handing her a piece to try. If she can't fit it anywhere, hand her another piece and offer suggestions about how to turn it until it fits. Stay with her until she finishes. As with cleanup, your help may be best appreciated just by being there, watching, or cheering her on.

Respect

You expect the children to show respect toward you. But how do you model this prosocial behavior toward the children? Respect entails treating others with consideration, speaking to them as if they matter and not speaking down to them, listening to them when they speak to you, not interrupting what they are doing or saying, treating their products as something important, asking for permission to add to or change something they have done, and asking their opinions on classroom matters. You also show respect when you refrain from talking about children to their parents when they are present. All children are worthy human beings who will act toward us in the same way that we act toward them. As McCloskey (1996) notes:

> Respect must be a two-way street. Teachers do deserve respect; however, so do children. Rules must be designed so that both you and your children can abide by them. Above all, mutual respect should prevail in all situations. When we are respected, we usually live up to the regard that another places upon us. (p. 15)

Don't forget to thank children for helping, cooperating, sharing, taking turns, and respecting one another and the materials. Giving such thanks to children is a respectful and necessary action for us to perform if we want them to learn to thank others and treat them well.

TEACHERS AS MODELS OF PROSOCIAL BEHAVIOR

Young children are perceptive observers of all that goes on around them. They are especially attentive to the teachers, teacher assistants, volunteers, and student teachers they meet in early childhood programs. The prosocial behaviors that these adults demonstrate as they interact with the youngsters are powerful cues as to how the children themselves should behave.

Social scientists call this behavior *social modeling* and describe it as being "the process of producing a model of social behavior that enables another to learn by observation and imitation" (Cartledge & Milburn, 1995, p. 75). An individual observes how a significant person in his or her life is behaving and imitates that behavior under similar conditions. Social modeling, in fact, is the principal method for teaching young children how to behave. When we say that parents are their children's first and most important teachers, we are not referring to formal instruction but to their informal social modeling that their children observe and imitate.

Children observe just as carefully their teachers' actions and reactions to people and situations. Do teachers show concern immediately for a child who is crying? Do they maintain control over their own emotions when a child has lost control? Do they speak firmly, not harshly, to a child who has hit someone? Do they allow children to resolve their own conflicts whenever possible? Do they help during pickup? Do they listen respectfully to parents and respond helpfully? Are they consistent in their prosocial behaviors, or do they employ them only occasionally?

If you want children to learn self-control, a concern for others, how to play with others, how to share and take turns, how to cooperate in group play, how to help with classroom tasks, and how to treat people and materials with respect, then you must demonstrate these behaviors yourself. You must display them again and again whenever the occasion arises. They must become a natural part of your social behavior. But there is one more aspect to modeling behavior that Eisenberg (1992) feels is important: nurturant modeling.

Nurturant Modeling

Teachers clearly serve as models of prosocial behavior; moreover, they are more frequently imitated by children if they are nurturant. In one study, nurturant adults who took part in preschool classes and who modeled prosocial behaviors had a relatively enduring influence on children's own prosocial behavior. In contrast, children did not model the prosocial behavior of cold, aloof adults in the classroom. (Eisenberg, 1992, p. 113)

What does it mean to be nurturant? It means you are warm, caring, understanding, and helpful. You enjoy having children around you and go out of your way to show how much you care for them. You express your positive feelings toward the children in your care through smiles, friendly touches, happy talk, and considerate listening. Children like you because you like them. They will show it by trying to behave like you do.

Is this how you truly feel about young children? Are you able to show your enthusiasm and respond to theirs? It is important to have nurturing teachers in preschool programs. If you feel uncomfortable around children of this age, or if you feel awkward expressing your emotions openly to the children, you may need to reconsider your working at the preschool level. Displaying open enthusiasm for your work and warm affection for the children should be top priorities for every person entering this field.

TEACHERS AS MIRRORS OF CHILDREN'S EMOTIONS

Helping children express a wide range of emotions by "mirroring" how children feel is a seldom discussed aspect of teacher behavior that can readily support children's prosocial development. When we look in a mirror, we see ourselves looking back at us. A preschool teacher can serve as that mirror for children's expression of their own feelings.

What purpose would that serve? It is important that children be allowed and encouraged to express a wide range of emotions. They must feel free to reveal loneliness, sadness, worry, grief, fear, and anger—and also joy, happiness, excitement, and enthusiasm. Teachers give permission for this expression when they mirror those emotions themselves. When they see a child displaying a worried expression, they can look worried themselves, at the same time identifying the emotion and empathizing with the child about it. "You look worried today, Jamie. Are you still concerned about your mother in the hospital?"

Our society tends to downplay the expression of emotions. Many adults have learned since childhood that it is bad to show anger, for example. Yet preschool children must be allowed to express and work through negative feelings to gain control over them. They should not be criticized for being angry but instead helped to work through the feeling.

When you feel anger or exasperation over a child's behavior of knocking down everyone's block buildings, for example, let it show on your face, but then be sure to talk to the child about it when things have cooled down. Ask the child whether he saw what your face looked like. Could he tell how you felt about his actions? Ask him what he was feeling when he displayed the behavior. What could he do to express this feeling without knocking down other children's buildings?

A teacher's mirroring of such emotions and then talking about them helps a child understand that he is not bad for displaying anger. It happens to everyone, even the teacher. But the teacher did not shout or knock down buildings—she talked about it. As Koplow (1996) advises:

> Instead of trying to minimize the expression of negative affects in the classroom, teachers might use naturally occurring expressions of affect to help children become better attuned to affects, to differentiate among them, and to develop strategies for affect regulation when necessary. (p. 25)

Accepting Strong Emotions

When a child is having a tantrum, for example, the teacher can talk to the other children calmly about feelings, asking how they think the child is feeling and whether they ever felt like that. This helps children know that it is all right and not terrible to feel so upset, that the teacher accepts their feelings.

Reading a book about feelings can also help children release some of their own discomfort about the tantrum child who may be crying or even screaming in the corner. *I Was So Mad!* (Simon, 1974) tells about a girl and then a boy who become upset over losing a kite, tying a shoe, having to pick up their room, having to play an unwanted role in dramatic play, having their block building knocked down, and finally how their mother and father handle it when they themselves get mad.

When children realize that the adults in the classroom accept their strong emotions, they may display them more freely. The mirroring of children's emotions on the faces and in the postures of the teachers thus helps youngsters recognize this acceptance. For "at-risk" preschool children (i.e., children who have been abused or neglected), it is essential to their development that their negative emotions be accepted in this nonverbal manner. As Koplow (1996) notes:

> At-risk children need to experience their affective expressions as understood and valued before they will be able to take in affective information from others. Without mastering this fundamental form of communication, children may have difficulty moving toward more sophisticated forms of communication and learning. (p. 17)

Reading Nonverbal Emotional Messages

Mirroring of emotions by the teacher needs to be encouraged as a form of nonverbal communication essential for children's further growth and development. Koplow (1996) believes that if a preschool child lacks the ability to project and read emotional messages, she will also lack the necessary tools for successful peer interaction. She may read another child's expression wrong or project an inaccurate expression of her own emotions.

For you to mirror children's emotions successfully, you will first need to be aware of what the expressions on children's faces really look like. Keep alert to emotional experiences in the classroom when someone is excited, sad, or upset. Attune yourself and the children to what certain emotions look like. Display posters of people smiling, frowning, crying, and showing anger. Talk about feelings and what they look like. Play games about feelings. For example, show children your frowning face and ask them to guess how you feel. Then show them a smiling face. Let them make a face, and you try to guess what it means. Bring in hand or pocket mirrors and have children make faces in them.

But when children display real emotions, your reflection needs to be genuine as well. Instead of pretending to feel as children do, you should truly empathize with them. Don't be afraid to show your own emotions, both negative and positive. Show enthusiasm if that's the way you feel. Show anger when you are upset. As Koplow (1996) points out:

> It is impossible for classroom adults to serve as healthy models if they are falsely cheerful, speak to the children in an unnatural or forced tone of voice, offer empty compliments, or interact with children in an effusive and undifferentiated manner. (p. 24)

Identifying and Naming Emotions

It is also important for children to be able to identify and name emotions as they feel them and see them on the faces and in the gestures of others around them. One way for them to learn what emotions look like and feel like is to read picture books with emotional themes and then look closely at the illustrations. Plan to read at least one book a week about children and their feelings to individuals and small groups. Then discuss what your listeners think about the book characters and their feelings. Here are some appropriate titles:

Don't Worry, I'll Find You, A. G. Hines (New York: Dutton, 1986) (fear, happiness)
Feelings, Aliki (New York: Mulberry, 1984) (excited, happy, angry, proud, jealous, sad, appreciation, bored, afraid, lonely, shy, quiet, impatient)

Feelings, J. B. Murphy (Windsor, Ontario: Black Moss Press, 1985) (happy, proud, frustrated, excited, quiet, noisy, fat, scared, mad, sad, surprised, clean, sleepy)

Fun Is a Feeling, C. M. Curtis (Bellevue, WA: Illumination Arts, 1992) (joy, happiness)

The Good-Bye Book, J. Viorst (New York: Macmillan, 1988) (upset, angry, sick, mad, sad, happy)

How Do I Feel? N. Simon (Morton Grove, IL: Whitman, 1970) (lazy, hungry, cozy, smart, stupid, strong, brave, scared, safe, tired, dirty, worried, better, special, happy)

Jamaica Tag-Along, J. Havill (Boston: Houghton Mifflin, 1989) (surprise, anger, sadness, hurt, happiness)

Jim Meets the Thing, M. Cohen (New York: Greenwillow, 1981) (fright, shame, worry, silliness, pride)

Kinda Blue, A. Grifalconi (Boston: Little, Brown, 1993) (sad, lonely, sorry, grumpy, happy, silly, sly, surprised, loved)

The Leaving Morning, A. Johnson (New York: Orchard, 1992) (sad, happy)

Sometimes I Feel Like a Mouse, J. Modesitt (New York: Scholastic, 1992) (shy, bold, sad, happy, scared, brave, excited, calm, mad, warm, ashamed, proud)

The Way I Feel . . . Sometimes, B. S. de Regniers (New York: Clarion, 1988) (mean, cooperative, rude, cross, surly, marvelous, terrific, thrilling, swell, glad, sad, silly, proud, jealous, bored, scared, friendless, sorry, commanding, surprised)

TEACHERS AS PROVIDERS OF PROSOCIAL GUIDANCE

As you interact with children on a daily basis, you will find that prosocial guidance fits in naturally with lesson plans, curriculum projects, and activities for individuals. Your goals for helping children learn to feel good about themselves, to control their behavior, to feel good about others, and to exhibit friendliness, generosity, cooperation, helpfulness, and respect can easily be integrated into your overall classroom plans.

As the youngsters learn new large- and small-motor skills, develop creativity, improve language production, and acquire cognitive concepts, they will also be learning to get along with one another, to share and take turns, to engage in group play, to help one another complete projects, and to respect people and materials. Your role in making sure these goals are accomplished is both a direct and indirect one. It can best be expressed in the following eight teacher responsibilities:

1. Provides a prosocial physical environment
2. Uses positive prevention to control inappropriate child behavior
3. Uses positive intervention to help children control their own behavior
4. Uses positive reinforcement to help children learn prosocial behaviors
5. Promotes children's self-esteem
6. Uses other-esteem conflict conversion

7. Promotes positive communication among children and adults
8. Promotes family involvement in prosocial guidance

The remaining chapters of this text take a closer look at each of these prosocial guidance components. To assess your own competence and to outline the actions necessary for implementing the program, a Teacher Prosocial Guidance Checklist is provided (Figure 3-1).

Spend time with the other staff members going over this checklist together. Are there components you have already provided? Are you unclear about some items? Read the appropriate chapters to make sure you understand the different strategies for implementing prosocial guidance in the classroom. Try some of the recommendations suggested. Add some of your own ideas. Then observe the children to see whether their prosocial behavior has improved in any way. Can their improvements be related to your activities? Be sure to keep a record of these changes along with suggestions for further improvements. Behavior change takes time. But following the guidelines proposed in this checklist will help you and the children make the necessary changes over time.

REFERENCES

Cartledge, G., & Milburn, J. F. (1995). *Teaching social skills to children and youth: Innovative approaches* (3rd ed.). Boston: Allyn & Bacon.

Eisenberg, N. (1992). *The caring child.* Cambridge, MA: Harvard University Press.

Kontos, S., & Wilcox-Herzog, A. (1997). Teacher's interactions with children: Why are they so important? *Young Children, 52*(2), 4–12.

Koplow, L. (Ed.). (1996). *Unsmiling faces: How preschools can heal.* New York: Teachers College Press.

Layzer, J. B., Goodson, & Moss, M. (1993). *Observational study of early childhood programs: Final report, Vol. 1: Life in preschool.* Washington, DC: U.S. Department of Education.

Lester, H. (1986). *A porcupine named Fluffy.* Boston: Houghton Mifflin.

McCloskey, C. M. (1996). Taking positive steps toward classroom management in preschool: Loosening up without letting it all fall apart. *Young Children, 51*(3), 14–16.

Ramsey, P. G. (1987). *Teaching and learning in a diverse world.* New York: Teachers College Press.

Simon, N. (1974). *I was so mad!* Morton Grove, IL: Whitman.

SUGGESTED READINGS

Bakley, S. (1997). Love a little more, accept a little more. *Young Children, 52*(2), 21.

Beaty, J. J. (1998). *Observing development of the young child.* Upper Saddle River, NJ: Merrill/Prentice Hall.

Greenspan, S. I. (1997). *The growth of the mind and the endangered origins of intelligence.* Reading, MA: Addison-Wesley.

Hyson, M. C. (1994). *The emotional development of young children: Building an emotion-centered curriculum.* New York: Teachers College Press.

Noori, K. (1996). Writing my own script: Pathways to teaching. *Young Children, 51*(3), 17–19.

Weinreb, M. L. (1997) Be a resiliency mentor: You may be a lifesaver for a high-risk child. *Young Children, 52*(2), 14–20.

Name _____

1. *Provides a prosocial physical environment*

_____ Arranges learning centers clearly for children's easy access and use

_____ Provides enough materials for children's use without conflict

_____ Allows enough time for children to become deeply involved with materials and activities

_____ Provides self-regulating devices for children to use learning centers and materials independently

_____ Models helpfulness by helping children keep environment in order without taking over

2. *Uses positive prevention to manage inappropriate child behavior*

_____ Anticipates inappropriate behavior and acts unobtrusively to prevent it

_____ Establishes clear limits and enforces them consistently

_____ Involves children in making rules

_____ Introduces new materials to everyone and sets up turn-taking arrangements

_____ Models generosity with book characters, puppets, and own actions

3. *Uses positive intervention to help children manage their own behavior*

_____ Intervenes when children get out of control without blaming or shaming

_____ Accepts children's negative feelings

_____ Helps children verbalize their negative feelings

_____ Redirects children's disruptive behavior into calming activities

_____ Models self-control by curbing own negative words and actions

4. *Uses positive reinforcement to help children learn prosocial behaviors*

_____ Looks for and reinforces with verbal and nonverbal cues the prosocial actions of disruptive children

_____ Makes eye or verbal contact with disruptive children only after their misbehavior has stopped

_____ Helps disruptive children find activities they can excel in

_____ Helps attention-seeking children learn to make friends

_____ Models friendship by developing friendships with every child

Figure 3-1   Teacher Prosocial Guidance Checklist.

Note: The publisher grants permission to reproduce this checklist for evaluation and record keeping.

5. *Promotes children's self-esteem*

_____ Helps every child feel accepted and wanted every day

_____ Accepts diversity in children and helps children accept it in one another

_____ Helps children become independent and self-directed

_____ Helps every child experience success

_____ Models respect by treating each child with respect

6. *Uses other-esteem conflict conversion*

_____ Helps each child verbalize what happened during interpersonal conflict

_____ Accepts what each child says without blaming or shaming

_____ Helps children in conflict to tell how the other child feels

_____ Assists each child in finding ways to help the other conflictee feel better

_____ Models other-esteem by demonstrating how to respond to feelings with book characters, puppets, and own actions

7. *Promotes positive communication among children and adults*

_____ Listens carefully to child's communication and responds with respect

_____ Helps each child engage in conversations every day

_____ Helps children learn what to say to avoid conflicts

_____ Carries out small-group role-plays about feelings and behaviors

_____ Models respectful speaking no matter what the situation

8. *Promotes family involvement in prosocial guidance*

_____ Involves family participation in prosocial guidance through ongoing, two-way communication

_____ Encourages family members to observe children's prosocial behavior

_____ Lends picture books with prosocial themes to families for reading to children

_____ Holds parent conferences for children based on prosocial behavior

_____ Models other-esteem by accepting differences in culture, lifestyle, and language of family

VIDEOTAPES

Educational Productions. (Producer). *Reframing discipline: Connecting with every child* (no. 2). (Available from Educational Productions, 9000 S.W. Gemini Drive, Beaverton, OR 97008)

Magna Systems. (Producer). *Guidance and discipline: Teacher/child interaction* (Early Childhood Training series no. 3). (Available from Magna Systems, 95 W. County Line Rd., Barrington, IL 60010)

LEARNING ACTIVITIES

1. Make a list of positive qualities you feel that you possess; then make a similar list of qualities you would like to possess. Choose one of these qualities, and discuss how you would go about acquiring it.

2. Make a list of the children in your classroom, writing something you like about each one. How can you let them know in a verbal or nonverbal manner the way you feel? Try it and record the results.

3. Keep track of the children you interact with on an individual basis for 3 days. Were they the same children? Was anyone omitted? What occurred during the interaction? How can you improve your interactions with everyone? Try it.

4. How do you express "nurturant modeling" to the children? Give examples for three specific children telling how you responded to them, what emotions you projected, and how you used verbal and nonverbal cues to express the emotions.

5. What emotions have you "mirrored" for a particular child? How did he or she respond? Read one of the recommended books to the child, and discuss the particular emotions described.

 **TWO**

Providing Prosocial Guidance

CHAPTER 4

Creating a Prosocial Physical Environment

□ Arrange learning centers clearly for children's easy access and use.

□ Provide enough materials for children's use without conflict.

□ Allow enough time for children to become deeply involved with materials and activities.

□ Provide self-regulating devices for children to use learning centers and materials independently.

□ Model helpfulness by helping children keep the environment in order without taking over.

Our goals for young children should be reflected in the physical environment of the classroom. The prosocial behavior goals discussed in Chapter 2 and outlined in the Child Prosocial Behavior Checklist can be implemented in the classroom (a) by carefully arranging learning centers, (b) by providing appropriate materials, (c) by using time wisely, and (d) by helping children choose activities independently.

As prosocial behaviors are strengthened, children feel better about themselves and thus treat others more considerately. Fewer possession disputes over toys and materials occur. Arguments over space and struggles over group access are also reduced, while children begin treating materials and one another with more respect.

For example, *self-esteem* is promoted when the classroom is set up so that children can choose their own activities and change to another activity on their own. *Self-control* comes into play when children feel an ownership in the learning centers and regulation of their use. *Other-esteem* and *friendliness* receive a boost when children work in areas set up for small groups to use. *Generosity* becomes a natural part of their behavior when enough of the favorite toys are available for several children to play with. *Cooperation* and *helpfulness* are fostered when children must work together to accomplish tasks. As children see themselves and their products treated with *respect* by everyone, they develop the same respect for the activities and products of others.

We realize that the physical arrangement of the classroom can have great influence on children's behavior. But are there specific arrangements that work better than others? How exactly should you set up your classroom to promote these behavior goals?

ARRANGE LEARNING CENTERS CLEARLY FOR CHILDREN'S EASY ACCESS AND USE

Balance is the key to classroom arrangement. There must be a balance between numbers of children and numbers of learning centers in the space available. For example, with 20 children in a medium-size classroom, there may be room for two large centers (dramatic play and blocks), four medium centers (art, water, books, and manipulatives), and three small centers (music, science, and writing). In addition, several cozy private areas for individuals who need to get away from the group for a while should be included (Figure 4-1). Here are the centers with approximate numbers of children:

Dramatic Play Center (6)	Science Center (2–4)
Block Center (6)	Manipulative/Math Center (4)
Art Center (6)	Writing/Computer Center (2)
Music Center (2)	Water/Sand Table (4)
Book Center (2–4)	Woodworking (2)

Obviously not all the children will fill each center to the maximum at the same time. In addition, space for eating and sleeping may need to be incorporated into several learning centers when the time comes. A space large enough for the total group to sit in a circle can be included in the block center. Pathways between the centers should be wide enough for easy access.

What is not included in the classroom described here is a large open space in the middle of the room. Open spaces invite children to run around wildly or mingle together aimlessly. If you observe such behavior in your own room, try pulling a learning center away from the wall and setting it up to prevent the running.

The classroom arrangement should speak to the children, inviting up to six of them to build blocks or play dress-up. Two can paint at the easels while four play with play dough from the four chairs set up for them at the art table. Four more can play at the four spaces around the water table, wearing the four plastic aprons provided, while two operate the computer from the two chairs placed in front.

Does this classroom sound too structured and regulated? Experienced teachers say it is not, for they are not doing the regulating. It is the physical arrangement of the room that regulates its use, giving children freedom to make choices and move around from one activity to the next on their own. Teachers have set up the room and provided the activities, so that children can see clearly what is available. Then they can become responsible for their own behavior within the areas.

Dramatic Play Center

When children see your arrangement, they should know immediately what exciting activities are available. The dramatic play "home center," for instance, has empty picnic baskets on the table today, and its shelves are full of plastic foods, paper plates, and utensils. A calendar on the wall at the children's eye level has a big red circle around a date—today's date—for the children to remember they have planned a pretend picnic out on the playground for one small group at a time.

Bunnett and Davis (1997) explain that "environments should be designed on what we know children love, and what we loved as children" (p. 43). Their unique arrangement of a home center is one that any preschool can adopt:

The home center enclosed by four walls (one formed by what can become a puppet theater at another time, another a storefront) is equipped with a doorbell, mail box, and Plexiglas windows that go up and down. The small lamp on the dresser inside the house allows

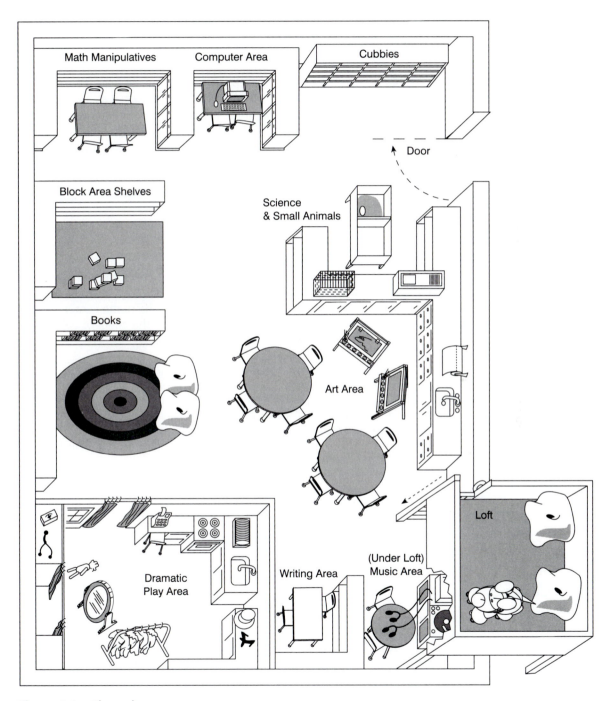

Figure 4-1   Floor plan

children to brighten or quiet the space. The pots, pans, utensils, cloth napkins and pot holders are real, "found" treasures from the secondhand store. The "soup pot" is on the stove. (pp. 42–43)

As you consider a dramatic play area arrangement like this, are you struck by the *feelings* it projects: warmth, coziness, welcome? Here is another key to successful room arrangement for prosocial development: feelings. A *positive emotional tone* should be projected by the learning centers. Children's behavior is highly influenced by the emotions they encounter. How would you have felt as a child playing in this area? What else might be added to enhance these feelings of a happy home?

Using Colors to Create Emotional Tones

What about certain colors? The use of colors is important in office buildings, for example, to create a calm atmosphere or in manufacturing facilities to increase production. Colors can also be used in preschool learning centers to generate an emotional tone. A red-checkered tablecloth invites children to sit down for a happy meal. Yellow curtains at the window give off a sunny, happy-day feeling. Pastel throw rugs and colored burlap wall hangings can add to the emotional tone of the center.

Early childhood educator Clare Cherry (1972) is aware of the effect of colors on a child:

As he becomes more socially oriented, and more aware of his own *self* and his own feelings and moods, he is more open to the impressionable effect of color. Color is magic, readily available to all and free for use by the young child. Experience it with him. Take him by the hand and plunge headlong into the very essence of its feelings and its affects. You can afford to be generous. Dish it out in liberal portions and let him know that it thrills you. Share with him its sparkle and its gloss, its quietness and its music, its smell and its touch. And watch him grow. (p. 34)

Put a colored light bulb in your home center lamp from time to time. Decorate the center for a party with colored crepe paper streamers. Ask the children what color napkins and paper plates they want for their picnic. Take several children with you to pick out the colored beanbag chairs you plan to purchase for the children's private places in the home center and book center.

Block Center

How can *balance* and *emotional tone* speak to children in the block center? Balance in this center means that you have provided enough unit blocks for the number of children the center can accommodate. They should be arranged *lengthwise* on the shelves of the center so that children can see what is available and can return them to the shelves easily during pickup. Label the shelves with outlines or cutouts of the different block shapes to help the children distinguish where particular blocks are located.

Storing unit blocks in a box or bin only leads to confusion and behavior problems. To find the blocks they want, children end up dumping out the whole box on the floor and scrambling to get them before someone else does—not a respectful situation for either the children or the blocks. Blocks stored lengthwise on shelves show children immediately what is available and help them choose their building materials without a struggle.

Accessories to be used with blocks are usually figures of people and animals, cars, and trucks. These too should be stored on shelves in the same area with their own labels. Other accessories can be added as children return from field trips and want to re-create the buildings they saw.

How can you generate the emotional excitement of building structures in the block center? Take a brief trip to a nearby construction site, and let the children see and photograph what is happening. Tape-record the sounds you hear. Afterward, mount the photos and other pictures of buildings in the block center at the children's eye level. Add to your shelves of accessories: strings for wire, plastic aquarium tubing for pipes, a box full of plastic golf tee "nails," and builders' tools such as toy hammers, pliers, and tape measures. Play the tape you made of the pounding, grinding, drilling, and shouting sounds you recorded. Be sure to take photos of the children's buildings both during and after their construction for display in the center.

Because children pretend and take roles in this area as well as in the dramatic play center, have some builders' props available: plastic hard hats, carpenters' aprons, tool belts, and tape measures. Then put out some books in the block center for the children to look at and you to read to any small group assembled there:

Building a House, B. Barton (New York: Penguin, 1981)
Hammers, Nails, Planks, and Paint, T. C. Jackson (New York: Scholastic, 1994)
How a House Is Built, G. Gibbons (New York: Holiday House, 1990)
This House Is Made of Mud, Esta casa esta hecha de lodo, K. Buchanan (Flagstaff, AZ: Northland, 1991)
This Is My House, A. Dorros (New York: Scholastic, 1992)
This Is Our House, B. Graham (Cambridge, MA: Candlewick, 1996)

If no construction sites are nearby, you can read one of these books as motivation for the children's building. Are your children excited yet? Can they access the materials easily? Is the block center itself arranged so that the block shelves are pulled away from the wall and serve as room dividers? Learning centers like this need to be clearly separated from the rest of the room. Put up colored burlap or colored poster boards to cover the empty wall for use in mounting photos, pictures, and posters. Have the children choose the color.

Are you wondering about the amount of effort you may have to expend to set up such a dynamic block center? If you are as enthusiastic about this learning opportunity as the children soon will be, then no amount of preparation should be too much. Think what prosocial behaviors you will be promoting by setting up a center like this:

1. Feeling happy to be a part of this exciting activity
2. Feeling good about themselves to be able to select building materials and contribute
3. Feeling good about others who build with them or let them join in
4. Experiencing a spirit of cooperation to create this new building that the teacher will photograph and display for all to see
5. Sensing pride of accomplishment and respect for those who helped

Other Learning Centers

Can other learning centers be arranged for children's easy access and use as creatively as the dramatic play and block centers? Use your own and your children's ingenuity. The **art center**, for example, needs to be set up ahead of time with easels ready with paper and paints, and tables near art materials accessible to children. Making children as independent as possible gives them confidence that the teacher trusts them with the materials. Stock the shelves with paper, paint, brushes, clay, chalk, glue, scissors, tape, pipe cleaners, ribbons, Styrofoam pieces, and other collage materials for them to use. Locate the center near a water source so children can clean up more easily.

A **music center** for two children at a time can be located at a small table against the wall with two chairs ready. Two tape recorders and headsets with an ever-changing selection of tapes are always available. A shelf containing a keyboard, drums, and other toy instruments, or a pegboard with hooks holding a changing selection of rhythm instruments made by the children, invites them to make their own music. Blank tapes are available for recording. On the wall are posters of rock musicians or photos of the children playing instruments. Several books on the shelf invite children into the lives of music makers:

> *Ben's Trumpet,* R. Isadora (New York: Mulberry, 1979)
> *The Bravest Flute,* A. Grifalconi (Boston: Little, Brown, 1994)
> *Charlie Parker Played Be Bop,* C. Raschka (New York: Orchard, 1992)
> *Little Lil and the Swinging Singing Sax,* L. M. Gray (New York: Simon & Schuster, 1996)
> *Love Flute,* P. Goble (New York: Bradbury, 1992)
> *Sing, Sophie!* D. A. Dodds (Cambridge, MA: Candlewick, 1997)
> *Willie Jerome,* A. F. Duncan (New York: Macmillan, 1995)
> *Wood-Hoopoe Willie,* V. Kroll (Watertown, MA: Charlesbridge, 1992)

To give children the freedom to make music on their own yet contain the boisterous behavior music making sometimes creates, tape two hula hoops onto the floor in the music center and let the children dance *inside* them as they play their instruments or tapes.

What about your **book center**? This is often a quiet, not rambunctious, center where children sit on pillows or chairs to look at books or listen to book tapes. Is your center being used, or is it usually empty? What will it take to bring children and books together in your program?

First, be sure children can see what books are available by placing them on low shelves with their covers, not spines, facing out. Or you can string a clothesline against the wall and hang books from it with clothespins. Or you can have a "book tree" made from a hat tree with books hanging from its "branches" in clear plastic baggies. Be original. Listen to how the children would like their books displayed. Make books exciting for them!

Then, as with the blocks, be sure numerous book accessories are available for children's pretending. Pretending in the book area? Definitely! Just as books have stories to tell, so do children. Let them act out stories with book accessories: hats like the book characters are wearing, puppets representing people and animal characters, stuffed animals, toy figures of people and animals, or character dolls that go with the books you have on display this week. Buy generic character dolls from educational supply houses or make your own: photocopy the character from the book, cut it out, and mount it on cardboard. Some books come with their own dolls:

Abuela, A. Dorros (New York: Dutton, 1991) (Rosalba doll)
Amazing Grace, M. Hoffman (New York: Dial, 1991) (Grace doll)
Baby Rattlesnake, T. Ata (San Francisco: Children's Book Press, 1989) (baby rattlesnake)
Mama, Do You Love Me? B. M. Joose (San Francisco: Chronicle, 1991) (Dear One doll)
Tar Beach, F. Ringgold (New York: Crown, 1991) (Cassie doll)
Whistle for Willie, E. J. Keats (New York: Viking, 1964) (Peter doll)

The **science/nature center** can be a centerpiece, too, if you also section it off clearly and provide enough space for the two to four children you expect to use it. Permanent features will be the classroom animals and plants: an aquarium for fish, a terrarium for pond plants, a guinea pig, a cactus dish garden. By changing activities once or twice a month, you can lure children into this center for the "float-and-sink" or "what can magnets pick up?" or "bark rubbing" experiments you set up. Use brightly colored backing paper for the experiments, contrasted with the colorful science posters mounted on the walls to attract participants. Can you feel the emotional tone this center radiates?

The **writing/computer center** can be set up like a little office, with the computer on a desk with two chairs in front. This arrangement says to children that two can use the computer at the same time, learning to take turns by pressing the keys and helping each other operate a program. Computers are thus excellent prosocial behavior teaching devices. But the two chairs at the writing table invite children to use paper and writing materials individually from the two in-baskets on top.

A **water or sand table** is not always considered a learning center, but it should be. Have it located near shelves of accessory materials to use in it. Children can be self-directed if four plastic aprons hang on hooks near the water table, as well as four pairs of goggles for children to use at the sand table.

A pair of goggles, a hammer, nails, and a tree stump make a fine woodworking center.

Children should also wear goggles (and they love to!) in the **woodworking center**. Two pairs mean that two children can use the center. If you don't have a workbench, bring in tree stumps for hammering. On shelves nearby store hammers, containers of nails, and golf tees, along with pieces of Styrofoam, soft wood, ceiling tiles, and even pieces of leather for pounding through.

The **manipulative/math center** also needs shelves near a table to hold baskets or plastic containers of sorting and counting materials, matching games, number games, table blocks of all kinds, a toy cash register, and an abacus or children's calculator. Four chairs at the table indicate the number of children the center can accommodate. Make the table large enough for blocks or games to be spread out so individuals need not struggle for space. Take photos of the children's creations, and have them enlarged and mounted in the area.

Still can't get children to use this area independently? Put a glass fishbowl on the table filled with colorful counters, tiny toy cars, or people figures. Next to it place a sign: "Guess How Many?" Then have a clipboard for children to record their guesses along with initials or scribbled name. Help these preliterate children to read the sign and record their guesses the first time through. After that, they can help one another. After everyone who wants to has made a guess, dump the contents out on the table and have the children help you count the objects. Whoever comes closest to the correct number can have his or her name displayed on the manipulative area bulletin board for the week. The children will tell you, "Let's do it again, Teacher," so be sure to have new materials ready to fill up the bowl every week: acorns, seashells, buttons, crayons—you name it.

All of your learning centers should be clearly separated from one another by room dividers such as shelves, tables, screens, or furniture if we want children to see what activities the program offers. To make your own dividers, cut a large cardboard carton apart for a screen, and have the children paint it. Put picture signs with center names at each of these areas. Sign-up sheets or hooks for name tags help children control their own use of the centers. Thus, behavior problems can be decreased significantly when the classroom is arranged for children's easy access and use.

PROVIDE ENOUGH MATERIALS FOR CHILDREN'S USE WITHOUT CONFLICT

Another simple method for reducing the most common classroom conflict, *possession disputes*, is to supply enough materials in each of the learning centers in the first place. How much is enough? It does not mean you need four eggbeaters in the water table for the four children using the center, but you will soon find that one is not enough. Once children see there are two of their favorite playthings as well as many other toys to choose from, they will take turns with the favorite ones without difficulty.

Unit Blocks

Just as you can help children control their own use of the learning centers by the way you have them arranged, you can also support their prosocial behavior by the number of materials you provide. Take unit blocks, for example. Many centers provide only a small set of blocks without realizing that several children may want to build *large* buildings. When they don't find enough blocks to complete their own buildings, they may take blocks from others or knock down all the buildings in frustration.

Blocks are important learning materials for preschool children as they experiment with the cognitive concepts of size, shape, space, bridging, and balancing. Just as important are the prosocial behaviors they can learn from sharing materials and space, learning to cooperate and help others, developing new friendships, and learning to respect the structures others have created. But they need enough blocks.

If you purchase in sets, plan to buy a large-group full set of unit blocks. Some teachers prefer to purchase blocks separately. For them it is more important to have many blocks of one shape rather than fewer blocks of many shapes. Units, double units, quadruple units, and half units are most important. Fill your block shelves with them. Pillars, double pillars, large cylinders, triangles, arches, and ramps are also necessary, but you won't need as many. Large hollow blocks and building boards are other choices.

Block Accessories

Block accessories should change as your curriculum for the children changes. Accessory shelves in the block area should support field trips to construction sites, as mentioned previously, or trips to a farm, gas station, zoo, museum, clinic, fire station, park, beach, airport, or railroad depot. Sometimes the only accessories you need are small figures of people (be sure they are multiethnic) and regular-size hats for the builders themselves. Then they can pretend to be the workers they saw on their trip as they now build block bridges, highways, houses, zoos, and hospitals.

How many hard hats should you hang on a hat tree in the block center? Be sure to have enough for each child. If six builders will be in a block center construction site, then provide six plastic hard hats. Otherwise expect a squabble. Sounds simple, doesn't it? But it is surprising how many teachers do not anticipate such conflicts. They do not realize that preschool children have not yet learned adult ways of sharing and waiting for turns. Nor do young children have the verbal skills to make their wants known. When they want something, they take it—even away from someone else.

How much simpler to have enough in the first place and avoid the conflict. Or to have enough different items to be able to trade with someone else for the one they want. A well-equipped classroom provides preschool children with this independence.

*How many hard hats should you
have in the block center?*

Book Center

Did you notice that this text advocates bringing materials from one learning center into another one to support special activities? Most of the hats and dress-up clothes will be located in the dramatic play center, but some can be left in the block center, as mentioned, as a follow-up of field trips. Some toy figures of people and animals can be taken from the block center to the book center to serve as characters for certain stories. Hats from the dramatic play area can also play a role as book characters along with the character dolls previously mentioned.

Since books will be occupying the most of the shelves in the book center, hang book accessories such as hats, puppets, and dolls from hat trees or pegboards with hooks so that children can see clearly what's available in the center and make independent choices. As Fayden (1997) notes, "When we honor children's choices, they gain confidence in their actions and view themselves as capable decisionmakers" (p. 16).

Changing Materials

Changing materials from time to time is another important consideration. When things stay the same from week to week, they lose their emotional appeal. Look around your room to see which learning centers attract the most and least children. When no new materials have been added to the sand table, for instance, children tend to ignore it. Novelty sparks interest that can quickly grow to enthusiasm with young children. Put the sand buckets, sieves, shovels, and hoppers away for a while, and line up a selection of little cars, trucks, blocks, and people figures on the sand table shelves. Another month put out dollhouse furniture and people, and watch what happens.

Change the materials in all of your learning centers from time to time to spark new interest among the children. Where will you obtain such materials? Don't put out everything the program owns at the beginning of the year. Save some for later. Complex puzzles, for instance, can be better used later in the year instead of at the beginning. Change your books from time to time by adding a few new ones but keeping out the favorites. Trade some of your games and toys with the class next door. They too may profit by a change.

 # ALLOW ENOUGH TIME FOR CHILDREN TO BECOME DEEPLY INVOLVED WITH MATERIALS AND ACTIVITIES

Most American preschools follow a schedule that allots a certain amount of time for certain activities. Children experience arrival time when they come in the morning, then circle time, free play, snack, outdoors, lunch, story time, nap, free play, circle time, and departure. When it is time for a transition from one activity to the next, children are expected to pick up and put away all the toys and materials they have been using. They may not have finished their block buildings, paintings, computer games, dramatic play, or the book or music tapes they were listening to. No matter. They must stop and switch to the new activity.

Most early childhood educators have followed such a schedule as long as they can remember. Is something wrong with this? Not necessarily. But little by little we are learning about other programs that do not enforce strict times. They allow children to finish what they have started. And these programs do not seem to experience the common "transition troubles" where children get out of hand, refusing to pick up, leave the first activity, or settle down to the next one. These programs also report that certain kinds of their children's learning seem far in advance of that from more highly structured programs. Is it time for us to take a closer look at schedules and times?

Reggio Emilia Preschools

American early childhood educators who have visited the acclaimed preschools of Reggio Emilia in Italy were surprised to see how accomplished the Italian children seemed to be in arts and crafts. Incredible paintings, sculptures, and collages filled the buildings. How could preschoolers produce such astounding products? Then they learned that individual children are given as much time as they need to complete their activities. They also have the opportunity to use the same materials over and over until they have gained control over them. As a result, the children get deeply involved in their activities—even to the exclusion of behavior problems. Seefeldt (1995) notes:

> Time is used differently in Reggio preschools than in preschools in the United States. Experiences and themes last months, as opposed to the one- or two-week units typical in the United States. And the children are never expected to move on to something new until they have exhausted their own ideas fully. Often, in Reggio, children were observed painting at easels for an entire morning or working with clay for hours. (p. 42)

Educators from both countries realize that it is the process of art and not the product that is most important for children. Because this process is treated so seriously in Reggio preschools by giving it so much time, the children's products are extraordinary. We also note that this philosophy is modeled by the teachers who treat their children's activity with such respect that time is allowed for them to complete it.

When children become deeply involved in their work or play, they have no time or interest in disrupting others. Even "challenging" children who see that others pay little attention to their disruptions eventually calm down and join in an activity of their own.

Flexible Schedules

Am I suggesting that you do away with your schedule and turn the entire day into one long free-play activity? No. I am suggesting that you first look carefully at the children's activities and the way the schedule seems to be working. Is there enough time for them to complete what they are doing before you call for cleanup or pickup? If not, why not postpone the cleanup time and allow the free-play period to continue? On the other hand, if children are not deeply involved or have finished their activities early on certain days, free play can be cut short and the next activity period begun.

Making time *flexible* is the suggestion. Make the activity periods flexible every day. Consider them to be "time blocks" in which a certain activity always occurs but at varying lengths of time, depending on children's involvement. You can be the one to determine when to end the activity period. On days when children need more time to finish their activities, allow the period to continue. See whether this makes a difference in their prosocial behaviors.

Computer Use Research

We know that time makes a definite difference in children's learning. The children from two preschool classrooms involved in my computer use research experienced very different outcomes because of how time was used. At the outset my colleagues and I asked the teachers involved to allow interested children to work on their own during the daily free-play period with the computer programs we supplied. These periods were the same length in both classrooms.

Children in the first classroom taught themselves to use several letter, number, drawing, and matching programs with ease during the 6 weeks of the research. However, most children in the second classroom did not learn how the programs worked and finally lost interest in using the computer altogether. What caused the difference? Both classrooms allowed interested children to choose to use the computer on their own, two at a time, by selecting "computer necklaces." It was a puzzling outcome for all of us.

Are you allowing children enough time to get deeply involved in their learning?

We finally discovered that children in the first classroom could remain at the computer as long as they wanted to. Children in the second classroom, however, were self-regulated by a kitchen timer that dinged every 5 minutes, at which time they had to give up their turns to the next two children. They learned to take turns on their own, but none of them ever had time enough to learn to use the computer programs (Beaty & Tucker, 1986)!

Time and Attention Span

The fact that young children have short attention spans has been misunderstood and misused by many preschool programs. By constructing daily schedules around brief activity periods followed by transitions to the next period, these programs unwittingly promote children's disengagement in learning. When children are disengaged, they tend to wander around, often creating disturbances among others. On the other hand, when children are deeply engaged in their own learning, their attention spans are stretched and their learning increases. Isenberg and Jalongo (1993) note:

> Many teachers erroneously believe that because children have short attention spans, activities must be changed constantly. When young children are engaged in meaningful activities, however, they are capable of concentrating for long periods of time. (p. 177)

Look at your own schedule to see whether you are allowing children enough time to become deeply involved in their own learning. When they are allowed to choose among many interesting activities and given enough time to complete them, children become self-directed in their learning. Behavior problems are decreased and may even disappear. As Isenberg and Jalongo conclude, "*Time* conveys a clear message about the importance of an activity. When children have long blocks of time, their play is more constructive, cooperative, and expressive than with short, interrupted time periods" (p. 176).

Transitions

On the other hand, transitions from one activity to another should take as little time as possible. Standing in line to go outdoors, sitting at a table waiting for lunch, and sitting in a circle waiting for a storyteller to appear are time-wasting situations. Young children are soon squirming, bouncing around, and pushing or hitting their neighbors.

You can streamline waiting time and eliminate disruptive behavior by flexibly scheduling trips to the playground or bathroom. Not everyone needs to go at once, so it is not necessary that everyone line up and wait. But when waiting time is necessary, spend it doing fingerplays, songs, stories, creative movement, and guessing games. When children are thus engaged, the time will fly by.

PROVIDE SELF-REGULATING DEVICES FOR CHILDREN TO USE LEARNING CENTERS AND MATERIALS INDEPENDENTLY

Children who are given the means for choosing classroom activities and materials on their own can become independent and entirely self-directed in their learning. They make choices based on their own interests, not the teacher's, and tend to stay with their choices for longer periods of time. They also learn how to trade off their choices with others without a fuss when their interest lags. Such self-directed children seldom engage in disruptive behavior.

Can 3- and 4-year-old children actually learn such self-control? They can if you provide them with interesting kinds of devices for making choices. For instance, you can furnish them with name tags hanging from a hook board or Velcro board near the total group area. When the time comes to choose an activity, every child can take their name tag and hook it on one of the hooks at the entrance to the learning center of their choice. Each learning center should display hooks for the number of children it can accommodate. When the hooks are filled up, children must look elsewhere. Or they can trade centers with someone if they can convince a child to change with them.

Some teachers prefer a second self-regulating method of equipping each area with "learning center necklaces" made of yarn and hanging from hooks at the entrance to each center. To play in a learning center, children take the necklace and wear it while they are in the center. When all of the necklaces are taken, other children must look for another center. Children quickly learn to trade necklaces with one another when they want to change.

Self-Regulating the Taking of Turns

Taking turns with equipment can be another fascinating experience for youngsters when they realize how grown-up they are being treated. For example, children who want a turn at using the computer or riding a tricycle can sign up for it on a clipboard. If they cannot print their name or initials, have them write their scribbled names one under another. Keep a pencil with a string attached to the board so that children can cross off their names when they are finished.

When a new toy or task is introduced into the classroom and everyone wants it at once, children can have the fun of drawing names out of a hat for the various turns. Taking numbered tickets (as in a bakery) is another method for determining turns. How do your children regulate their turns? So many different methods abound that children soon learn they are in charge of their activities. When this happens, space conflicts and possession disputes may disappear altogether.

Three-minute egg timers and kitchen timers are other devices children can use for turns with equipment. Some children may become more concerned with the timers than with their turn. If this is the case, have them draw a name or take a ticket instead. Equal time is actually not as important for young children as it is for adults. Personal acknowledgment of their problem is what they need from you.

Although most children enjoy being in charge of their activities and space like this, a few may try to push in without using a tag or waiting a turn. Your observations will tell you who has learned to control such impulsive behavior and who may need more help.

MODEL HELPFULNESS BY HELPING CHILDREN KEEP THE ENVIRONMENT IN ORDER WITHOUT TAKING OVER

Your behavior in the classroom is its most important aspect—even more important than the physical arrangement itself. You lend a definite emotional tone to every learning center by the way you treat the children as you interact with them. Your prosocial helping behavior tells them that you care about them and will assist them when necessary.

Your assistance must be diplomatic so that children understand that they are still in charge of their activities. In other words, do not barge into a learning center during cleanup time and begin helping children to pick up the toys. Show your respect for them and their activities by asking permission. "May I help you with the pickup, Greg and Ramon? You have a lot of blocks to put back on the shelves. How can I help you?"

Treat the children just as you would an adult friend whose house you are helping clean. You can certainly make suggestions about how it can be done most easily, but wait for the friend's response before you start in. Children are worthy people who deserve our respect. From our treatment of them, they learn how to treat others.

No 5-Minute "Warning"

Tell children ahead of time that they need to finish their activities because it will soon be time to clean up. Many teachers give a 5-minute "warning." It is not necessary to present this timing information in the form of a warning to everyone in a loud voice. The concept of "5 minutes" has little meaning for preschool children. A more respectful way to inform children to get ready for the next activity is to visit each group in their learning center and tell them personally, "Larue and Jessica, you need to get ready for outdoor time. Can you pick up the dress-up clothes by yourselves, or do you need help?"

For children who have not finished the project they are working on, you should discuss its completion with them. Can they finish it now if you give them extra time on their painting, building, or counting game? Or is this a project that needs to be left standing and finished at another time?

For activities children want to continue another day, help them make signs for their block buildings saying, "Please Leave Building Standing." Incomplete art products can be placed in a storage area. Science experiments can be moved to one side with a sign that reads, "Please do not touch Jeff's seed experiment." If you have enough room, you can encourage children to work on projects for more than one day, as in the classroom Bunnett and Davis (1997) visited:

The block area feels and looks more like a construction site in progress than a daily play area. Children are encouraged to continue projects, it appears, from the "Children at Work" and "Construction in Process" signs in the area. There are loose parts such as blocks, tape, cardboard and plastic cylinders available in different kinds of containers, encouraging ongoing projects. (p. 43)

This is your classroom, of course, but it is also the children's. Just as you delegate authority to other adults, you can also entrust children with some of the operation of their classroom by asking their opinions and taking their suggestions. You have set up the physical environment to help the children learn prosocial behaviors as they work and play with one another. As they learn these behaviors, you will be able to entrust them with more responsibility. As you learn to trust them, they will learn to trust you. It is a "delicious," not a vicious, cycle.

REFERENCES

Beaty, J. J. (1997). *Building bridges with multicultural picture books*. Upper Saddle River, NJ: Merrill/Prentice Hall.

Beaty, J. J., & Tucker, W. H. (1987). *The computer as a paintbrush: Creative uses for the personal computer in the preschool classroom*. Upper Saddle River, NJ: Merrill/Prentice Hall.

Bunnett, R., & Davis, N. L. (1997). Getting to the heart of the matter. *Child Care Information Exchange, 114*, 42–44.

Cherry, C. (1972). *Creative art for the developing child*. Belmont, CA: Fearon.

Fayden, T. (1997). Children's choice: Planting seeds for creating a thematic sociodramatic center. *Young Children, 52*(3), 15–20.

Isenberg, J. P., & Jalongo, M. R. (1993). *Creative expression and play in the early childhood curriculum*. Upper Saddle River, NJ: Merrill/Prentice Hall.

Seefeldt, C. (1995). Art—A serious work. *Young Children, 50*(3), 39–45.

SUGGESTED READINGS

Barclay K., Benelli, C., & Wolf, J. M. (1997). "Is it time yet?" Getting more *time* out of daily routines. *Dimensions of Early Childhood, 25*(1), 22–26.

Beaty, J. J. (1996). *Skills for preschool teachers* (5th ed.). Upper Saddle River, NJ: Merrill/Prentice Hall.

Edwards, C., Gandini, L., & Forman, G. (1993). *The hundred languages of children: The Reggio Emilia approach to early childhood education*. Norwood, NJ: Ablex.

Greenman, J. (1988). *Caring spaces, learning places: Children's environments that work*. Redmond, WA: Exchange.

Hyson, M. C. (1994). *The emotional development of young children: Building an emotion-centered curriculum*. New York: Teachers College Press.

Isbell, R. (1995). *The complete learning center book*. Beltsville, MD: Gryphon House.

Shepherd, W., & Eaton, J. (1997). Creating environments that intrigue and delight children and adults. *Child Care Information Exchange, 117*, 42–47.

Youcha, V., & Wood, K. (1997). Enhancing the environment for ALL children. *Child Care Information Exchange, 114*, 45–49.

VIDEOTAPES

Dodge, D. T. (Producer). *New room arrangement as a teaching strategy.* (Available from Redleaf Press, 450 N. Syndicate, Suite 5, St. Paul, MN 55104)

Educational Productions. (Producer). *Space to grow.* (Available from Educational Productions, 9000 S.W. Gemini Drive, Beaverton, OR 97008)

High/Scope. (Producer). *Setting up the learning environment.* (Available from High/Scope Press, 600 N. River St., Ypsilanti, MI 48198)

Magna Systems. (Producer). *Learning environment.* (Available from Magna Systems, 95 W. County Line Rd., Barrington, IL 60010)

National Association for the Education of Young Children. (Producer). *Places to grow: The learning environment.* (Available from NAEYC, 1509 16th St. N.W., Washington, DC 20036-1426)

Self-Dimensions & Creative Educational Video. *Discipline and the physical environment.* (Available from Redleaf Press, 450 N. Syndicate, Suite 5, St. Paul, MN 55104)

LEARNING ACTIVITIES

1. How can you arrange your dramatic play center to project the emotional tones of coziness, warmth, and welcome? Describe in detail.

2. What prosocial behaviors can children learn in the block center after a field trip? How does your arrangement promote such learning? Make a floor plan drawing and record how children use the center.

3. Count the number of children in each learning center during free play for 3 days. What centers attract the fewest children? Why do you think this

is so? Rearrange one of those centers to make it more attractive. Record the results.

4. Rearrange your schedule to allow more time for children to complete their activities. Inform children in each center separately when it is time to clean up, and help them when necessary. Does this make a difference in children's behavior?

5. Try a new self-regulating method for your children to learn to take turns. Use tags, hooks, necklaces, name drawing, or another method and record how it works.

CHAPTER 5

Using Positive Prevention to Manage Inappropriate Behavior

□ Anticipate inappropriate behavior, and act unobtrusively to prevent it.

□ Establish clear limits, and enforce them consistently.

□ Involve children in making rules.

□ Introduce new materials to everyone, and set up turn-taking arrangements.

□ Model generosity with book characters, puppets, and your own actions.

What is *positive prevention,* and how do you use it? This type of prosocial guidance calls on you to anticipate how children may behave under various circumstances and to take the necessary precautions to ward off inappropriate actions.

Healthy preschool children are naturally curious, often fearless, and frequently rambunctious. They love to take things apart but haven't yet figured out how to put them back together. They often climb as high as they can but can't seem to get back down. They may take a toy from a playmate but don't understand why the other child hits them when they won't give it back. In other words, they have trouble anticipating the consequences of their actions. Their impulsive behavior sometimes gets them into trouble.

You, on the other hand, can learn to anticipate children's behavior if you pay attention to their actions on a daily basis. Once you know what to expect in the way of inappropriate behavior, you can act to prevent it in a positive manner before it gets out of hand. With 20 lively youngsters in attendance, you quickly come to understand that an ounce of prevention is truly worth a pound of intervention.

ANTICIPATE INAPPROPRIATE BEHAVIOR, AND ACT UNOBTRUSIVELY TO PREVENT IT

Let's look at a typical daily schedule for a preschool program with the idea of anticipating any disruptive behavior that could be prevented (see Figure 5-1). Such a schedule might occupy the time blocks described in the following subsections.

Arrival

Children's arrival in the morning can be a time of happy greetings and excited engagement in the array of activities that await them. Or it can be a time of pushing and

Figure 5-1   Daily schedule

A.M.: Arrival	P.M.: Story time
Circle time	Nap time
Free choice	Free choice
Snack	Closing circle
Outdoor play	Departure
Lunch	

shoving, of "It's mine!" or "I got here first!" as children surge into the classroom and struggle to assert their claims over materials and space. How is it in your program?

Observe to see what happens when the children arrive each day. If they come by bus, you can anticipate a large group of children pouring in all at once. Are activities set up and awaiting their arrival? Do certain children fight over toys or space every time they come in? Are you or other staff members able to greet every child every day? Step back and watch what happens.

If your arrival time is chaotic, then analyze what happens to make it so. Young children who ride a bus for lengthy periods are often ready to burst into loud and wild activity as soon as they enter the room. Trying to calm them down may be futile. Why not spend 10 minutes or so of the arrival period out on the playground, letting the youngsters run around and release some of their pent-up energy?

On the other hand, your arrival periods may be calm except for a few children who have not yet fully waked up and may act grumpy and uncooperative. Some programs serve a breakfast or breakfast snack for children on their arrival. As soon as their outside garments have been hung in their cubbies, children have the choice to sit down at the breakfast table or go directly to a learning center. Food or juice may be all it takes to get them going in the morning.

Observe children when they arrive in the morning using the Child Prosocial Behavior Checklist to see which feel good about themselves, abide by the classroom limits, and play with others in a friendly manner. For individuals who do not display this behavior, you may want to interact with them on a friendly one-to-one basis to get them involved in a classroom activity rather than roughhousing with their peers. "C'mon, Frank, see if you can make this puzzle. I put it out especially for you. Maybe you can make it and maybe it's too hard for you. Want to try it and see?"

Circle Time

Many programs start the morning with a circle time for greeting individual children and introducing them to the activities on hand for the day. Be sure to keep this period short. This is one time that preschool children's short attention span comes into play with a vengeance. They are ready to engage in activities right away and not to sit quietly in a circle listening to someone talk. If you cannot keep this period under 10 minutes long, expect some children to act inappropriately. It is not their problem. It is yours. As Wald, Morris, and Abraham (1996) point out, "A fatal flaw of circle time often lies in planning activities that tax the attention span of children" (p. 27).

Circle time must not only be short, it must engage everyone rapidly. When you sing your welcome song, name each child quickly. When you describe what activities are waiting for them, be brief. Pass a sample of the materials around the circle. This is not the time for each child to "show and tell," an activity better suited to older children. Instead, after introducing the activities, you should send children off in small groups to make their choices.

Use a concept transition game, such as this: "All the children with blue and white shirts can go to a learning center," or "All the children with a picture on their tee shirts can go." Don't use the same game every day. Use your ingenuity to invent different

*If hands are involved in circle-time
disruptions, put them to work
clapping or doing fingerplays.*

transition games: "Close your eyes and wait for a tap on your shoulder. When you feel a tap, get up and go choose your activity. No peeking!"

If you anticipate that a certain child may be disruptive, sit next to her and help engage her attention toward the person in charge. If some children seem to be poking others, start a clapping game such as "Let's clap out everyone's name. One clap for each sound. Here we go. Chris-tin-a Mar-ti-nez, clap-clap-clap, clap-clap-clap. C'mon, Christina, you clap too!"

Positive prevention like this is so much more effective and even fun for everyone than scolding the disrupter. If hands are involved in the disruption, put them to work clapping. If children are talking too loud, then go around the circle whispering to them, "I can't hear you. I'm whispering your name. Can you hear me whisper your name? Now you do it." Or have everyone "play a horn" with their hands when you give the signal. Can they play softly?

Free Choice

Free choice should be the longest period of the day, for it is the time when children have chosen an activity in one of the learning centers and need time enough to complete it. If they can see clearly what is available and make their own choices, most children are likely to stay deeply involved with the activity and not act in a disruptive manner.

To make a choice and become involved is not so easy for some children. Some may not want to make a choice, and others just have trouble settling down. You can anticipate which ones have difficulty by the informal observations you make from time to time. If you know who these children are, you can help them get started:

"Roberta, you can't seem to find anything to do this morning. Would you like to help me look through these old magazines for some pictures to put in our class scrapbook? I need pictures of children and animals. Do you think you could find some?"

In anticipation of finding such children at loose ends, be sure to have a pile of old magazines on hand. Have some scissors and glue ready, too, if children want to cut out and paste the pictures. Another strategy teachers find successful is to assign the wandering child to a partner or a project: "Jabal is making a blue background for the wall in the block center, Anthony. I'm going to push this table next to his and put out another piece of cardboard so you can help him. You decide what color you want. Thanks a lot."

Cleanup

Cleanup can be one of the most disruptive times for preschoolers. You can always anticipate some out-of-bounds behavior whenever you announce, "Time to clean up. Let's start picking up and putting away all the materials you got out." DeVries and Zan (1994, p. 221) mention three problems a teacher must deal with during cleanup: coercion, transition, and distraction.

Motivating Children to Clean Up

Children often feel *coerced* into cleaning up. They feel that they are being forced into doing something they don't want to do, even though they are the ones who pulled all the blocks off the shelves or scattered the clothes in the dress-up area. In some instances, as soon as the teacher announces cleanup time, children quickly leave an area so they won't have to pick up the blocks or toys there. How can you entice children into cleaning up willingly?

As mentioned in Chapter 4, it is better for you and the other staff members to visit each learning center privately, informing its occupants that it is time to get ready for snack (or outdoor play), and they need to begin cleaning up. Ask them if they need help with the cleanup. If they do, tell them they can get started and you will be back to help them in a few minutes. Mention that you hope they will make their center look really nice for the next children to use. It is important to emphasize the reason for cleaning up. Children may be more willing to pick up and put away dolls, dresses, and play house materials if they know why it must be done. Can they make their center look as neat as it did when they entered it? Even neater? You will be back to see.

Making Transitions Easy

A second problem with cleanup involves children's difficulty in making *transitions*. If children are deeply involved in their activity, they resent being pulled away from it and having to put the materials away. If you visit each center personally you can sometimes offer an alternative: "Do you need more time to finish your painting, Audrey? Why don't you clean up the brushes and put away the paints for now, and leave your painting on the table to finish later."

Cleanup should not be any less interesting for children than the activity itself unless you make it so.

A third problem involves *distraction*. As children begin cleanup, they may become so distracted by the materials that they start new activities with them instead of putting them away. If you have suggested some sort of game for block pickup, for instance, the children may want to take blocks *off* the shelves to play the game. You will need to help with the pickup yourself, if this is the case, to keep the children on task. Once again remind them that they need to clean up their area so the next children can use it.

Making Cleanup Fun

You can overcome many of these problems if you make cleanup fun. Too often it is the teacher who makes cleanup an onerous chore by loudly announcing a dismal warning "Five minutes to cleanup!" This already sounds like something bad to children, and they may try to escape. Try not to use your voice like a drill sergeant ordering people around. Cleanup should not be any less interesting than the activity itself unless you make it so. Change your own mind-set, thinking of cleanup as another fun activity that everyone will want to engage in.

Have a basket of magic "cleanup puppets" for everyone to choose to put over one of their hands to make it work like magic. "Do you want a dog puppet or a shark puppet to help you today, Rinaldo?" Or stick "magic" peel-off stickers on the back of every hand that wants to work like magic. "What color stickers do you want today, Sondra? I've heard that red can really get your hands moving!" Cleanup can be just as much fun as any activity in your program. Use your creativity to make it so.

Snack

Children need nourishment in the middle of the day, it's true, but should you pull them away from their unfinished activities to sit down together at a snack table? Every transition like this is not only time-consuming but also disruptive on your part. If you really want a flexible schedule with children free to enter and exit learning centers as the need arises, then consider having an ongoing snack table at one side of the room.

Put out the snack at the same time every day on a table with four chairs. Children can come for a snack when they feel like it and then return to their activities. Keep track of children who have not had a snack and remind them privately: "Ron and Sarah, last call for snacks." Children can dispose of their own paper cups and plates in a nearby trash can.

Outdoor Play

Can you anticipate any disruptive behavior associated with outdoor play? If children need to wait in line to go out or come in, there is sure to be some turmoil, especially if the wait is a long one. Perhaps one of your coworkers can take those who are ready outside while you remain inside with those who are getting dressed. If everyone must wait in line together, then be prepared with a fingerplay, song, or story to keep them occupied.

Once out on the playground, a principal concern may be possession disputes. Do you have only one tricycle or wagon? Be prepared for daily conflicts unless you have set up a turn-taking method ahead of time. Children can sign up on a clipboard for a turn or use a kitchen timer. Most programs prefer to have several trikes available.

Lunch/Story Time

As children come in from outside and wash up for lunch, they will usually go either directly to their lunch table or to the circle for story time. Some teachers prefer to help children calm down like this after a strenuous playground experience, before they eat lunch. Others prefer to have children become quiet just before nap time. Sitting and listening to the teacher tell or read a story serves either purpose.

Teachers need to wait until everyone has settled down before beginning a story. Interruptions by disruptive children make listening hard for everyone. Don't start until you have everyone's attention. If you're using a book, hold up the cover and point to a picture. If you're telling the story orally, go around the circle holding a finger to your lips till everyone is ready, or start out by whispering until everyone is quiet enough to hear.

Telling rather than reading a story helps a teacher keep her eyes on the children rather than on a book. This creates a great deal of interest for children as well, since they must now keep their eyes on the teacher. You can make any story exciting, suspenseful, funny, or scary just by the tone of your voice. You can whisper or growl, or slo-o-ow down the words. Children love it—and there are few disruptions.

As for lunch itself, children like to find their own name tags at their lunch tables. Change them around from day to day. Be sure to place the most "challenging" children next to youngsters who will not be bothered by them. Have all get involved by pouring their own milk from a small pitcher, taking small portions of food from the serving bowls, and passing them along to the next person. They can come back for seconds. When they are finished, everyone can clean up their own place.

Nap Time

How do you get the children in your program to take a nap? Going to bed has always been difficult for lively youngsters even at night. So why should they have to do it in the middle of the day? We understand they need a rest period after a full day of activity, but most children resent having to stop playing and lie down on cots. You can anticipate disruptive behavior during nap time from many children, especially at the beginning of the year.

How will you handle it? First, you yourself may need to change your mind about nap time. It should be considered as another classroom activity and not just a chance for the teacher to get away from the children. Some children need a great deal of individual help to get settled down. You need to be there for them. But all of the children need your help in preparing for rest. You can do it if you take nap time seriously, and not as an escape for you.

Children need to be in the mood for nap time, before they allow themselves to fall asleep. *It is up to you to establish a sleepy-time mood.* How will you do it? First, you need to signal nap time in some special way. After the cots are in place, some teachers turn off the lights. Others put on a quiet tape or record. They talk in whispers. They help children lie down on their cots and may cover them with a sheet or blanket. Some programs offer children a stuffed animal or a little car or person figure to hold.

Many teachers read a sleepy-time book in a sing-song voice. Choose a quiet nighttime story or one with repetition. Do not show children the pictures. Have the lights off and tell the children to close their eyes and make pictures in their minds of the story you are reading. Read in a whispery or sing-song voice. Here are some books to choose from:

Abuela, A. Dorros (New York: Dutton, 1991)
Dreams, E. J. Keats (New York: Collier, 1974)
First Pink Light, E. Greenfield (New York: Scholastic, 1976)
Goodnight Moon, M. W. Brown (New York: Scholastic, 1947)
Moon Rope, Un Lazo a la luna, L. Ehlert (San Diego: Harcourt Brace, 1992)
Octopus Hug, L. Pringle (Honesdale, PA: Boyds Mill, 1993)
On the Day I Was Born, D. Chocolate (New York: Scholastic, 1995)
Tar Beach, F. Ringgold (New York: Crown, 1991)

Through Moon and Stars and Night Skies, A. Turner (New York: HarperCollins, 1991)

Tucking Mommy In, M. Loh (New York: Orchard, 1987)

For children who have difficulty going to sleep and tend to disrupt the sleep of others, you may want to direct them quietly to another part of the room after the room has quieted down. There they can read a book, make a puzzle, or play with quiet toys. But remember, one of the most disruptive sounds for everyone is a teacher's loud voice speaking across the room: "Andrew, it's time for you to be QUIET!" Instead, you can whisper privately to Andrew that he is disturbing those who want to sleep, and he can play in the "quiet corner" if he can't sleep. Some guidelines to make nap time less stressful are as follows:

1. Establish a quiet, peaceful environment.
2. Make the napping environment as comfortable as possible.
3. Establish specific nap-time rituals.
4. Emphasize that children need rest in order to be healthy and happy children.
5. Empathize with children's struggles in falling asleep.
6. Respect children's physiological and emotional needs.
7. Take the attitude that you are there to help the children rest.
8. Use problems at nap time as opportunities to help children take the perspective of others. (Adapted from DeVries and Zan, pp. 244–249)

Afternoon Free Choice

As children awake from their naps, they can once again choose an activity. Have quiet activities on tables for children to sit down and get themselves oriented. Some children sleep very deeply and are cranky when they wake up. They may want to sit quietly until they feel better. Then they can work on a puzzle, draw with colored markers, play a matching game, or read a book. Put out new games and materials different from the ones available in the morning to engage children's interest. This may be the time to open the water or sand table if they weren't in use in the morning. As long as you have enough materials for everyone, things should go smoothly. At the same time, you may want to serve snacks once again. Many children need this nourishment to help get them going after a long nap.

Closing Circle

Keep the free-choice period going as long as children are comfortably engaged. When they begin to get restless, you can call them over to the closing circle. Sing some songs together that the children already know, and teach them a new one. This is also the time to ask what they did today that they liked. You can begin the transition to departure by talking about what will happen in the program tomorrow. Who can guess what new toy will be waiting for them in the block center? They'll just have to come tomorrow and see what it is.

Departure

Many programs lend books for children to take home overnight. A coworker can begin circulating around with a basket of books from the lending library for children to choose from and sign up for. Other children can begin putting on their outside garments. Do you anticipate any disorderly behavior from particular children? Sit down with these individuals before it can happen and read them a story.

Some programs open their playgrounds at the end of the day and have the children play outside until their parents come or the bus arrives. Be sure that you or another staff member says a personal "So long, see you tomorrow!" to each child.

ESTABLISH CLEAR LIMITS, AND ENFORCE THEM CONSISTENTLY

Children are used to having the adults around them try to make them behave. When outbursts occur, adults often swoop down on the perpetrators and inform them in no uncertain terms, "I told you not to do that!" or "What's the matter with you? You know the rules!" Chances are, however, that the children do not know the rules. They may have heard adults talking about rules, but what do they really mean? Preschool children learn most effectively from acting (trial and error) or from seeing others act.

Words do not have the same effect for these preliterate youngsters as they do for adults. Children must hear the same words repeated over and over and applied to actions they have witnessed or participated in for them to become meaningful. Nevertheless, words need to be used to help the teacher set the tone for what is acceptable behavior in the classroom and what is not.

We call these words *limits* rather than rules. They tell children what is allowed. They need to be few, simple, and to the point:

1. No one can be hurt by anyone.
2. No one can destroy any materials. (Demaree, 1995, p. 32)

Teachers need to be committed to enforcing these limits with firmness, consistency, and compassion. They do not need to announce the limits before something happens. When children get out of bounds with inappropriate behavior, teachers need to stop the behavior and say aloud, "No one can be hurt by anyone in the classroom, Sondra. Your yelling is hurting Stephanie. Please stop it." Or "No one can destroy any materials in this classroom, Rodney. Please get a sponge and you can scrub off the crayon marks you made on the wall."

These should be the only firm limits. When the rules are few and simple, children will come to accept and respect them. But you must enforce them every time when child behavior gets out of hand. How you do it makes the difference in prosocial guidance. Be firm but compassionate. Don't lose your temper or shout. Limits like this should make children feel safe and secure, not threatened. As Demaree (1995) points out, "Every child in the class wants to behave appropriately; some children just do not know how or do not feel safe and therefore act out" (p. 32).

These limits are concerned with safety for everyone, not punishment for individuals who do not behave. The first limit, "No one can be hurt by anyone," means that children are safe from others and even from themselves. The teacher won't let them jump from a moving swing, for instance, or walk too closely behind it because they might hurt themselves. The second limit, "No one can destroy any materials," means that children are safe from having their products destroyed—that means block buildings, paintings, and even puzzles. It also means that toys, games, and equipment are safe from being damaged or destroyed by others. Such limits should give everyone a sense of relief that appropriate behavior by everyone is expected and inappropriate behavior will be stopped. Such limits are a definite form of prevention of irresponsible behavior.

INVOLVE CHILDREN IN MAKING RULES

Rules, on the other hand, are on-the-spot agreements involving an immediate concern that requires some kind of control. The children who will be affected by them should be involved in making some of them. For example, Justin is standing on a chair in the block corner to build his tower "up to the ceiling." The other children are worried that it will crash into their buildings when it falls. The teacher has her own concern about enforcing the limit of no one being hurt. Justin's building may indeed fall on another child, or Justin himself may fall off the chair.

The time is ripe to talk things over with the builders. Have them each express their concerns and listen to yours. Then ask them, "What do you think the rule should be about how high a block building can be built?" One may say, "As high as your head." Another, "Three feet high" (although he may not know how high that is). Justin wants the rule to be "as high as you can reach when you stand on a chair," but the others say no to this. You can offer a compromise: "What about as high as you can reach while standing on the floor?" Yes, everyone agrees, including Justin who sees that he is outnumbered. At this point you can record the block-building rule on a sign to be displayed in the area: "Height of buildings: as high as builder can reach while standing on floor."

Obviously, you could have made this rule yourself without asking the children. But you realize they need to feel an ownership of the program, too, and they are more likely to obey a rule they have made themselves. When children understand that you will listen to them and respect their ideas, they are also more inclined to listen to you and follow the limits you require.

Going on field trips, for instance, requires that children stay together and not cross a street until directed to. Safety rules are especially important here. Talk with the group about how they should walk down the sidewalk. Ask them what rules they should follow when walking. Can they decide to walk with a partner, holding hands and walking two by two in a line? Before they leave the building, have them practice following the "walking rule" as they walk around the classroom.

Teachers who do not understand the reasoning behind child involvement in rule making sometimes have difficulty putting it into practice. As DeVries and Zan (1994) point out:

> Rule making presents a clear opportunity for children to exercise autonomy. Many teach-ers feel nervous at first about turning the rule-making process over to children. They may believe children cannot make rules. They may fear that children will make unacceptable rules, or worse yet, no rules at all. These fears have not been realized in our experiences of observing young children participate in rule making. (p. 126)

As you have seen in the examples previously described, by allowing children to participate in making rules that affect them directly, you help children develop the following prosocial attitudes:

1. Learn safety concerns and empathy for others
2. Feel an ownership in classroom decisions
3. Feel a shared responsibility in what happens in the classroom

It is important, however, that you do not overdo the rule making. Because the children themselves asked your help in resolving their block-building dilemma, it was appropriate to record the solution in the form of a rule. But too many rules can make life unpleasant and oppressive for everyone in the classroom. When a child runs around wildly, for instance, you can stop him and apply the safety limit already estab-lished, saying, "No one can be hurt by anyone, Mark, not even you. You could hurt yourself and others with your running"—rather than scolding Mark or posting a rule saying, "No running in the room."

Prosocial guidance asks you to take this positive stand regarding children's behav-ior. The children themselves come to understand that you are not blaming them for being bad but protecting them from being hurt. Having children help make certain rules is still another form of positive prevention against inappropriate behavior.

INTRODUCE NEW MATERIALS TO EVERYONE, AND SET UP TURN-TAKING ARRANGEMENTS

Here is the opportunity for you to teach turn taking directly with materials the children are sure to enjoy. Plan to bring in a new material to be used in a different learning cen-ter *every week*. It can be an African-American character doll such as Cassie to go with the book *Tar Beach* or Rosalba, a Hispanic doll, to go with the book *Abuela* for the book center; it can be a new red fire truck for the block center, an electronic keyboard for the music center, or a pair of binoculars and a bird book for the science center.

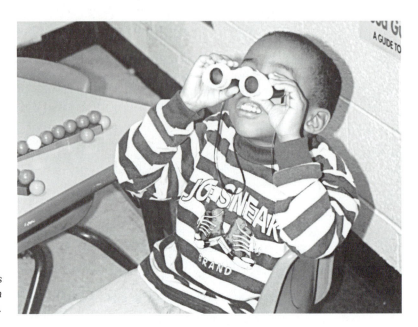

Help children learn to take turns by bringing in a new toy each week.

Children will be more excited than ever to participate in circle time on the days you bring in a "surprise." Once again, be sure to hold back some of the new toys and materials at the beginning of the year so you will have these surprises to offer later. Keep each weekly surprise in a bag. Tell the children which learning center it belongs to and have them try to guess what it is. Give them some hints. Then reveal the new toy and pass it around. Next comes setting up the turn taking.

Have the children decide how to take turns with the new material until everyone gets a chance to play with it. You can introduce new turn-taking methods every week and then let the children vote on which one they will use on that particular week. Figure 5-2 lists some possibilities.

Using Turn-Taking Devices

Children like the idea of putting all their names in a hat and then drawing out a name for a turn. Have all who want a turn write, print, or scribble their name or initials on a

Figure 5-2   Turn-taking devices

1. Name tags drawn out of hat
2. Learning center necklaces
3. Sign-up sheet
4. Numbered tickets
5. Kitchen timer or egg hourglass for controlling amount of time

sheet of paper from a little pad, fold it, and put it in the hat. Choose someone to draw out the name of who comes first, second, third, and so on. It is not necessary to draw all the names at once. Write those drawn on a numbered list for turns. If more turns are needed, more names can be drawn later.

For certain items, teachers will want to put them in their particular learning centers and let children choose learning center necklaces to play in the area with the item. In case not everyone wants to play with an item, a sign-up sheet may be a more convenient way to take turns for those who do.

Numbered tickets work like drawing names out of a hat. Whoever gets number 1 gets the first turn, and so on. If everyone wants to play with the item right from the start, this may be the fairest method. How long should they play before it is the next person's turn? A kitchen timer can be used to keep track of whatever time the group decides.

Once the children have decided how turn taking should be regulated, put the new item on a certain shelf or spot in the learning center so they can find it easily and return it when finished. Now it is up to the children to regulate their own turns. By allowing them to decide how to manage their own behavior, you send a positive message of trust to the children, as well as reducing or even eliminating possession disputes over favorite toys. It is time well spent, and for some children this *process* of setting up turns is even more interesting than actually playing with the item.

MODEL GENEROSITY WITH BOOK CHARACTERS, PUPPETS, AND YOUR OWN ACTIONS

Taking turns and waiting for turns are aspects of the prosocial behavior *generosity.* Giving a gift, giving a turn, or giving something meaningful to another person are also forms of generosity. Young children learn generosity by seeing people giving gifts to others, by giving something to others themselves, and by being complimented for their generous actions. Children who have learned to give are less likely to be involved in disputes over toys or turns.

In this possession-oriented world of ours, mainstream American culture focuses more of its time on getting rather than giving. Television programs bombard us with ads about what we must buy to make our lives complete. Stores offer discounts on every imaginable item. Junk mail floods our homes with deals we have trouble refusing. Few messages come to us about giving. As I have mentioned:

> We send children mixed messages. We tell them it is a good idea to give to people in need, but then the youngsters see us turn away charity solicitors at our front doors. Children hear us refuse to lend a lawn mower or power tool to a neighbor who has a need. "Let him buy his own," we say, "Let him work as hard as we did to buy this one." (Beaty, 1998, p. 157)

Not every culture values material possessions as highly as mainstream America does. Native American people and Pacific Islanders, for instance, teach their children the importance of giving. At social gatherings they have "giveaways" when valuable gifts of food, money, and craft items are given away to certain people in attendance by those sponsoring the event. Others willingly give a personal possession to a neighbor or relative who admires or has need of it. Such cultures believe that the givers are enhanced by the person accepting something from them.

As a preschool teacher, you need to help young children learn the importance of giving as well as sharing possessions, regardless of society's confusion over this issue. One way you can help children experience such generosity is by involving them with stories about book characters who give things to others.

Act Out Stories About Characters Who Give Gifts

In *Pablo's Tree* by Pat Mora (1994), a little Hispanic boy makes his birthday visit to his grandfather's house where his special birth tree is growing, to hear once again the story of his first four birthdays and find out what gift his grandfather Lito will hang on the tree for this, his fifth birthday. On his first birthday, it was yellow, orange, and red streamers; second birthday, balloons of every color; third birthday, paper lanterns; fourth birthday, tiny birdcages; and fifth birthday, bells and chimes.

Talk to the children about the gifts made by the grandfather. Do they understand that these simple gifts represent love? Make a birthday tree in your classroom by standing a large tree limb in a bucket filled with dirt. When someone's birthday comes, have the children make surprise paper gifts to be hung on the tree. For children whose birthdays come on days when the program is closed, have them choose a day to be their pretend birthday.

A Birthday Basket for Tia by Pat Mora (1992) has a little girl, Cecilia, making up a birthday basket of gifts for her great-aunt Tia's 90th birthday. In the basket she puts a book, a mixing bowl, a flowerpot, a teacup, and a red ball to remind her of all the things the two of them have done together.

Have your children cut out pictures from old magazines of things they would like to give to someone. They can paste them on cardboard backing. Take a basket around to collect their "gifts." Can they tell why they are giving a gift like this?

Alejandro's Gift by Richard E. Albert (1994) is about an old man who lives by himself in the desert and feels so lonely he plants a garden to occupy his time. When a ground squirrel comes to drink water from his garden, he feels less lonely. Soon other desert birds and animals visit the garden, and Alejandro decides to dig a water hole for the animals and fill it with water from his windmill. At first he puts the hole so close to his house that the animals are afraid. But then he moves his gift water hole farther away, and soon they all come for water.

Have your children find each animal in the wonderfully detailed illustrations as you read its name. Can they also give gifts like this to wildlife? What about starting a bird feeder or a birdbath near the classroom?

The Rainbow Fish by Marcus Pfister (1992) is about the most beautiful fish in the ocean with its blue, green, purple, and sparkling silver scales. The other fish try to get Rainbow Fish to play with them, but he only glides past them, letting his scales sparkle. One day a little fish asks Rainbow Fish for one of his sparkling scales, but Rainbow Fish refuses in such anger the little fish is shocked. He tells the others, and they soon turn away from the proud Rainbow Fish. Now Rainbow Fish has no friends. He goes to the wise octopus for advice. She tells him he must give away one of his glittering scales to each of the other fish if he wants to be happy. Reluctantly Rainbow Fish begins to give away his scales. As he does so he feels better and better. At last he has only one silver scale left, but the other fish are calling him to play and off he goes.

You can purchase a rainbow fish with removable scales, but better still, make your own cardboard fish or puppet fish from a sock covered with peel-off stickers of various colors. Children love to play the Rainbow Fish Giveaway game when they have cardboard or puppet fish of their own to paste their stickers on. Have children take turns being Rainbow Fish. Afterward ask them how they feel about giving away something they treasure. Ask them how they feel when they see someone else enjoying their treasure.

Whenever you see children giving or sharing something of theirs with someone else, make a comment about how they remind you of Rainbow Fish or Cecilia or Alejandro. Let them see you giving something to someone in need: an article of clothing, a book, food, or even money. By promoting prosocial behaviors such as giving and sharing like this, you will find that children are less likely to squabble over toys and materials.

REFERENCES

Beaty, J. J. (1998). *Observing development of the young child.* Upper Saddle River, NJ: Merrill/Prentice Hall.

Demaree, M. A. (1995). Creating safe environments for children with Post-Traumatic Stress Disorder. *Dimensions of Early Childhood, 23*(3), 31–33.

DeVries, R., & Zan, B. (1994). *Moral classrooms, moral children: Creating a constructivist atmos-* *phere in early childhood.* New York: Teachers College Press.

Wald, P., Morris, L., & Abraham, M. (1996). Three keys for successful circle time: Responding to children with diverse abilities. *Dimensions of Early Childhood, 24*(1), 26–29.

SUGGESTED READINGS

Beaty, J. J. (1996). *Skills for preschool teachers.* Upper Saddle River, NJ: Merrill/Prentice Hall.

Beaty, J. J. (1997). *Building bridges with multicultural picture books: For children 3–5.* Upper Saddle River, NJ: Merrill/Prentice Hall.

Cartledge, G., & Milburn, J. F. (1995). *Teaching social skills to children and youth: Innovative approaches.* Boston: Allyn & Bacon.

Fields, M. V., & Boesser, C. (1994). *Constructive guidance and discipline: Preschool and primary* *education.* Upper Saddle River, NJ: Merrill/Prentice Hall.

Honig, A. S., & Wittmer, D. S. (1996). Helping children become more prosocial: Ideas for classrooms, families, schools, and communities. *Young Children, 51*(2), 62–70.

Miller, D. F. (1996). *Positive child guidance.* Albany, NY: Delmar.

CHILDREN'S BOOKS

Albert, R. E. (1994). *Alejandro's gift*. San Francisco: Chronicle.

Mora, P. (1992). *A birthday basket for Tia*. New York: Simon & Schuster.

Mora, P. (1994). *Pablo's tree*. New York: Macmillan.

Pfister, M. (1992). *Rainbow fish*. New York: North-South Books.

VIDEOTAPES

Magna Systems. (Producer). *Guidance and discipline: The curriculum* (no. 2). (Available from Magna Systems, 95 W. County Line Rd., Barrington, IL 60010)

National Association for the Education of Young Children. (Producer). *Discipline: Appropriate guidance of young children*. (Available from NAEYC, 1509 16th St. N.W., Washington, DC 20036-1426)

LEARNING ACTIVITIES

1. Look at each of the time blocks in your daily schedule. What kinds of disruptive behavior can you anticipate happening in each? How can you prevent it? Develop a plan and implement it for one time block.

2. What behavior limits are used in your program? How do your children come to learn about them? How to you enforce them? How are they working? What do you suggest doing to help them work better? Try it and record the results.

3. Have you ever involved children in making rules in the classroom? Describe what happened. What kinds of rules would you want children to be involved in making in the block center, for example? Try it and record what happens.

4. Introduce a new material to the children as described in this chapter, and set up a turn-taking arrangement with the children. Describe what happens.

5. Read a book that features giving, such as those discussed here, and have children get involved in the story through puppets, dolls, or dramatic play. How can you tell that they understand the concept of being generous?

CHAPTER 6

Using Positive Intervention to Help Children Manage Their Own Behavior

☐ Intervene when children get out of control, without blaming or shaming.

☐ Accept children's negative feelings.

☐ Help children verbalize their feelings.

☐ Redirect children's disruptive behavior into calming activities.

☐ Model self-control by curbing your own negative words and actions.

Some of children's out-of-control behavior can be warded off before it begins by your alert anticipation of their actions, as discussed in Chapter 5. You notice that Anthony has not said a word to anyone since he entered the room. You also know that he possesses quite a temper when he feels out of sorts. Now you step in before the other boys, who are beginning to tease him, set him off. "Let's look at a book together, Anthony. You choose one."

But more often than not, your attention may be focused elsewhere in the classroom, and Anthony's temper suddenly explodes with yelling and hitting before you are even aware of the situation. Now you must intervene swiftly, effectively, and compassionately. *Positive intervention* means stopping out-of-control child behavior such as yelling, name-calling, hitting, pushing, biting, fighting, crying, running wildly, damaging materials, or acting dangerously—in a calm, not angry manner, without blaming or shaming the children involved.

USING CONFLICTS AS LEARNING OPPORTUNITIES

Teachers need to look upon such outbursts as *learning opportunities* for the youngsters, not as episodes children will be punished for. Do you have trouble coming to grips with such a notion? To look at conflicts as learning opportunities is a real "paradigm shift" in the mind-set of many teachers. Consider Crosser's (1992) valuable insight:

> Conflict is a natural part of living and working together in groups. It is good that conflicts arise in the early childhood classroom because it is only through facing conflicts that children can learn the skills necessary to resolve real-life problems. (p. 28)

It is up to you to intervene in such a conflict as Anthony's, but not to punish him or his aggressors. Instead, you will be helping him learn *self-control*, as well as helping the other boys learn *empathy*. This is the real lesson of prosocial guidance: learning to get along with one another in a humane manner right from the earliest years. If children can learn this skill in preschool, then they can carry such lessons with them throughout life. Imagine what a difference this learning can make as these boys (and girls) grow older. Imagine how important your own role becomes in helping youngsters develop such prosocial behavior. If you really believe this to be true, you will come to welcome conflict and never want to punish a child again!

INTERVENE WHEN CHILDREN GET OUT OF CONTROL, WITHOUT BLAMING OR SHAMING

The majority of child conflicts in preschool can be resolved by the children themselves without teacher intervention. It is when things get out of hand—when children cry or scream or become physically abusive—that the teacher must step in to stop the behavior. Children expect this of you. The youngster who is out of control needs your help to bring him back to normal. Other children involved may need your assistance to prevent injuries. Once more the issue is safety rather than "bad" behavior.

Halting Out-of-Control Behavior

Move quickly to the site of the disruption, and halt the out-of-control child's behavior with a calm but firm voice. Do not call out across the room. That only disturbs everyone else. Try to keep emotional outbursts as private and contained as possible. It is not the others' business. They can go on with their own activities.

You may need to halt physical aggression by putting an arm around the child and moving him away from the others. If he is kicking, you may need to remove his shoes. You can hold him until he calms down, all the while speaking in low, repetitive words: "Calm down, Anthony, calm down, calm down. It's all right now. You're safe now, Anthony. Calm down, calm down. I'm going to hold you until you feel calm enough to control yourself. I'll ask you when I think you're ready." Then you can wait quietly until you feel the child relax. Ask him again if he feels calm enough. If he does not answer, he probably is not ready.

Some programs have an adult-size rocking chair in a corner that children use as a private space and teachers use to help upset children calm down by holding them on their laps and rocking. This is not a time-out chair but a quiet and comfortable refuge in the busy classroom. It is important to have such a private, comforting retreat, especially if you have children in the program who lose control easily.

When the child is calm enough to talk, let him tell you what happened if he wants to. You can listen to his remarks impartially, not blaming or shaming him or anyone else. If the child does not want to be held after he has regained control, have him rock himself until he feels better. You should also talk with the other children involved in the incident. The boys who teased Anthony need to know how he feels. They need to think about how they would feel if it had happened to them.

No Blaming or Shaming

Most children are well aware of what it means to be blamed for doing something. They or their siblings have been blamed for accidents and incidents at home. They have seen other children trying to avoid being blamed for something they did. They understand that the person who gets the blame also gets the punishment or humiliation. A great deal of effort is thus exerted by children to escape being blamed: "He did it!" "It's her fault!" "He started it!" "It wasn't my fault!"

Whether or not they are the ones to blame, young children vociferously deny their guilt and vigorously blame someone else when things go wrong. Being blamed for doing something wrong creates a powerful feeling of shame or guilt within a person. Damon (1988) describes it well:

> Shame is a feeling of embarrassment that is experienced when one fails to act in accord with perceived behavioral standards. Some believe that the capacity for shame is generated in early confrontations with parents over affect-laden issues like toilet training. Whether intentional or not, parents often humiliate children in the process of inducing them to use the potty. (p. 21)

As a teacher or student teacher, you can relate to such feelings. No one wants to be blamed or feel the shame of having an accident or doing something wrong. When such a feeling of shame is internalized, it takes the form of guilt. For preschool children just beginning to sort out the ways of the world, that is where the danger lies: feeling guilty. As Damon (1988) notes, "Guilt poses the greatest danger to the preschoolers' emerging sense of initiative. . . . It can curb children's pride in their achievements and their exuberance in the face of their new-found physical and mental powers" (p. 23).

Whereas adults may be able to swallow their pride and accept their guilt for causing something unfortunate, young children tend to let guilt erode their self-esteem. No children's blame or guilt should be involved in the positive intervention you employ with out-of-control youngsters. They have not done anything wrong. They have merely lost control. They need your help to regain their sense of equilibrium, not to be blamed for trying to harm others, not to feel shame for exposing themselves to the ridicule of others. When they have calmed down, you can begin to work with them on redirecting their anger in acceptable ways. As Greenspan (1997) points out:

> To feel secure, they must believe that adults will help them keep their anger, greed, frustration, and other negative emotions in check. This must be done, however, through positive means that impose rigor yet protect the child's self-esteem. (p. 224)

ACCEPT CHILDREN'S NEGATIVE FEELINGS

Feelings are powerful stimulants of behavior for both the children and you. Can you feel it in the pit of your stomach when Kendra starts yelling angrily at the girls in the dramatic play center and then throws her purse at them? Are you yourself upset about the situation? Are you prepared for something like this to happen?

Don't wait for a negative outburst to occur and then be forced to act inappropriately. Decide what to do ahead of time. You need to be prepared for children to express negative feelings just as you yourself do from time to time. It is natural for children to feel angry or frustrated. Your acceptance of their feelings, however, does not mean approval of their actions. It means that you recognize they are feeling bad and that you will help them deal with these emotions in a positive, prosocial manner. Your acceptance helps children control the inappropriate aspects of their behavior.

If you believe that conflicts are learning opportunities, then it should not upset you when a conflict does arise. Tell yourself that this is another learning situation for a child. Approach the conflict with a calm acceptance, knowing that you are there to help the child learn to deal with negative feelings.

Displaying Acceptance of Feelings

Display your acceptance by not becoming angry yourself. You must neutralize your own emotions before dealing with a child's negative feelings. Your unruffled behavior will have a calming effect on the child. Start by communicating nonverbally to Kendra that you are not upset with her. You may not like her angry yelling and throwing of the purse, but you realize that children's inappropriate actions can be redirected once their emotions have calmed down. That is your first task: to help diffuse Kendra's anger.

Your facial features should remain unruffled and not project anger or distaste. Your body language and gestures should display the same calmness as you approach her. No rushing to her side or flailing of your arms is necessary. Take it easy. Your calm, matter-of-fact approach tells the child you are not angry at her.

Your words and tone of voice should also project calmness. "Kendra, Kendra, calm down. What's wrong? Can you tell me about it? It's all right now. It's all over. Can you tell me what happened?"

Give Kendra a chance for your demeanor and words to sink in. She will eventually understand that you are not scolding her and that you want her to tell you what happened. She should already know you accept her as a person by your previous treatment of her. You have given her personal attention, listened with serious intent to whatever she had to say, helped her get involved in activities, displayed her work attractively—all of the nonverbal forms of acceptance you provide for every child.

Now it is time for the next step: helping her verbalize her negative feelings in an acceptable manner.

 # HELP CHILDREN VERBALIZE NEGATIVE FEELINGS

Not all upset children shout out angry words like Kendra. Some display emotions inappropriately by hitting, kicking, biting, pushing, or damaging materials. Their anger, frustration, or rage need an acceptable outlet. Expressing such feelings out loud helps diffuse them. But it must be done in an acceptable manner, not shouted at someone. And it must be done with acceptable words, not name-calling. This is your next task: to help children diffuse their anger by putting it into acceptable words.

When children are able to say things like "You make me really mad!" "I am so-o-o angry!" "I am furious!" it not only stops the inappropriate action on the part of others but also helps the child get control of her feelings. Putting strong feelings like this into words helps diffuse such negative emotions. It enables the child to think about what she feels. If she can think about it, she has more control over the emotion. She can take other actions such as leaving the scene of the conflict, or going to a private area to calm down, or getting help from the teacher.

Help children learn to express in words by reflecting what you observe in your voice and body language for the child to see.

If the emotion is strong enough, the child may end up crying. Rather than telling Kendra to stop crying, you should let her continue. Crying, like saying the words aloud, is a catharsis for many children. You can help her find a private spot to pull herself together. After she has calmed down enough to listen, you can talk with her about feelings.

Reflecting Children's Feelings in Your Words

To help a child learn to express negative feelings in words, you might begin by reflecting what you observe in your own words, saying something like "Kendra, you seem to be very angry at the other girls. Your face has a mad look. What do you feel like?"

Little by little, the child may be able to respond about her feelings, perhaps only with one word at a time. "Mad!" You can repeat her word: "Yes, mad. I can see by your face that you are mad. How else do you feel?"

Some children will only want to blame others for whatever happened. Let them express anything they want to say about the affair to you. This also is cathartic for children. You can accept whatever they say, whether or not you agree. Once again, the focus should be on feelings, not blame: "Yes, Kendra, I hear what you are saying. How does that make you feel? Tell me how you feel about that."

Helping Children Verbalize Feelings

Finally, you may be able to ask Kendra to put her feelings into more words. "You say you are very angry about the girls in the dramatic play center. You feel very bad about it. Can you tell them that? Can you tell them how you feel? Saying things about feelings is better than shouting. Telling people how you feel is better than throwing things. Let's see if you can tell them how you feel. I'll go over there with you. Want to try it? It will make you feel better."

By intervening in negative actions this way every time they happen, children will begin to understand what is acceptable in the classroom and what is not: that you expect them to talk, not hit. Talking rationally is not always easy for children (or anyone) in the throes of a temper explosion; but youngsters like Kendra will eventually have plenty of help. Her peers will begin saying to her, "Tell them. Don't throw things," or "Tell her. Don't hit her!" When you hear other children using your words like this, you will know your prosocial approach is beginning to be effective.

Teaching Children Feeling Words

What about children who do not know the words for expressing emotions? Three-year-olds, especially, may have a limited vocabulary. They can learn such words by hearing you and the others use them, but in addition, plan to arrange learning activities focused on "feeling words."

For example, read an appropriate "feelings" book to a small group at a time, and have them act out the roles of the characters. *I Was So Mad!* (1974) by Norma Simon shows brief episodes of a girl or boy character getting angry at other children because of the things they do:

1. The boys try to make the girl character play the role of mother while they play fireman and astronaut;
2. a boy kicks down a girl's block building;
3. a boy gets blamed for something he didn't do;
4. a little boy runs over a bigger boy's toy and breaks it;
5. others point their fingers at a girl and tease her.

These episodes show the children becoming angry but not how they resolve the conflicts. Go around your small group, asking each child to tell what he or she would do and say to the other child. Youngsters who do not know the words soon learn them when they hear them repeated by their peers.

Feelings (1984) by Aliki has a situation on every page or two with tiny cartoon-like characters enacting a feelings episode to illustrate the words that go with the feeling. For example, on the "How Do You Feel?" page, a little boy demonstrates a series

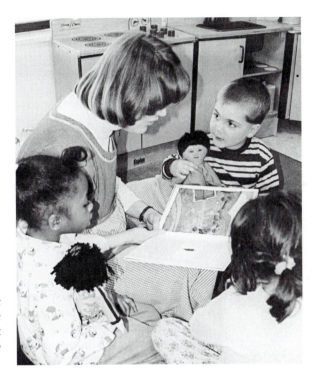

Children can identify with book characters like Carlos from the story Carlos and the Squash Plant *and thus learn what it feels like to be embarrassed.*

of different feelings to a little girl, who must guess what they are. Children learn words like *angry, sad, happy, lonely, brave, shy, insulted, scared, furious, excited, impatient, proud, selfish, quiet,* and *fine.* Have your children guess what feeling the boy is demonstrating each time. Then have them display a feeling of their own and let the others try to put words to it.

In the book *Carlos and the Squash Plant* by Jan Romero Stevens (1993), Carlos, who comes home dirty from working in the field, refuses to wash his ears. Overnight a squash plant begins growing out of one ear. The boy is so embarrassed he hides the plant under a large hat. Children enjoy identifying with the characters in books like this, telling how they would feel or what they would do. Feeling words such as *embarrassed* and *ashamed* take on real meaning when the children pretend to be the book character or when they reenact stories with character dolls.

Dealing with Name-Calling

On the other hand, some children know too many words and may use them inappropriately whenever the occasion arises. Name-calling is a case in point. Preschoolers may not know the meaning of certain words, but when they see an angry response from adults or other children whenever they use certain words, it only encourages them to continue. Teachers need to recognize that words can hurt just as much as fists do. As Essa (1990) notes, "Children, like adults, want to feel good about themselves, so anything that does not reinforce a positive self-image is hurtful. The child who calls other children unpleasant names has found a way of hurting them" (p. 76).

Name-calling only works when someone responds. If everyone ignores it, it stops. You can help stop this inappropriate practice, first, by ignoring it yourself. Do not make eye contact with the caller. Ask the recipient not to look at or respond to the caller. Have the child turn her back or walk away. This time it is you, not the recipient, who needs to verbalize feelings.

Read privately to the child who is doing the name-calling a book such as Johanna Cole's (1990) *Don't Call Me Names!* The characters are animals who have the same problems as children. Nell is a frog who loves where she lives on Pond Street except for Mike (a fox) and Joe (a pig) who always tease her and make fun of her name ("Nell, Nell, dumbbell!"). Nell's porcupine friend Amy helps her turn the tables on the teasers, and soon they run away. Have your listener talk about how each of these characters feel when names are called. Can she relate to these feelings?

Read the same book to the victim of the name-calling. Have this child pay attention to the various characters' responses when the name-calling focuses on them. What happens to the name-callers when the characters respond by running away, crying, or hiding? What happens to the name-callers when the characters don't run away but stand up to them and even try to scare them? Ask your listener how she would handle the situation.

Other children's books featuring name-calling include these:

Bootsie Barker Bites, B. Bottner (New York: Putnam, 1992)
Fighting Words, E. Merriam (New York: Morrow, 1992)
Emily Umily, K. Corrigan (Toronto: Annick, 1984)
Move Over, Twerp, M. Alexander (New York: Dial, 1981)
My Name Is Not Dummy, E. Crary (Seattle: Parenting, 1983)
Oliver Button Is a Sissy, T. DePaola (San Diego: Harcourt Brace, 1979)
Willy the Wimp, A. Browne (New York: Knopf, 1984)

Use any of these books the same way, reading them on an individual basis to the name-caller and asking how the book character felt when names were called. Then read the same book to the victim of the name-calling, asking this child what the book victims did to end the name-calling. Children learn about articulating feelings from the characters in the books.

REDIRECT CHILDREN'S DISRUPTIVE BEHAVIOR INTO CALMING ACTIVITIES

When children's emotions are so out of control that they have great difficulty composing themselves, try redirecting them to a calming activity. If their misbehavior involves their use of hands in pushing, pinching, throwing, or hitting other children or being destructive of materials, they may be able to work off this negative energy with clay, play dough, finger painting, water play, sand play, or dolls and stuffed animals. If their voice is out of control, music or the tape recorder may help them regain their composure.

Don't force out-of-control children into an activity, but calmly offer it to them. This is not a punishment. You know your children well enough to predict the kind of activity that will calm them down. If they refuse one activity, try another one. Always set some materials aside for this use—something not available every day but only for a special occasion like this.

Using Art Materials

Many disruptive children find relief in working with clay or play dough. If their negative energy is being expressed through their hands, have them push and pinch and punch clay or plasticine. These materials are somewhat difficult to work with at first. Children need to exert strength in their hands and fingers to mold the materials. Play dough responds more easily. If you note that upset children get frustrated with the stiffer materials, switch them to play dough.

On the other hand, some out-of-control children respond best to finger painting. They can get their whole bodies involved in swishing arms and hands around and around in the paint. Releasing energy through these movements helps calm them down. Painting with a brush at an easel can achieve the same results. Such children are not painting a picture but processing emotions. It is a therapeutic activity that can be used by a child as long as the emotions last.

Using Water Play

Most preschool classrooms contain water tables of some kind. If yours does not, bring in a plastic tub and place it on a low table the children can reach easily. Have plastic aprons hanging nearby, a sheet of plastic underneath to protect the floor, and water play accessories in the water or on nearby shelves.

Most children love to play with water. They love its feel on their hands: the way they can swish it, splash it, pour it, and squirt it. As Crosser (1994) notes:

> Water is intriguing. It seems to draw children to explore its structure and properties. Because water is naturally fascinating, the thoughtful teacher can structure the environment and materials in the water center to make the most of water play. (p. 28)

When using water play for therapeutic purposes, you may want to keep the water table private for the upset child to use alone. Or set up a special plastic tub for the child's individual use. He may want to use his hands to turn an eggbeater or squeeze a baster. Some teachers provide a set of sponges of different sizes and shapes for such children to squeeze. Outside the classroom, give the child a bucket of water and a wide paintbrush for painting a wall, fence, or sidewalk with water.

Running water also has a calming, almost mesmerizing effect on children. Upset children can play in your sink, filling and emptying containers with running water. Ask the children what water activities will make them feel better.

Most children love to play with water and find it to be a very calming activity after a classroom disruption.

Using Sand Play

Sand play can be an especially important therapeutic activity for emotionally distraught children. Wheat (1995) mentions:

> The very process of working with the sand tray regularly has helped some children immensely. Teachers have discussed how they have watched children work through sadness, anger, and disappointment and finally return to the group in a relaxed state. (p. 82)

In addition to working off negative energy through moving sand with their hands, distressed children can play with the toy figures you provide to create and manipulate their own world. Wheat (1995) notes that sand play like this can "help children who *feel* violent find *non*violent ways of dealing constructively with their distress" (p. 82). Her teachers provide 70 little figures of people, animals, trees, buildings, and vehicles for children to construct their own world in the sand. They work by themselves for 30 to 60 minutes at a time. Children who come from dysfunctional families with little sense of order at home can create their own world of harmony in such a sand table. It is a highly satisfying activity for them.

Most classrooms have only one table that is used by a small group for either water or sand play. Make an additional individual sand table from a plastic tub placed on a table and partly filled with fine-textured sand. Dollhouse figures of people, animals, and vehicles available from school supply catalogs can be kept separate from block play accessories and used only in this sand table. Reserve the table for regular use by one child at a time, but keep it ready for "emergency" use when a child needs to be redirected into a calming activity to work through his emotions.

Using Doll Play

Have you noticed how some children cling to a stuffed animal or cloth doll when they are out of sorts? Keep a basketful of special dolls and animals for a child to choose and play with when he is feeling bad. Be sure to have both boy and girl doll figures so that both boys and girls will have a special doll they can identify with whenever things are upsetting for them. Book character dolls make good doll playmates for children who may remember them from the stories you have read. Stuffed dogs, cats, and teddy bears are also comforting toys to hold and carry when things are not going well for children.

Keep special dolls available for children to play with when they get out of sorts.

Using Music

You remember that music can "soothe the wild beast" in all of us. Be sure to provide at least one tape cassette player, quiet tapes, and a headset for children who need something to calm them down. Making music with rhythm instruments or an electronic keyboard may be too loud at this particular time. But if children have been using their voices aggressively, they can record their talking or singing with the tape recorder. This may be all that is necessary to release tension for them. Even drumming can be used if you substitute plastic spoons for drumsticks.

Most people know of an activity that is calming for them when they get upset. It may be playing a computer game, looking at a book, digging in dirt, or tearing paper and making a collage. You can redirect your children to one of the described activities, but be open to their own suggestions as well.

No "Time-Out"

The so-called "time-out" period used in many preschool classrooms when individual children get out of hand is not a positive intervention. Sending a child to a time-out chair until he feels he can return to classroom activities without causing a disturbance is, in fact, an outright punishment. The child has behaved inappropriately. The teacher has pointed to a chair where he must sit until she releases him. In some cases she must physically take him to the chair and sit him down. She calls it "time-out." In reality it is punishment for a child's misbehavior.

Although most teachers do not discuss time-out with the class, children soon come to know what it means. It is what happens to them when they misbehave. The child sitting in the chair feels all eyes on her. She may feel really bad and even cry about her punishment because she is being humiliated in front of everyone, or she may smirk and show off because everyone is looking. As Duffy (1996) notes:

> Many a child sits on that time out chair deciding: I am a bad person; no one likes me; or she even sits there smiling because she is now the center of attention. Are those the messages we want children to receive? (p. 61)

When a particular chair is referred to and used as "the time-out chair," it becomes just like the old-fashioned "dunce chair": a threat to all and a damper on preschoolers' exuberance. When a teacher uses the word *time-out* as a threat—as in "If you don't behave, I'm going to send you to time-out!"—she further underscores its punishment intention.

Being ostracized from the other children and activities may be an effective temporary measure for stopping unwanted behavior, but it is not a prosocial act. Children feel worse because of it, not better. Their overall behavior patterns are not changed, merely stopped temporarily. These ostracized children would go right back to misbehaving except for the threat of time-out.

Real changes in behavior come from within a child. Prosocial guidance as discussed in this text helps children focus on what is right about themselves, not what is wrong. They learn how to handle negative feelings in acceptable ways. They are not punished for the behavior mistakes they make but redirected into acceptable actions. When they are guided consistently in this prosocial manner, true changes occur in their behavior. But it comes from within.

Should time-out, then, be banished totally from the classroom? No. The concept as it was originally intended can be used if teachers themselves become involved along with the out-of-control child who needs a moment away from things to gain control of herself. "C'mon, Sherry. Let's sit over here until you calm down," says the teacher. "Let me know when you feel better."

There is nothing threatening about these statements. The word *time-out* is not mentioned. No special chair is used. But the biggest difference is *the teacher remains with the out-of-control child*. The teacher is there to give comfort, support, and help for the child to gain control over her own behavior. There is no hint of being punished or ostracized. The teacher's presence makes the entire experience one of concern for the child rather than chastisement. It is time for preschool teachers to return to this original purpose for time-out.

MODEL SELF-CONTROL BY CURBING YOUR OWN NEGATIVE WORDS AND ACTIONS

Often the person who needs time-out when things get out of hand is the teacher. A preschool teacher in a boisterous group of youngsters is sometimes "pushed to the wall" by children's out-of-control actions. It is important that you take a break at this time and give yourself a chance to regain your own composure. One of the other staff members can take your place until you are calm enough to continue. As Gartrell (1994) tells us:

> Because the skills of expressing strong emotions acceptably and getting along with others are difficult even for educated adults, teachers occasionally do express anger in ways that hurt. Perhaps a first step in learning to recover from a bad episode is to recognize our feelings and *forgive* ourselves. Only then can we figure out how to make the best of a situation and to forgive the other. (p. 275)

Talk with other staff members about this problem of self-control at a staff meeting. Ask for suggestions about how to handle it for everyone. Teaching is a reciprocal occupation in which sensitive teachers learn as much as they teach.

Using a Puppet

Curbing anger is not easy for anyone. Once you feel it rise up in your throat, you must stop before you release it in the form of irate and hurtful words. Take a deep breath. Take another one. Count to 10 or use whatever other ploy seems to work for you. Some teachers immediately head for the book center to get a "feelings puppet" to be used by anyone who has strong feelings to express. Then you can say firmly, but calmly, what needs to be said through the mouth of the puppet. "Curtis, Curtis, I am really angry to see you upsetting that paint again. How can we get it cleaned up?"

The time it takes to get the puppet and return to the scene of the spill should be enough to help you gain control. Instead of yelling at Curtis, you can express your anger in an acceptable manner. Yelling at a child puts you in the same position as the child who is out of control. Anger is not helpful to either of you when expressed violently by yelling or saying hurtful words. Instead, you need to model for children how to handle anger. By using the feelings puppet, you demonstrate to Curtis and other nearby children an appropriate way to handle anger. They too can use the feelings puppet when they have strong emotions to express.

Coach them in the use of such a puppet after incidents like this have happened. Read the book *I Was So Mad!* again, and this time role-play how you would respond to the anger-causing incidents in the story by speaking through the puppet. Then pass the puppet to one of the children for him to try his own controlled expression of anger.

Identifying the Trigger That Sets Off Anger

If you can identify the trigger that sets off your anger, you may be better able to contain it when it happens. Perhaps it is a child who whines, or a child who talks back, or children who won't clean up the mess they've made. Some teachers get angry when children show little interest in an activity they have spent long hours in planning. Once you recognize such a recurring cause of your anger, you may be able to deflect your inappropriate response.

But if one should occur—if you should speak harshly or bang a book or slam a door—be sure to talk calmly to the children afterward. Tell them that teachers sometimes get angry, too, and that you are sorry you spoke so loudly or slammed the book. Apologies are also appropriate behaviors for you to model.

Modeling Self-Control

Adult modeling of self-control may be more important in the lives of young children than we previously realized. Research shows that children pay close attention to the behavior of adults when upsetting things happen. Hyson (1994) notes, "Children's observation of adults' emotion-related behavior influences many aspects of their behavior and development" (p. 129). Even babies imitate emotional facial expressions of their mothers. They also look to their caregivers to see how they will act in difficult situations before taking action themselves. But the good news is that "children who observe many instances of adults modeling empathy, generosity, and frustration tolerance are more likely to develop these qualities themselves" (Hyson, p. 129).

When frustrating situations occur for you in the classroom, remember that children are watching to see what you will do. Try not to take your frustration out on the children. Instead, turn the situation around by modeling patience or verbalizing your feelings in an acceptable manner. "Oh, no, it happened again. What are we going to do about that hitting of yours, Charlene?"

Your own behavior may well be the key to the children's behavior in the classroom. Many children will imitate the way you act. Others will imitate the words you use. Listen and you may hear yourself talking when children encounter a frustrating situation. "Tell him—don't hit him, Charlene!" Then you'll know you've made a real difference by using prosocial guidance.

REFERENCES

Crosser, S. (1992). Managing the early childhood classroom. *Young Children, 47*(2), 23–29.

Crosser, S. (1994). Making the most of water play. *Young Children, 49*(5), 28–32.

Damon, W. (1988). *The moral child: Nurturing children's natural moral growth.* New York: Free Press.

Duffy, R. (1996). Time out: How it is abused. *Child Care Information Exchange, 111,* 61.

Essa, E. L. (1990). *A practical guide to solving preschool behavior problems.* Albany, NY: Delmar.

Gartrell, D. (1994). *A guidance approach to discipline.* Albany, NY: Delmar.

Greenspan, S. I. (1997). *The growth of the mind: And the endangered origins of intelligence.* Reading, MA: Addison-Wesley.

Hyson, M. C. (1994). *The emotional development of young children: Building an emotion-centered curriculum.* New York: Teachers College Press.

Wheat, R. (1995). Help children work through emotional difficulties—Sand trays are great! *Young Children, 51*(1), 82–83.

SUGGESTED READINGS

Bailey, B. (1996). Understanding temper tantrums. *Children Our Concern, 21*(1), 22–23.

Beaty, J. J. (1995). *Converting conflicts in preschool.* Fort Worth, TX: Harcourt Brace.

Beaty, J. J. (1996). *Skills for preschool teachers.* Upper Saddle River, NJ: Merrill/Prentice Hall.

Betz, C. (1994). Beyond time out: Tips from a teacher. *Young Children, 49*(3), 10–14.

DeVries, R., & Zan, B. (1994). *Moral classrooms, moral children: Creating a constructivist atmosphere in early education.* New York: Teachers College Press.

Furman, R. A. (1995). Helping children cope with stress and deal with feelings. *Young Children, 50*(2), 33–41.

Koplow, L. (Ed.). (1996). *Unsmiling faces: How preschools can heal.* New York: Teachers College Press.

CHILDREN'S BOOKS

Aliki. (1984). *Feelings.* New York: Mulberry.

Cole, J. (1990). *Don't call me names!* New York: Random House.

Simon, N. (1974). *I was so mad!* Morton Grove, IL: Whitman.

Stevens, J. R. (1993). *Carlos and the squash plant (Carlos y la planta de calabaza).* Flagstaff, AZ: Northland.

VIDEOTAPES

Educational Productions. (Producer). *Reframing discipline: Doing the groundwork* (no. 1); *Understanding difficult behavior* (no. 3). (Available from Educational Productions, 9000 S.W. Gemini Drive, Beaverton, OR 97008)

National Association for the Education of Young Children. (Producer). *Discipline: Appropriate guidance of young children.* (Available from NAEYC, 1509 16th St. N.W., Washington, DC 20036-1426)

National Association for the Education of Young Children. (Producer). *Painting a positive picture: Proactive behavior management.* (Available from NAEYC, 1509 16th St. N.W., Washington, DC 20036-1426)

LEARNING ACTIVITIES

1. How can you halt the out-of-bounds physical aggression of one child against another without blaming or punishing? Why should you not call out the child's name across the room? Record what happens next time you stop a physically aggressive child.

2. How can you display acceptance of a child's angry feelings, while at the same time helping diffuse the anger? Try it and record what happens.

3. How does helping a child verbalize negative feelings diffuse the feelings? How can you get a child to verbalize? Try it and record what happens.

4. What kinds of calming activities does your program offer for redirecting out-of-bounds children? Try out one of the materials suggested here and record what happens.

5. How is time-out used in your program? What is the result? Is there a better way to help children stop misbehaving? Try it and record what happens.

CHAPTER 7

Using Positive Reinforcement to Help Children Learn Prosocial Behaviors

- Look for and reinforce with verbal and nonverbal cues the prosocial actions of disruptive children.

- Make eye or verbal contact with disruptive children only after their misbehavior has stopped.

- Help disruptive children find activities they can excel in.

- Help attention-seeking children learn to make friends.

- Model friendship by developing friendships with every child.

Positive reinforcement is the strategy that helps teachers focus on children's desirable behaviors and ignore, as much as possible, their undesirable ones. It helps children learn which of their behaviors are acceptable in the classroom and which ones are not. We often assume that young children know the difference, but that is not necessarily the case. Behaviors that are tolerated in the home may not be appropriate in the classroom.

For children who are desperately trying to gain the attention of the adult in charge, almost any behavior seems right as long as the teacher recognizes them. Teachers often focus on inappropriate behavior because it is so attention getting. When a child yells or hits or damages another child's work, we rush over to stop him. Yet when we respond to such behavior with punishment, we do not change it. We only halt it temporarily. Instead, the unwanted behavior is reinforced by our action and will probably occur again. To the attention-seeking child, even punishment is better than no attention at all. Rather than learning how *not* to behave, the disruptive child instead learns what he *must do* to gain our notice.

Both child and teacher can learn a better way to behave in the classroom. But both will need to make a change in the way they deal with attention getting. As psychologist Rollo May (1972) discovered some years ago, "Deeds of violence in our society are performed largely by those who are trying to establish their self-esteem, to defend their self-image, and to demonstrate that they, too, are significant" (p. 23).

Although May was describing society in general, his words apply to preschool children who are trying to demonstrate their significance, too, in this new world of the classroom. Preschool teachers, on the other hand, need to find a better way than punishment to stop disruptive behavior. Punishment makes many children feel unworthy or angry and ready to strike out again. Attention seekers seem to be able to accept punishment as long as it makes them the center of attention.

LOOK FOR AND REINFORCE WITH VERBAL AND NONVERBAL CUES THE PROSOCIAL ACTIONS OF DISRUPTIVE CHILDREN

Shifting attention from children's undesirable behavior to their desirable actions is no simple task for most preschool teachers. It calls for a definite changing of mind-set on the part of you and your coworkers. Is it possible for you to pay more attention to children's prosocial actions than their disruptions? Why should you, you may want to know?

Psychologists and sociologists who have studied human behavior suggest that "children who feel incompetent or incapable of influencing others will resort to extremes in control behavior" (Smith, 1982, p. 160). To compensate for their own negative feelings, they strike out at their peers, shoving or hitting them, disrupting their activities, or damaging their products. Even when they are reprimanded or punished, they may repeat these actions for no apparent reason except to say, "Look at me! I am somebody that can cause things to happen."

Some such children may have been mistreated like this at home, so they strike out at others in the same manner. Others seem to be children who do not know how to make friends. They may push their way into play groups but find few children who will play with them. The more they resort to force, the more the others reject them. These are children who can learn important lessons from positive reinforcement.

Children who feel good about themselves have no need to resort to such attention-getting ploys. Children who know that the teachers feel good about them, too, tend to interact with others in harmony, not disruption. Your role is to focus on their positive behavior until they come to understand that in the preschool classroom it is their prosocial behaviors that will gain them the most attention. Do any disruptive children in your class know that you feel good about them? Your positive reinforcement of their helpful behaviors with nonverbal and verbal cues will let them know.

Nonverbal Cues

Nonverbal cues that adults can use to communicate their feelings to children consist of the natural body language all of us use daily almost without thinking. Greenspan (1997), who has spent a great deal of time studying human emotions and their expression, notes, "Our emotions are created and brought to life through the expressions and gestures we make with the voluntary muscle systems of our faces, arms, and legs—smiles, frowns, slumps, waves, and so forth" (p. 22).

When we smile at children, we often elicit a smile in return. This nonverbal expression tells children we approve of them. A frown signals our disapproval. Eye contact tells them we see them and note that they see us as well. Avoidance of eye contact may mean that all is not well with one or the other.

Greenspan's studies have found that nonverbal cues are a child's first and most important form of communication with others. Long before they talk, infants learn to elicit smiles from their mothers by smiling themselves. From infancy on, youngsters keep close track of expressions on the faces of their caregivers to see how adults feel about them and their actions. As Greenspan (1997) notes in his "Levels of the Mind" (See Table 1–1), between 12 and 18 months the child learns to distinguish facial expressions and body postures and is able to deal with them in social interactions. He explains:

> For the rest of her life, this ability will serve as a kind of radar she can use to navigate through her social universe. . . . [T]he child learns more vividly and precisely than through any language what is good and bad, what is done and not done, what is acceptable and unacceptable in the social world she inhabits. (pp. 64–65)

Teachers can use such nonverbal cues very effectively to let youngsters know that they are on the right track, that the teacher approves of them and what they are doing, that she likes them. Facial expressions such as smiles, laughs, twinkling eyes, looks of delight, or winks; gestures such as nods, thumbs-up signals, claps, hand-shakes, blown kisses, victory signs, hugs, or touches of encouragement—all are signs of approval that children understand even better than words.

Some attention-grabbing children just need to be shown a little love and affection. A hug, an arm around the waist, a hand on the shoulder are as important as food to an affection-starved child. Just standing close to such a child is a nonverbal cue of acceptance. Perhaps no one has ever shown him affection before. No wonder he behaves so disruptively to get your attention. Do not allow the current concern about "good touches and bad touches" to alter your display of affection toward all your children. "Good touches" like yours can help heal the hurt behind a child's unruliness and open his heart to joy.

Verbal Cues

Words of encouragement and congratulation are also important reinforcers of children's positive behavior. But do not offer empty praise. Your words should be related specifically to what the child is doing or has accomplished, telling him *why* you like it. "I like the way you've put the blocks together in your building today, Emory. I've never seen a pattern like that before."

The tone of your voice should also convey approval or enthusiasm. How do you sound to this child who has caused so much disruption? Be careful that your tone of voice does not convey annoyance or disapproval. If you do not know how you sound, put a blank tape in your tape recorder and switch it on when you are talking with the child. Later when you play it back you can decide whether your voice needs an overhaul.

Recognizing Prosocial Behaviors

To see any of the prosocial behaviors a disruptive child may exhibit, we must first look for them. Although this seems obvious, in truth we almost never look at disruptive children in this fashion. We do not see them acting prosocially because we are not looking for this type of behavior in such children. In changing our mind-set about reinforcing the positive in youngsters instead of the negative, we must also change what we look for. This is the time to use the Child Prosocial Behavior Checklist as an observation tool. Its eight different components of prosocial behavior look only at positive aspects of children's actions.

Observing Jessica

As a case in point, the teachers in Jessica's class were hard-pressed to find any positive behaviors they could reinforce for this 4-year-old. From the moment she walked in the door in the morning until her mother came to pick her up in the afternoon, she seemed surrounded by turmoil. The children complained that she "stole" things from their cubbies, messed up their paintings, hid the books they wanted to look at, pushed to the front of the line, always got the first turn on the trike or slide, always had to be the mother in dramatic play, wouldn't pass the food at lunch time, and on and on.

The teachers agreed that her voice was too loud, her pushy way of interacting with others was too aggressive, and her violent shoving, hitting, and even spitting when anyone crossed her were completely unacceptable. What could they possibly reinforce that was positive? They did, however, agree to spend 3 days observing Jessica using the checklist, not only checking off items they saw her performing but also noting in the margin her specific behaviors. At the next weekly staff meeting, they reported their findings (Figure 7-1).

Everyone was surprised. Both the teacher and teacher assistant, as well as the student teacher, all checked more positive behaviors than they had predicted. Under *self-esteem* they noticed that Jessica smiled many times during the day. She never expressed fear of other people, and she always stood up firmly for her rights. Under *self-control* they noted that she liked using the self-regulating learning center necklaces, and although she "expresses strong feelings in words," it was "too loud."

What about *other-esteem*? Jessica seemed to get along with the few children she played with, at least; but she did not act that concerned for other children in distress, especially since she created much of their distress. She also had trouble telling how another child felt because of her strong self-centeredness. For *friendliness* the observers were surprised to note that Jessica did have several followers as friends who seemed to be attracted to her overbearing ways. She played with them peacefully as long as she could be boss. *Generosity* was also checked, at least when she played with her friends. On the other hand, she was just as likely to take a toy or a turn from someone not in her inner circle.

Because "getting her own way" loomed large over much of Jessica's behavior, the items under *cooperation* and *helpfulness* could be checked only when she was in charge. None of the items under *respect* was checked. She did not treat toys or people with much respect most of the time. Nor did she respond well to adults' intervention in her behavior—and that happened a great deal of the time. Her usual response was to pout, turn her head, or sometimes talk back or walk away.

The checklist record produced by the staff showed an entirely different picture of Jessica because only positive and not negative items were recorded. Now discussion centered around her many prosocial behaviors that the staff admitted having overlooked before. What if a substitute teacher came in one day and had only this checklist to go by? Would she treat Jessica differently than they had? Yes, they agreed, and it was time for them to change, too.

Using Checklist Results

They began by picking out the most noticeable of Jessica's prosocial behaviors and listing them as follows:

Smiles when she is playing with friends

Name_____Jessica_____ Age____4_____

1. *Self-Esteem: Feeling Good about Self*

__√__ Smiles, seems happy much of time

__√__ Is not afraid of people or things

__√__ Stands up for own rights

2. *Self-Control: Developing Control over Own Behavior*

_____ Abides by established limits most of the time

__√__ Uses classroom self-regulating devices

__√__ Expresses strong feelings in words rather than actions (too loud)

3. *Other-Esteem: Feeling Good about Other Children*

__√__ Gets along with other children (her friends only)

_____ Shows concern for another child in distress

_____ Can tell how another child feels

4. *Friendliness: Making Friends among Other Children*

_____ Seeks other children to play with

__√__ Makes friends with other children (a few)

__√__ Plays with others in congenial manner (when she is boss)

5. *Generosity: Giving and Sharing Things with Others*

__√__ Shares toys and materials with other children (her friends only)

_____ Takes turns without a fuss

__√__ Gives something (a toy, a turn) to another child (her friends only)

6. *Cooperation: Doing Things with Others*

__√__ Engages in cooperative play in group activity (when she is in charge)

__√__ Allows others to enter ongoing play without a struggle (when she is in charge)

_____ Complies with adult requests

7. *Helpfulness: Doing Things for the Common Good*

__√__ Picks up and puts away toys and materials (when she is in charge)

__√__ Helps another do a task (only her friends)

_____ Takes on classroom chores willingly

8. *Respect: Treating People and Materials Considerately*

_____ Uses toys, materials in constructive manner

_____ Treats other people's materials with respect

_____ Listens and responds to adults with consideration

Figure 7-1   Jessica's checklist

Note: The publisher grants permission to reproduce this checklist for evaluation and record keeping.

Does not show fear of new people or things
Stands up for own rights
Uses learning center necklaces
Knows how to make friends
Plays with friends harmoniously
Shares toys with friends

Next they decided that they would respond to Jessica *every time* they saw her demonstrate any of these behaviors for the next week. They would use both verbal and nonverbal responses and later record what happened. Only the teacher would intervene should Jessica misbehave, and then only when absolutely necessary. The other two staff members were to turn away.

At the staff meeting the following week their reports stirred excitement all around. Jessica's behavior had changed dramatically! She had stopped pushing other children around. There were no reports of her taking things from the other children's cubbies. She did not interfere with anyone's activity. She allowed "outsiders" to play in the house corner, and she even gave up her turn on the trike. Yes, she still talked too loud, but now there was more of Jessica's laughter to be heard. Furthermore, she now approached the teachers happily rather than hurrying away when she saw one coming. What was going on? How could she have changed her behavior so dramatically in a week?

Each staff member then reported how she had responded to Jessica's prosocial behavior. The teacher assistant told about smiling at Jessica every time she saw her with her friends. In fact, she ended up smiling at Jessica every time she looked at her, and soon Jessica was smiling back. It was the first time either had smiled at the other. The student teacher told Jessica, "I like the way you always remember to take a learning center necklace, Jessica. Some children forget." She also found occasion to tell her, "You really know how to share your dolls today, Jessica."

The teacher said she had thanked the girl several times for helping pick up the dramatic play center, for playing so well with her friends, and for smiling so much ("You really light up the room with your smile, Jessica. Thanks for being here."). She also thanked the girl for waiting so patiently to use the computer.

Jessica had pushed one boy the first day and taken another child's crayons. The teacher did not respond to her, only to the victims. She had also poured milk on one of the children's plates of food. The teacher cleaned it up without comment. But by the third day of the week, most of her misbehaviors were beginning to vanish. Was this really possible? Had Jessica actually changed that much?

Staff Conclusions

Yes, she had changed, they decided. But it was not just Jessica who had changed. The real change came from the staff members. They had behaved differently toward Jessica than they ever had before. Would it last? Yes, they decided. They would make it last by continuing to reinforce Jessica's prosocial actions with both verbal and nonverbal cues. Next they would begin observing another child whose behaviors (or theirs?) needed to change. It was an exciting prospect.

MAKE EYE OR VERBAL CONTACT WITH DISRUPTIVE CHILDREN ONLY AFTER THEIR MISBEHAVIOR HAS STOPPED

Attention-seeking children want the teacher to look at them or speak to them when they cause a disturbance, even if it is to scold them. When teachers do not respond to their disruptive actions in this manner, the actions lose their effect. Often such children will repeat one disturbance after another to make themselves the center of attention for the teacher.

If the behavior becomes too extreme, the teacher may be forced to step in and halt actions that cause harm to another child or damage to materials. He should do it quickly, not making eye contact but telling the child matter-of-factly, "Rodney, we don't damage art materials like that. You can sit down in the book center and look at a book, or sit right here and work on this floor puzzle. I'll be back later to see how you're doing."

Once the out-of-bounds behavior has been stopped and the child not scolded but redirected to another activity, the teacher should keep alert to Rodney's further actions. As soon as he notes that Rodney has settled down to looking at a book or making a puzzle, he can return to Rodney's side, giving him positive reinforcement: "Rodney, you really know how to make puzzles, don't you? How did you finish that

The teacher reinforces Rodney's appropriate behavior by giving him his undivided attention and complimenting him on his puzzle making.

one so quickly? Did you ever try to make a puzzle when all the pieces are upside down? Want to try it? I'd like to see if you can do it. Then maybe I'll try."

This time the teacher should make eye contact, giving Rodney a big smile. He is also giving Rodney his undivided attention, something the boy seemed to be striving for. But now the teacher's attention is focused on Rodney's accomplishment, not his misbehavior. The teacher does not refer to the misbehavior at all. He has removed the boy from it, redirecting—not ordering—him to other activities, but then allowing him to retain some control by giving him a choice between two activities.

Giving Choices

Giving a child a choice like this is important in any emotion-charged situation. For one thing, it averts any power struggle that might occur between child and teacher. Some children have learned at home to argue with adults. But there is no need for a teacher to become involved in such a struggle with a child. Instead, offering a choice distracts the child from his former disruptive behavior and makes him consider something new. As Wittmer and Honig (1994) suggest, "Toddlers and preschoolers struggling to assert newly emergent autonomy cooperate more easily with caregiver requests if they feel empowered to make choices. Adults can decide on the choices to be offered" (p. 11).

Afterward, the teacher gives verbal reinforcement by complimenting Rodney's puzzle making and telling the boy he will watch and maybe even get involved himself. These verbal and nonverbal actions deliver a powerful message: that the teacher will pay attention only when you become involved in an activity, not when you are disruptive.

Asking Rodney either to sit in the book corner and look at a book or sit on the floor and work on a floor puzzle is not the same as sending him to a time-out chair. Neither of these areas is associated with punishment or being ostracized. Other children may be playing in them alongside Rodney. This type of adult response to his actions is one Rodney can accept without feeling shame or blame. Eventually he should realize that the only way to gain teacher attention is to become involved in activities. You, of course, must do your part by remembering to pay special attention to Rodney's involvement.

No Eye Contact

For children who cause disturbances to get the teacher's attention, it is important not to make eye contact with them. Making eye contact with disruptive youngsters only reinforces their inappropriate behavior by showing them that you noticed what they were doing. If you catch yourself doing this, look quickly away. If you must intervene as Rodney's teacher did, simply go to the child without looking him in the eye and give him the necessary guidance. Shortly afterward when you note that the child is involved in an acceptable activity, return to his side and look him in the eye while complimenting him with your positive reinforcement about his work. Be sure when you speak to him like this that you get down to his eye level. Making eye contact while squatting or sitting down, rather than looming over a child, is a form of nonverbal body language that tells the child you now approve of him and what he is doing.

If one child is in the act of pushing or hitting another youngster, you may need to step between the two with your back to the aggressor. Make sure the victim is not hurt before you turn and address the aggressor. Once again make as little eye contact as possible, but tell him you can't let anyone be hurt like that in the classroom. He can choose one of the two areas you mention where he can work.

Attending to the victim first is often more difficult for a teacher than stepping in to stop the aggressor. It is hard not to rush in immediately to stop the aggressive child. But this reinforces his negative actions. Instead, you must concentrate on the child being hit or pushed. It is another mind-set you and your coworkers may need to change.

Try doing a role-play of such a situation at your next staff meeting. Have two volunteers act out the scene you describe, and have another as teacher rush in to attend to the victim first. Can the "teacher" address the aggressor with as little eye contact as possible? Ask the volunteers afterward how each one felt about what happened. Did the victim feel better that the teacher went to her first? Did the aggressor get the nonverbal message that the teacher was more concerned with the victim? Switch roles and try it again. Soon you will be prepared to try it when such a disturbance happens in the class. It is important that staff members practice these new prosocial guidance techniques ahead of time to learn what to do and say with children and how to make the approach work best for them.

HELP DISRUPTIVE CHILDREN FIND ACTIVITIES THEY CAN EXCEL IN

Everyone is an expert in something. Think of yourself. What do you excel in? Smiling, saying nice things to people, baking cookies, throwing a party, walking the length of the block and back every day, being on time, doing crossword puzzles, taking photos, identifying birds, growing flowers, making quilts, inventing creative activities for children, making a difference in the lives of young children? Whatever people excel in gives them a wonderful sense of accomplishment. They feel good about themselves and their expertise and often want to share it with others.

What about the children in your classroom who seem to delight in disrupting others? Do they have special skills that they perform with dexterity or interests they would like to develop? Do you know? More often than not, teachers avoid the so-called "trouble-makers" in the class and may know little about their interests. But you could take the time to find out.

One teacher found that a boy who ran around wildly in her classroom could shoot a basket every time he had a basketball in his hands: no mean accomplishment for a 4-year-old! Another teacher brought in her autoharp for all of the children to try and found that the child who showed the least impulse control was the best autoharp strummer. The first teacher set up a little basketball net in a corner of the room to be used with Nerf balls. The second teacher had her expert strummer strum the accompaniment to the songs she played daily on the autoharp. When children are engaged in an activity they do well, they have little time or interest in disturbing others.

Using Books

One way to learn more about children and their interests is to read a particular book to them and discuss it as you go along. If you have already noticed a learning center that a certain child seems drawn to, you might start with a book featuring characters involved in similar activities. Books written from a first-person point of view help children identify with the main characters.

For example, the Caucasian girl Debbie Dundee, the main character in *If I Ran the Family* by Lee and Sue Kaiser Johnson (1992) tells in her own words what she would do if she were in charge of her multiethnic family of four children and two parents. A girl from your class who spends a great deal of time in the housekeeping center but has trouble getting along with others might benefit from hearing what Debbie has to say.

Debbie tells in rhyming verse and large, colorful, double-page illustrations how she'd make sure that everyone in her family had a say-so when problems come up,

One way to learn more about children and their interests is to read certain books to them and ask about the story as you go along.

that everyone would be allowed to cry as long as they wanted if they got hurt and no one would say "big kids don't cry," that you can share your feelings without fear, that you wouldn't have to eat foods you didn't like, and that it's okay if you feel down in the dumps at times without blaming anybody. Then Debbie asks the readers whether grownups and kids get the same treatment in their families or whether kids get all the blame, whether kids can just be themselves and not always have to be perfect, and whether kids get to make any choices.

Let your listener talk about any of Debbie's feelings and ideas, giving her own opinion if she wants. You might bring in a new set of family figures for her to play with in your sand table or in a dollhouse you have just acquired. Later talk with her about how the family figures she is playing with are getting along. Encourage her to make up stories about them that you can tape-record or transcribe in a little booklet for the child. Help her become a family interaction expert just like Debbie.

If you don't know what a child is interested in or good at doing, you might read *I Want to Be* by Thylias Moss (1993) about an African-American girl who runs, walks, hopscotches, dances, twirls, swings, and daydreams through the large, color-filled pages of this story after neighbors ask her what she wants to be. She pretends to be a dancer, a fiddle, a firefighter, a singer with "the oxygen choir." Finally, she lets her imagination loose in poetic lines about being big, strong, old, fast, wise, beautiful, green ("but not so green that I can't also be purple"), tall, quiet, a sound, in motion, invisible, weightless, eyes, ears, hands, mouth, heart, and life. Does your listener

Children can pretend to be characters from the stories you have read when they play with book character dolls.

know what she wants to be? Would she like to play with a character doll like the girl from the *I Want to Be* book?

Other books that may help you discover the interests of a child include these:

> *Abuela*, A. Dorros (New York: Dutton, 1991) (about Rosalba, a Hispanic girl in New York City who takes her grandmother on an adventure to the park and teaches her to fly above the city)
>
> *Kofi and His Magic*, M. Angelou (New York: Clarkson/Potter, 1996) (about an African boy who weaves beautiful Kente cloth)
>
> *Max Found Two Sticks*, B. Pinkney (New York: Simon & Schuster, 1994) (about an African-American boy who finds two sticks and uses them to beat out rhythms on the front steps of his apartment building)
>
> *Zoom! Zoom! Zoom! I'm Off to the Moon!* D. Yaccarino (New York: Scholastic, 1997) (about a Caucasian boy who puts on his space suit and blasts off on an adventure to the moon and back)

Using Magazines

If you still do not know how to get a child interested in an activity he can explore or how to develop his talents, bring in some back issues of magazines full of pictures. Even catalogs are fascinating to children. But be sure they know you are not ordering toys from them. Show them to one child at a time, letting the child turn the pages and tell you about items he is interested in or knows something about. Does this give you a clue about his interests? Have him cut out pictures and paste them in a scrapbook about "Things I Like."

No Material Rewards

Preschool children can learn prosocial behaviors without external rewards such as stickers, stars, raisins, peanuts, popcorn, or candy for "good behavior." The activities you set up to help them excel can divert their attention from misbehavior to eager involvement. Then follow up with your own attention: positive reinforcement for their prosocial behavior and accomplishments in the form of compliments and displays their work, rather than material rewards such as stickers. As Wittmer and Honig (1994) note, "Commenting on positive behaviors and attributing positive characteristics to children rather than using external rewards help young children internalize prosocial responses" (p. 6).

Take photos of the child playing house with her family figures, strumming the autoharp, making a basket with a basketball, weaving with yarn on a simple loom, drumming with homemade drumsticks, or making a space ship from play dough. Such pictures can be mounted on the classroom walls, pasted in a child's personal scrapbook along with a story about them, or shared with parents during a parent conference. The teachers' recognition of their accomplishments in their special activities makes children's former attention-getting disturbances unnecessary.

HELP ATTENTION-SEEKING CHILDREN
LEARN TO MAKE FRIENDS

How does one make a friend? For many young children it is as simple as running up to another child full of smiles and laughter and an exclamation of "C'mon! Let's play together with the blocks today!" But for others the task is not so simple. They seem to have no idea how to connect with another child in a peaceful manner. They are more likely to push a child out of the space they want or take someone's toy. The more vigorously they try to force themselves into group play, the more other children reject them. No one wants to play with them because of their aggressive behavior. They are outsiders.

But they must have someone's attention. So they seek yours. They seek it by causing disruptions in other children's activities wherever they go. They may knock down a block building, mess up an easel painting, or wreck someone's science project. But each time they cause another child to retaliate with yells, pushes, or even hitting, they take a quick look your way to see if you are noticing. Do you notice their look? They are calling out for your attention in the only way they know how.

You can help them find friends in a more appropriate manner once you have identified disruptive children as outsiders. How can you tell? Friendships among preschool children are not the same as those of older children. Edwards (1986) points out that preschooler concepts of friendship are

> self-centered, present-bound, and focused on the concrete and external. A friend is someone whom the self likes "right now." Friends play together and share food, toys and other valued resources. They are close in terms of physical proximity or even looking alike. (p. 117)

In other words, preschool friends are playmates. They may change from day to day or grow stronger as the same children continue to play together, but in any case the youngsters accept one another as playmates. Thus, the most important aspect of this type of friendship concerns whether a child is *included* in the play of other children.

Observing to Determine Who Is Included

To help children make friends in preschool, the teacher must first observe to determine who is included and who excluded from group activities. Some who are excluded may be shy children who play by themselves. Others may be newcomers to the class who have not yet become acclimated to their surroundings. Still others may be in the "parallel play" stage of social play development as discussed in Chapter 2. What about the disruptive child? Does she ever play peacefully with another child? Does she try to enter group play only to be rebuffed?

Pairing Children Who Are Excluded

If you notice an excluded child, you can begin to help by pairing that child with another youngster. Choose a child who is friendly and outgoing. Ask the two children to perform a task for you, perhaps helping clean the guinea pig's cage. One can hold the guinea pig, and one can hold the trash can while you dump out the tray. Would they now like to build a house for the guinea pig out of blocks? Or what about looking at a guinea pig book together, such as *Guinea Pigs Far and Near* by Kate Duke (1984) or *Guinea Pigs: A Practical Guide to Caring for Your Guinea Pigs* by Mark Evans?

If you note that this activity has caught their interest, try extending it in other ways. They can keep track of filling its water and food containers, get lettuce from the kitchen for the animal, tape-record its squeaks, paint a picture or dictate a story about it, model a guinea pig out of play dough. If other children want to join them, let it be their decision whether to include others. Keep track of this budding friendship from day to day. If it breaks down, try pairing the first child with one or two others. Read a story to all three children, such as *Where Is Gah-Ning?* by Robert Munsch (1994) about a very determined little girl and her hilarious attempts to get to the store and go shopping. If they like the story, could they have fun acting it out with puppets? Ask them what else they would like to do together.

Because the staff of a preschool program consists of more than one teacher, someone is always free to pursue such important tasks as working with individual children to help them develop friendships.

MODEL FRIENDSHIP BY DEVELOPING FRIENDSHIPS WITH EVERY CHILD

You are the principal model of friendship in your class. The children look to you to see how to make friends and how to behave toward friends. Are the children your friends? A friendship on adult terms is a relationship between two people who come to know one another, respect one another, and like one another. You may know the children rather well, but what do they know about you? If they see you as an aloof teacher-figure who tells them what to do and what not to do, then they can hardly consider you as a friend. Carter (1995) calls out to all of us when she says:

> Children desperately need meaningful, not perfunctory relationships. Their world is full of stress, danger, and commercialism. They have little time to cultivate friendships or to engage in imaginative work at their own pace. Instead of real role models, children have media created super-heroes and celebrities. . . . Children need adults around them who provide examples of how to make friendships, handle mistakes, use a variety of tools, and pursue one's passions. (p. 68)

How do you make friends with a child, you may ask? Ask yourself how you go about making friends with your peers. The same process applies (see Figure 7-2). First, you approach them with an *attitude of friendship,* using smiles, body language, and a happy tone of voice to convey your feelings. You carry on a real, not patronizing, conversation by *listening* to what they have to say and trying to find some *commonalities* of experience ("Oh, I've been there, too," or "Did you like that film, too? I thought it was terrific"). You *tell them* something *about yourself* and listen to what they have to say about themselves. You *spend time together* and *help one another.*

Figure 7-2   Developing a
friendship with a child

1. Approach child with attitude of friendship.
   Smile.
   Use happy tone of voice.
   Get down to child's level.
2. Carry on real conversations.
   Listen to child.
   Tell about yourself.
   Comment on commonalities of interest.
3. Spend time together.
   Have one-to-one experiences.
4. Help one another.
   Assist child and ask for assistance.

Is it possible to develop friendships with so many children, you may ask? Many teachers do it every year. Your own attitude toward the children in your group sets the tone. If you see yourself as a superior being apart from these little inexperienced ones, then you may not be successful. You must think of children as young human beings with as much potential as you have. We are all in this life together. Those who have been here longer have an obligation to assist those who are just getting started.

Would you like to become friends with the children? Do you want them for your friends? Think seriously about these questions. If your answer is yes, then you will find ways to do it. If your answer is no or "I'm not sure," then you may need to talk it over with coworkers and associates. Can you change your mind-set? Is early childhood really the best field for you? Think about it.

What can preschool children possibly bring to a friendship with a teacher, some child caregivers have asked? Think about this, too. Some answers have been love, affection, excitement, a new lease on life, a new way of looking at things, a song in the heart. Have you experienced any of these feelings from the children you work with?

Sharing Yourself with the Children

Share yourself with your children, says Carter (1995). Bring in photos of yourself when you were young. Tell them about some of the places you have visited and what you like to do after school. If you have a family, talk about your own children. For real friendship to begin, children need to see you as a person and not just a teacher.

Is there any child you would not want as a friend? Then you have some work to do on yourself, first. It is important that you accept unconditionally each of the children. You also remember about not choosing favorites among the children. The opposite also applies. You do not reject certain children because of their looks, behavior, background, ethnicity, or any other quality. Do not be swayed by gossip about the children or their families. Make it your professional obligation to find something to like about every child in your group.

What if you are rejected by one of the children you are trying to befriend? This is an important experience for you. This child may well be repeating his own rejection by others. Both he and the other children will be watching for your reaction. Remember that you are their model for friendship. Be kind to the child, but do not give up. Try again, always without pressure, when he is in a better mood. You may not succeed. Don't take it personally. Not everyone becomes a friend to everyone else. As long as you keep yourself open to this child, you give him permission to change his mind.

As Montagu (1995) reminds us:

> A teacher of young children, more than anything else, must be able to love children unconditionally, to be able to communicate to them, without any patronizing and without any strings attached, that she is their friend—for friendship, it must be understood, is just another word for love. (pp. 42–44)

REFERENCES

Carter, M. (1995). Being real for children. *Child Care Information Exchange, 106,* 68–70.

Edwards, C. P. (1986). *Social and moral development in young children.* New York: Teachers College Press.

Greenspan, S. I. (1997). *The growth of the mind: And the endangered origins of intelligence.* Reading, MA: Addison-Wesley.

May, R. (1972). *Power and influence.* New York: Norton.

Montagu, A. (1995). Friendship—Loving: What early childhood education is all about. *Child Care Information Exchange, 106,* 42–44.

Smith, C. A. (1982). *Promoting the social development of young children: Strategies and activities.* Palo Alto, CA: Mayfield.

Wittmer, D. S., & Honig, A. S. (1994). Encouraging positive social development in young children. *Young Children, 49*(5), 4–12.

SUGGESTED READINGS

Beaty, J. J. (1998). *Observing development of the young child.* Upper Saddle River, NJ: Merrill/Prentice Hall.

Bukowski, W. M., Newcomb, A. F., & Hartup, W. W. (1996). *The company they keep: Friendship in childhood and adolescence.* New York: Cambridge University Press.

Cartledge, G., & Milburn, J. F. (1995). *Teaching social skills to children and youth: Innovative approaches.* Boston: Allyn & Bacon.

Kohn, A. (1993). *Punished by rewards: The trouble with gold stars, incentive plans, A's, praise, and other bribes.* Boston: Houghton Mifflin.

Lawhon, T. (1997). Encouraging friendships among children. *Childhood Education, 73*(4), 228–231.

Ramsey, P. G. (1991). *Making friends in school: Promoting peer relationships in early childhood.* New York: Teachers College Press.

Wilt, J. V. (1996). Beyond stickers and popcorn parties. *Dimensions of Early Childhood, 24*(1), 17–20.

Wolf, D. P. (1986). *Connecting: Friendship in the lives of young children and their teachers.* Redmond, WA: Exchange.

CHILDREN'S BOOKS

Duke, K. (1982). *Guinea pigs far and near.* New York: Dutton.

Evans, M. (1992). *Guinea pigs: A practical guide to caring for your guinea pigs.* New York: Dorling Kindersley.

Johnson, L., & S. K. Johnson. (1992). *If I ran the family.* Minneapolis, MN: Free Spirit.

Moss, M. (1993). *I want to be.* New York: Dial.

Munsch, R. (1994). *Where is Gah-Ning?* Toronto: Annick.

VIDEOTAPES

Educational Productions. (Producer). *Reframing discipline: Connecting with every child* (no. 2). (Available from Educational Productions, 9000 S.W. Gemini Drive, Beaverton, OR 97008)

Magna Systems. (Producer). *Guidance and discipline: Teacher/child interaction* (no. 3) and *Preschoolers: Social and emotional development.* (Available from

Magna Systems, 95 W. County Line Rd., Barrington, IL 60010)

National Association for the Education of Young Children. (Producer). *Discipline: Appropriate guidance of young children* and *Painting a positive picture: Proactive behavior management.* (Available from NAEYC, 1509 16th St. N.W., Washington, DC 20036-1426)

LEARNING ACTIVITIES

1. Look for any prosocial behaviors displayed by an attention-seeking child, and reinforce them with verbal and nonverbal cues. Record what happens.

2. Make eye contact with a disruptive child only after the misbehavior has stopped. Then give the child a choice of two activities to become involved in. Record the results.

3. Find an activity that an attention-seeking child can excel in and motivate him or her to try it with a story or magazine pictures. Record what happens.

4. Help an attention-seeking child make a friend of one other child by asking the pair to help with a task or do an activity together. Record the results.

5. Using the guidelines in Figure 7-2, develop a friendship yourself with a child who has displayed behavior problems. Record what you did and what happened.

Specific Strategies to Promote Prosocial Behavior

CHAPTER 8

Promoting Children's Self-Esteem

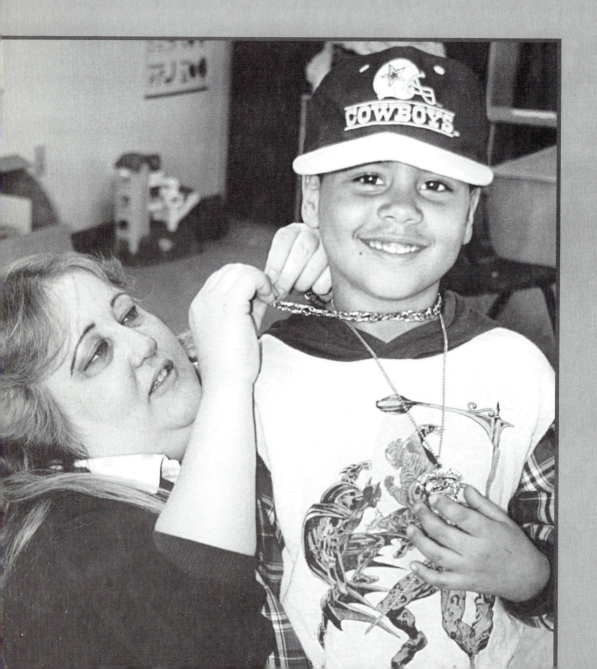

- Help every child feel accepted and wanted every day.
- Accept diversity in children, and help children accept it in one another.
- Help children become independent and self-directed.
- Help every child experience success.
- Model respect by treating each child with respect.

Self-esteem refers to children's feelings of worthiness about themselves and how acceptable they are in the eyes of others. It develops out of their early relationships with others as well as the verbal and nonverbal messages they receive about themselves from the significant people in their lives. You as a preschool teacher can affect the self-esteem of every child in your class by the way you accept them and respond to their behavior. As Ferber (1996) notes:

> Self-worth rests upon the experience of being loved, accepted, and cared for unconditionally. Adults can help improve children's self-esteem by giving them the message that they are fundamentally valuable in the eyes of others and worthy of care regardless of their behaviors or affects. (p. 38)

Preschool children are in the process of building their own self-concepts. These do not come ready-made at birth. Little by little the young human learns who she is, what she looks like, what she can or cannot do, and what others think of her. This self-concept consists of two aspects that we call *self-image* (the child's inner picture of herself) and *self-esteem* (her sense of self-worth).

She derives her self-image from interacting with people and materials in her environment. She learns about her looks, her gender, her ethnicity, her abilities, her role in her family, and more. The child's self-esteem, on the other hand, is an evaluation of everything she has internalized about herself. She acquires this sense of self-worth from what others say about her, how they act toward her, and the comparisons she continuously makes between herself and the others around her. Self-image and self-esteem together form the child's self-concept. As Kosnik (1993) explains:

> These two areas combine to form our self-concept. Throughout our lives a continuous dialogue exists between these two aspects of self. Our self-concept determines who we are, what we think we are, what we think we can do, and what we think we can become. (p. 32)

All of us are in a continuous process of becoming, especially at the beginning of our lives. But once the self-concept has taken on a definite form, it is more difficult to change as the child grows older. For example, if the child feels good about herself because of the way her family has treated her, she will see a teacher's good treatment as a confirmation of what she already knows about herself. She, in turn, will act in a cooperative manner toward others and receive good treatment in return.

On the other hand, if the child has been treated harshly or neglected by her family, she may feel she is bad or not worthy. Even a teacher's good treatment may not affect the child's self-concept at first because she may rationalize that the teacher is being nice because she feels sorry for the child since she is so bad. She may continue to cause disruptions in class just to prove how bad she really is.

But you know better. And your persistence in accepting a child, but not her inappropriate actions, will eventually win the day. Positive messages delivered day after day by significant adults do have a positive effect on a child's self-esteem.

HELP EVERY CHILD FEEL ACCEPTED AND WANTED EVERY DAY

Most preschool teachers have no problem with this concept of accepting all the children. Of course you accept the children in your class. It is not only your professional duty but also a personal pleasure to be involved with the youngsters. The difficulty lies not with the concept but with how it is implemented. As Kosnik (1993) points out:

> For children to believe that they are valuable members of the community, they must feel individually noticed and they must feel wanted. By getting to know the children and highlighting their abilities, the teacher validates the children. . . . She is one step closer to increasing the children's self-esteem. (p. 36)

Do you show all your children that you notice them every day? Making eye contact is not enough. Greeting each child in the morning is not enough. You and your staff must plan carefully and then diligently carry out an agreed-on procedure for helping children be aware that you notice them and appreciate their presence.

Using Photos

Some teachers take a photo of each child at the beginning of the year and have duplicate copies made for self-esteem activities. One of the photos they laminate with clear plastic to an attendance card. When a child enters the room in the morning, one of the teachers greets her with her own photo card, makes a positive comment about how nice it is to see her this morning, and gives the card to the child to hang on the attendance board under her name.

One of the photos is pasted to the front of each child's daily journal. She is encouraged to write, scribble, or draw something in this stapled-together booklet every day. You will want to look at the booklet with her from time to time, making positive comments on her entries.

Make an enlargement of each photo to be converted into a personal photo puzzle for each child. Glue it to cardboard and cut it into four or five pieces for the child to reassemble. Keep the pieces in manila envelopes with another photo of the child and her name on the front of each. They can be placed in the manipulative center. But wait until one has been prepared for every child before putting them out, so no one needs to feel left out.

Some programs use photo cards for place cards at the lunch tables from time to time instead of name cards. Children find their seat by recognizing their picture. Attendance photo cards can also be used in drawing out of a hat for turns.

Children need to see themselves like this as well as having you and other children recognize their likenesses. Having photos taken of them makes children feel important. What other uses can you make of children's photos? With the inexpensive technology available these days, it is within every program's budget to duplicate such a valuable resource as a child's photo either by having reprints made or by photocopying the pictures.

Take pictures of each child during the week, too, showing them working on a block structure, completing a painting, dressing up to play a role in the dramatic play center, reading a book, playing with a puppet, climbing on the monkey bars, or riding a trike. Ask the children what pictures they want you to take of themselves. Keep a photo check-off list of children's names, so you are sure to take pictures of everyone. Let them also take their own picture of something they would like to include in their journal. Would they also like to start a class photo album and keep it in the book center for everyone to look at?

Picture taking can be just as important in promoting your children's prestige as it is for film stars. When it is someone's birthday, display a framed photo captioned "Celebrity of the Week." For children whose birthdays fall in weeks you are not in session, let them pick their own "pretend birthday" to celebrate, as mentioned previously.

Using Mirrors

Another way children can see themselves is with mirrors. Be sure to have a full-length mirror in the dramatic play area for children to use when they dress up and play roles. Hand and pocket mirrors are also important self-esteem tools. Research supports the use of mirrors with young children. Ferber (1996) says, "Not only is visual self-recognition a reflection of the acquisition of self-concept, but vision is also an important source of feedback contributing to the development of self-image" (p. 29). Fraiberg's (1987) study of blind children found that because they couldn't see themselves, they were delayed in using the pronoun *I*.

Be sure to bring in enough hand or pocket mirrors for every child in a small group to use when you talk about feelings. Can they make a face showing happiness, sadness, anger, fear, and surprise? When they make happy faces, tell each one by name how much you enjoy seeing their smiles.

Read the book *Kelly in the Mirror* by Martha M. Vertreace (1993) about an African-American girl who hears her family talking about who her brother looks most like in the family. Kelly looks in a mirror but can't see that her features resemble anyone in her family. Then she finds an old photo album and in it is a picture of her mother as a little girl—looking just like Kelly.

Using Children's Names

Children's names are just as important to them as their features. They feel good about themselves when they hear you using their names. Be sure you say each child's name when you talk with her. Have written names displayed on children's cubbies, under their artwork, on name cards at lunch tables, on their toothbrushes, on their blankets, and as name tags when visitors are present. Use children's names as substitutes for a character's name from time to time when you read them a story.

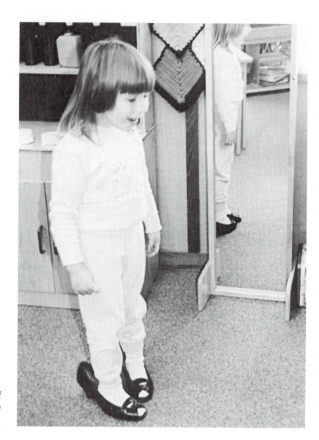

Full-length mirrors help young children develop a self-image by showing them what they look like.

During circle time every day, be sure to use each child's name. Go around the circle and thank the children for coming, making some kind of positive comment about their clothes or shoes or hair or smile or energy. Make up words to various nursery songs that include each child's name and sing them as a welcome song at circle time daily. Here are some suggestions:

Kendra Matta will you stand up,
Will you stand up, will you stand up;
Kendra Matta will you stand up,
Let's everyone give a clap. CLAP!
  (*Tune:* Lazy Mary Will You Get Up)

Zackary Brooks, Zackary Brooks,
There you are, there you are:
It's so nice to see you,
It's so nice to see you;
Come again, come again.
  (*Tune:* Are You Sleeping?)

On the other hand, try not to use a child's name in a negative manner by calling it out across the room when you see that child doing something inappropriate. If you must intervene because someone is being hurt or materials damaged, go to the child privately without using her name at first and redirect her to another activity. Afterward, when she is involved in that activity, you can talk with her quietly using her name.

Using Art Projects

Art projects involving a child's body, hands, feet, and face can give that youngster a feeling that he is indeed an important part of the program. Have each child lie on his back on newsprint or butcher paper while you trace around him. He can draw in his face and paint on his clothing any way he chooses. When everyone has completed a body picture, cut them out, have children label them, and mount them at eye level around the classroom or in the hall.

Children also enjoy hand and foot tracing with markers or stamping with poster paint against a light background. A total group mural can be produced this way with every child putting his own name next to his prints. If someone is absent, be sure to have him add his prints when he returns.

Face tracings can be produced by a teacher who holds tissue paper against a child's face and lightly traces its outline including eyes, nose, and mouth. Children fill in the details afterward. Another favorite personal art project is making sneaker rubbings. Place thin paper over the bottom of a sneaker and have the child rub the side of a crayon over it until the pattern appears. Hand rubbings and mitten rubbings can be produced in the same way. All of these products can be cut out and mounted on the classroom walls or pasted in a class scrapbook. Be sure each artist signs his name. It is up to you to make favorable comments about the children's products as they are completed.

Playing with Individual Children

Perhaps the most supportive function a teacher can perform for an individual child is to play or interact with her personally in an activity the child has chosen. Children recognize that a teacher has many other children besides themselves to deal with. If she chooses to spend time playing with them individually, then she must really like them and want them to be there. As the teacher plays a computer game with Raphael, builds a block tower with Nathan, counts colored pegs with Breanna, puts the baby doll to bed with Karen, or holds the autoharp for Roger to strum, she definitely imparts a nonverbal message of liking and supporting to the child. As Eaton (1997) tells us, "Research suggests that an adult's sensitive, personally attentive, genuinely focused relationship with a child increases the child's self-esteem and the strength of the child's ability to control impulses or hurtfulness toward others" (p. 44).

We must all find time to devote to every child in this manner. If we keep our free-choice periods long enough for children to become deeply involved in the interesting activities we have provided, then we give ourselves the opportunity to interact one to one with individual children but without taking over their play. Once again keep track

One of the most supportive functions a teacher can perform for an individual child is to interact with her in the child's chosen activity.

on a name check-off list to make sure you spend some individual time with *every* child during the week, but especially those who have a tendency to disrupt things.

ACCEPT DIVERSITY IN CHILDREN, AND HELP CHILDREN ACCEPT IT IN ONE ANOTHER

If you expect children to accept diversity in others, then you must demonstrate your own acceptance of everyone no matter how different they seem to be. By *diversity* we mean anyone who *looks different*, *talks different*, or *acts different* from most of the other children. Different appearances may relate to skin color, hair style, clothing, or even physical impairments. Speech differences can include different languages, dialects, or speech impairments. Different actions may be aggressiveness, shyness, hyperactivity, or physical limitations. It is up to you as teacher to treat each of the children with the same respect and affection as you do everyone else. As Ramsey (1987) notes, "It is the teacher who makes the goals of accepting, respecting, and appreciating oneself and others an honest and authentic dynamic in the classroom" (p. 40).

Children who are made to feel different from others because they are treated differently usually feel they are somehow not as good. Such children may express their low self-esteem by striking out against others. These actions only turn other children against them, creating a self-fulfilling prophecy for the "different" child: "They treat me bad because I am not as good as they are."

If teachers keep the following guidelines in mind, their treatment of every child should help improve the child's self-esteem:

1. Stress similarities, but honor differences.
2. Build on strengths.
3. Help every child succeed.

Stressing Similarities, but Honoring Differences

One child may look different from another, but they all have hair, they all have feet, and they all wear clothing and shoes. Take a look at how different the hair color and styles are among your children. Isn't diversity wonderful? Wouldn't sameness be boring? Imagine a classroom where everyone's hair was the same! If this is the way *you* feel, then your book center will surely feature Virginia Kroll's (1995) *Hats Off to Hair!* with its marvelous close-up illustrations of 36 children's faces, each with a different hairdo. Your children will want to hear over and over about Laura and Maura, Seth and Beth, Abe and Ahmed and their bangs, buzzes, cornrows, coils, dreadlocks, Mohawks, shags, corkscrew curls, and more than two dozen other do's in this cleverly rhyming celebration of differences.

Lynn Reiser's (1996) *Beach Feet* takes everyone barefoot to the beach where their feet—including those of animals, birds, crabs, and starfish—scrunch, squash, squish, and splash together in an incredible foot frolic. Talk about differences! Take your children to a nearby beach or, if that is impossible, to a wading pool outside the classroom, and snap some photos of just feet in the water or wet footprints on the sidewalk. This is the time to make foot stampings with poster paint or foot tracings with markers. Aren't feet wonderful? And everyone's are different.

The book *Bein' with You This Way* by W. Nikola-Lisa (1994), narrated by an energetic African-American girl, leads all the children on the playground in an exciting follow-the-leader rap, as they point out and sing out about straight or curly hair, big or little noses, brown or blue eyes, thick or thin arms, long or short legs, and light or dark skin. If your youngsters respond as enthusiastically as the playground children, they will surely want to activate their own follow-the-leader people parade around your classroom afterward.

All people have eyes, and noses, and faces, and skin. Some are different from one another, but all are beautiful to those who love them. That should be your focus rather than pointing out individual differences in children that might embarrass them. Think how it would feel if it happened to you, and use this as your guide.

Beauty may be only skin deep, but it can be decidedly different for different people—thank goodness! In Maryjean Watson Avery's (1995) unique book *What Is Beautiful?* each child finds one thing beautiful on the face of someone else: ears, hair, beard, smile, eyes, nose, mouth, or dimples. Then that someone points out the beauty on someone else's face, and so on, to the last page where a silvery paper mirror asks the reader to look and find "What's beautiful about you?" Your children should learn what beauty can mean to others by participating in this unique experience.

Whether or not the youngsters come from different ethnic or racial backgrounds, the equipment and materials you provide should feature as many multicultural groups as possible. Be sure there are Asian, Caucasian, African-American, Hispanic, and Native American baby dolls in the housekeeping area. Multicultural figures of people as well as figures showing disabilities should also be available in the block center and sand table. Plastic models of food available for children's play in the dramatic play center can include tacos, enchiladas, egg rolls, sushi, rice, dim sum, kabobs, and pitas.

Your bookshelves, of course, should display many of the latest children's books featuring multiethnic characters. Purchase character dolls to go with as many books as possible, such as an Asian doll to represent the Chinese-Canadian girl Gah-Ning in *Where Is Gah-Ning?* by Robert Munsch (see Beaty, 1997, for more ideas).

Building on Strengths

Everyone has certain abilities to be proud of. Kristin, a shy and quiet girl, can count almost to 100. Carlos, a Hispanic boy, can sing several songs in Spanish. Livia, a hear-

Children can learn about other children different from themselves but alike in their interests, such as the Chinese girl from the book Where Is Gah-Ning?

ing-impaired girl, knows many words in sign language. Help everyone focus on such skills rather than on differences. As you learn more about the special abilities of each child, help them share these skills with others. Read stories to the children about other girls and boys with special talents.

In Berneice Rabe's (1981) *The Balancing Girl,* little Margaret, a girl in a wheelchair and leg braces, has developed a special skill in balancing things. In Judith Caseley's (1991) *Harry and Willy and Carrothead,* Harry, who was born without a left hand, wears a prosthesis but plays ball as well as anyone. Your children may want to dictate a story about their own strengths for their daily journals or have you photograph them performing their specialty. For as Ramsey (1987) notes, "Viewed from a multicultural perspective, self-concepts of children relate not only to their racial, cultural, and class identification but also to their feelings of power in the school environment" (p. 118).

When you as a teacher recognize each child's strengths and help them build on them, you empower your children to feel good about themselves as worthy people.

HELP CHILDREN BECOME INDEPENDENT AND SELF-DIRECTED

Children also feel good about themselves when they can act in an independent fashion in the classroom and don't have to rely on teachers' directions for everything they do. Be sure the classroom is arranged as discussed in Chapter 4 so that learning centers are clearly visible and materials in each are ready and available. Check each of your own learning centers to make certain children can use it without your help.

Dramatic Play
Dress-up clothes hanging on hooks or hangers, not stuffed in drawers; baby dolls dressed; plastic food and utensils stored in cupboards or bins

Block Center
Blocks stored lengthwise on shelves with outlined signs for each type of block; block accessories stored on block shelves with labels; figures of people, animals, and vehicles available; books and special accessories for field trip follow-up available; books showing buildings or construction available

Art Center
Easels ready with paper and paints; art materials on low shelves next to art tables; special art activities out on art tables; art storybooks available; water for cleaning brushes and hands available

Music Center
Tape recorder, record player, and headsets ready; tapes rewound and stored near recorder; instruments hanging on hookboard or stored on shelves; music storybooks available

Book Center

Books arranged neatly on shelves with covers facing out; torn books repaired or removed; books for special themes or projects arranged separately; puppets and character dolls stored attractively; book tapes and books, recorders, and headsets on nearby shelf; books and book posters changed periodically

Science Center

Science project available with tools and activity arranged in inviting manner; science books nearby; animal cages and aquarium clean; feeding schedule posted; plant experiments in good shape; watering schedule posted

Manipulative/Math Center

Manipulative and counting activities in labeled boxes on shelves near center tables ready for use; puzzles in puzzle rack or out on table ready to use; puzzles and games complete with no pieces missing

Writing/Computer Center

Writing material on shelves near table or in desk drawers; good supply of pencils, pens, markers, paper, tablets, envelopes, stampers, stamp pads, paper punches, and brads; children's daily journals stored on nearby shelves; computer programs stored next to computer; two chairs in front of computer for use by pairs of children

Water/Sand Tables

Water table with clean water; water play equipment in water or stored on nearby shelves; aprons on hooks near table; sand table or box clean and ready for use; safety goggles and figures of people and vehicles stored nearby

Self-Regulating Devices

Learning center necklaces, name tags, or tickets ready for use at entrance to each center

Giving Children Choices

Some teachers believe that children's self-regulating devices are too restrictive and not necessary for a free-flowing schedule. If their priority for the program is to keep the centers completely open and available for all, they may be correct. However, if their goals include giving children independence and empowering them to make their own choices of what activities to engage in, then self-regulating devices are important. Otherwise the teacher must step in to control what happens (see Chapter 4). As Eaton (1997) explains, "Allowing young children to make choices daily encourages them to learn about responsibility and enhances their independence" (p. 44).

It also shifts ownership of the class from the teachers to the children and teachers together. This helps children become more self-directed and responsible for their actions. They begin to understand that this is their class, too, and they can make a difference in what happens here. What kinds of choices do you allow children to make daily in your program? Some teachers include these options:

1. Choosing activities to pursue during free-choice period
2. Picking tasks to be performed by pairs of children (mail deliverer, animal attendant, safety inspector, table setter, meal server, sleep supervisor, librarian, lighting supervisor)
3. Deciding where on the wall to place own art products
4. Choosing where to place cot at nap time
5. Picking what photos the teacher should take of him and his activities
6. Selecting personal science project
7. Choosing books for teacher to read at story time
8. Picking songs to sing at circle time
9. Choosing where to go for a nature walk
10. Choosing books to borrow for overnight reading

This type of independence also empowers children to settle their own disagreements and resolve many of their own conflicts over materials and space without the teacher's intervention. But its most important result may be the boost it gives to children's self-esteem when they learn that they can make a difference in this classroom.

 ## HELP EVERY CHILD EXPERIENCE SUCCESS

All children can experience success in the program, although some may need your help to get them started or see them through. Each child needs this feeling that she can be successful in order to boost her own self-esteem. What is success for a child 3 to 5 years old? One measure of such a child's success is the completion of an activity she has started. Some children give up almost before they get started and thus rarely have the satisfaction of succeeding even at simple tasks.

Keep your eyes open for children who wander from one activity to another without finishing any. They may not understand how something works or what they are supposed to do. You can help by sitting next to them for support or even offering suggestions or help. "Sit over here, Brad. I've got something to show you that I think you'll like. Have you seen this new puzzle of a working man in a hard hat? Want to try it?" When Brad sits down, hand him a puzzle piece to get him started. Then ask him to find another that fits. Can he turn the piece around and try it? Some children give up without understanding how to twist a puzzle piece around and try it in different places. You may have to place one yourself to give him the idea, but try not to take over.

Stay with Brad until he completes the puzzle. Then offer your congratulations: "You did it, Brad! Look how well you made this puzzle! Want to try it again?" Or you might ask him if he'd like you to take a photo of him with his puzzle for his daily journal, a record of his accomplishments.

With another child you may only need to get her started on a project and not have to stay until it is done. Ask the child, "Kristin, I can see that you really know how to do this yarn weaving now. Is it okay if I go? I'll be back when you're finished, and you can decide if you want me to take a picture of it. Okay?"

For the boy with the short temper who has just knocked down his block structure because he couldn't get the top blocks to balance, you might try sitting on the floor next to the blocks to encourage him. "Josh, I saw what you were building, and you almost had it finished. Want to try it again? I bet you'll get it right this time." Help him move the tumbled blocks aside and give him one or two blocks to start with. Have him tell you what blocks to hand him until he is well on his way again. Then offer to come back when he is almost finished to see how he solves the balancing problem. When teachers take children's play seriously like this, they bestow adult importance on children's self-chosen tasks, thus motivating them to succeed.

Make a list of children's individual activities on a daily basis, and check off which ones they complete. For youngsters who are not involved on their own or do not complete something they start, be sure to offer a suggestion for something new to try, or give your support to help them finish a project successfully. Can you motivate them by reading a book?

Try reading *Cleversticks* by Bernard Ashley (1991) to individual children or a small group about Ling Sung the Chinese boy who can't seem to do anything right the way the other children do in his new preschool. He tries to tie his shoes, but his fingers get tangled in the laces. He tries to write his name, but the lines go every which way. He tries to button his jacket but it always ends up crooked. He can't even seem to fasten the Velcro tabs on his painting apron.

When he drops the cookies off his snack dish, he doesn't try to pick them up with his fingers but instead inverts a pair of paintbrushes and uses them as chopsticks to retrieve the broken cookie pieces. The other children watch in amazement and want him to show them how. Soon there are cookie pieces everywhere as teachers and children follow Ling Sung's directions on how to eat with chopsticks. Everyone claps when the teacher takes his picture eating with paintbrush chopsticks. His dad, who has come to pick him up, calls him "Cleversticks."

Can your children eat with chopsticks? Perhaps one of them can demonstrate for the rest. The real moral of this story is that success for a child can be such a simple thing as zipping up a jacket or writing his name. Not so simple for many youngsters, you realize. Perhaps you should start your children's "success campaign" with their names. You can help individuals print one letter at a time if you show them what it looks like and how to hold a crayon or marker. For a child who does not know how, this can be a real success story.

MODEL RESPECT BY TREATING EACH CHILD WITH RESPECT

Your principal task for enhancing each child's self-esteem is to treat everyone with respect at all times. Do not think of them as "good" or "bad," "nice" or "naughty" children but simply as children who have come to your program to grow and learn. One of the important lessons they must learn is how to get along with others. This lesson starts with themselves. To feel good about others they need to feel good about themselves—that is, possess positive self-esteem. You can help them feel this way by the way you treat each one, no matter how he or she may behave. It is their inappropriate actions you do not accept, not the children.

You model respect for each of the children most effectively when you speak to them with respect no matter what the situation. You do not criticize mistakes or scold misbehavior. Instead, you give positive reinforcement to their successes and redirect their inappropriate actions. As Kosnik (1993) tells us:

> By far the most important way in which a caregiver or teacher can boost a child's self-esteem is by talking to him respectfully, encouraging him to make appropriate decisions, expecting him to choose between meaningful activity options, assisting him in solving a social problem, and helping him learn something specific without criticizing his mistake or insulting his intelligence. (p. 33)

REFERENCES

Beaty, J. J. (1997). *Building bridges with multicultural picture books*. Upper Saddle River, NJ: Merrill/Prentice Hall.

Eaton, M. (1997). Positive discipline: Fostering the self-esteem of young children. *Young Children, 52*(6), 43–46.

Ferber, J. (1996). A look in the mirror: Self-concept in preschool children. In L. Koplow (Ed.), *Unsmiling faces: How preschools can heal*. New York: Teachers College Press.

Fraiberg, S. (1987). Self-representation in language and play: Observations of blind children. In L. Fraiberg (Ed.), *Selected writings of Selma Fraiberg*. Columbus: Ohio University Press.

Kosnik, C. (1993). Everyone is a V.I.P. in this class. *Young Children, 49*(1), 32–36.

Ramsey, P. G. (1987). *Teaching and learning in a diverse world*. New York: Teachers College Press.

SUGGESTED READINGS

Garcia, E. E. (1997). The education of Hispanics in early childhood: Of roots and wings. *Young Children, 52*(3), 5–14.

Gordon, S. A. M., Green, K. M., & Morris, S. L. (1995). Creating an environment that supports the developing social skills of all children. *Child Care Information Exchange, 105*, 47–50.

Haugen, K. (1995). Using technology to help children with diverse needs participate and learn. *Child Care Information Exchange, 105*, 58–62.

Katz, L. G., & McClellan, D. E. (1997). *Fostering children's social competence: The teacher's role*. Washington, DC: National Association for the Education of Young Children.

Milner, S. (1996). Helping children develop healthy self-concepts. *Children Our Concern, 21*(1), 24–25.

Russell-Fox, J. (1997). Together is better: Specific tips on how to include children with various types of disabilities. *Young Children, 52*(4), 81–83.

Teaching Tolerance Project. (1997). *Starting small: Teaching tolerance in preschool and the early grades*. Montgomery, AL: Author.

Winter, S. M. (1994/1995). Diversity: A program for all children. *Childhood Education, 71*(2), 91–95.

CHILDREN'S BOOKS

Ashley, B. (1991). *Cleversticks.* New York: Crown.

Avery, M. W. (1995). *What is beautiful?* Berkeley, CA: Tricycle.

Caseley, J. (1991). *Harry and Willy and Carrothead.* New York: Greenwillow.

Kroll, V. (1995). *Hats off to hair!* Watertown, MA: Charlesbridge.

Munsch, R. (1994). *Where is Gah-Ning?* Toronto: Annick.

Nikola-Lisa, W. (1994). *Bein' with you this way.* New York: Lee & Low.

Rabe, B. (1981). *The balancing girl.* New York: Dutton.

Reiser, L. (1996). *Beach feet.* New York: Greenwillow.

Vertreace, M. M. (1993). *Kelly in the mirror.* Morton Grove, IL: Whitman.

VIDEOTAPES

Australian Early Childhood Association. (Producer). *We all belong: Multicultural child care that works.* (Available from Redleaf Press, 450 N. Syndicate, Suite 5, St. Paul, MN 55104)

Magna Systems. (Producer). *Diversity, independence, and individuality* (no. 1). (Available from Magna Systems, 95 W. County Line Rd., Barrington, IL 60010)

Magna Systems. (Producer). *Teacher/child interaction* (video 3). (Available from Magna Systems, 95 W. County Line Rd., Barrington, IL 60010)

National Association for the Education of Young Children. (Producer). *Building quality child care: Independence.* (Available from NAEYC, 1509 16th St. N.W., Washington, DC 20036-1426)

National Association for the Education of Young Children. (Producer). *Painting a positive picture: Proactive behavior management.* (Available from NAEYC, 1509 16th St. N.W., Washington, DC 20036-1426)

LEARNING ACTIVITIES

1. Take photos of several children, make copies, and use them with the children in several of the ways suggested to help improve their self-esteem. Or, bring in enough hand or pocket mirrors to be used in self-esteem activities for everyone in a small group. Record the results.

2. Use children's names every day in written form, spoken form, and songs and stories. Be sure to include children who have caused disruption. Record what you do and how the children respond.

3. Do a self-esteem art project such as body tracing or sneaker rubbing. Record the results.

4. Read one of the children's books suggested in the section on diversity, and do a follow-up activity with an individual or small group. Record the results.

5. Make a list of the choices that the children in your class can make every day. Describe in what other ways the children can express their independence. Make a daily chores chart and have children volunteer for chores. Record the results.

CHAPTER 9

Using Other-Esteem
Conflict Conversion

▢ Help each child verbalize what happened during interpersonal conflict.

▢ Accept what each child says without blaming or shaming.

▢ Help children in conflict tell how the *other* child feels.

▢ Assist each child in finding ways to help the other conflictee feel better.

▢ Model other-esteem by demonstrating how to respond to feelings with puppets, book characters, and your own actions.

As discussed in Chapter 2, *other-esteem* refers to feeling good about another person. It is an invented term used to counterbalance the oft-used word *self-esteem*. Its inventor, M. Ann Gilchrist (1994), has this to say about it:

> In our world today much emphasis is given to the development and enhancement of one's self-concept. We are continually reminded that we need to maintain and improve our self-motivation, self-esteem and self-development. . . . And yet, is there something missing from this idea of self? Perhaps we need to consider more seriously the fact that we do not live in a self-contained world. The *others* are out there and they are going to stay. So we not only have the challenge of learning about ourselves but also about other *selves*.
>
> If one has been continually self-absorbed, self-focused and self-contained, can he/she develop a working concept of *other*? Perhaps as we are developing esteem for ourselves or teaching it to others, we can balance these ideas and concepts with considering the esteem for *others*.
>
> Is *other-esteem* the counterpart of *self-esteem*? (pp. 1–2)

I think it is. I also believe that the time is at hand to help young children develop this essential aspect of their social nature in order for them to learn to resolve interpersonal conflicts and to get along with others in harmony.

It is true that early childhood programs have concentrated on promoting children's self-esteem. Young children need to feel good about themselves before they turn their attention to others. But have we perhaps gone overboard with our stress on self-esteem? How many programs have followed up on the next step in children's social development, that of concern for another person?

We teach preschoolers about the classroom limit that they are not allowed to hurt another child. But do we help them learn *why*? Why should they not hurt someone else? To an adult the reason is self-evident. Not so to a youngster at the beginning of his experiences in dealing with others. Why not hit someone who has taken his toy? Maybe that will make him give it back. Some teachers quickly intervene with "Stop it, Rodney! You'll hurt Josh!" But this is not enough.

What does Rodney really learn from the teacher? Words from a teacher tell her side of the story. The teacher's presence also stops him from his action—this time. But if we want Rodney to learn a more powerful lesson about not hitting another child, then he also needs to hear directly from the *other* child.

Hitting is more than physical harm; it also involves the emotions of the other child. Josh is feeling hurt not only physically but emotionally. If he cries, he often attracts other children who may express *sympathy*, an emotional response to another person's emotional state. Some may also feel *empathy* toward Josh—that is, feeling the same as another person.

What we would like them to learn is *other-esteem*: feeling good about another person, so that you will treat the person like you want yourself treated. It is the old but often neglected Golden Rule: do unto others as you would have them do unto you. Didn't we used to teach that to children, you may ask? What made us stop? Did we become so involved in promoting children's self-esteem that we forgot to take the next step, as Gilchrist suggests?

To learn other-esteem, a child needs to hear how another child feels *directly from that child*. We tend to assume that the hitter will know that the child he hits is feeling bad because he is being hurt. That is not necessarily the case. Egocentric young children see things mainly from their own point of view until they learn otherwise. Interpersonal conflict situations like this give them a valuable learning opportunity. As Eisenberg and Mussen (1989) note:

> Children are initially self-centered and become more oriented toward others as they achieve greater cognitive maturity and gain more experience. The control of moral behavior shifts from external rewards and punishments (by parents or other authorities) to internalized motives or individual principles. (p. 30)

One of the most effective ways we have found that young children can learn this moral behavior, this other-esteem, is by one child hearing from the other child how he feels after interpersonal conflict. Then he should have the chance to express his own feelings in return. Most of us have neglected to direct children's attention to other children's feelings. It is a serious omission but one that is easily remedied through a strategy we call other-esteem conflict conversion.

OTHER-ESTEEM CONFLICT CONVERSION

As previously noted, interpersonal conflicts among children in preschool are natural occurrences to be expected when one child interferes with something another child is doing or wants to do. Justin grabs Tony's toy truck. Maura wants to play in the housekeeping area and Larue won't let her. Morris knocks down Noah's block building. Rinaldo is a superhero who hits Andrew with a "karate chop" and makes him cry. We can expect such clashes to occur whenever egocentric youngsters get together with little experience in how to deal with one another.

Chapter 1 pointed out that such conflicts should be considered learning opportunities for both children and teachers. Through interpersonal conflicts children learn what to do when confrontations with peers occur. Katz and McClellan (1997) concur:

> Conflict is inevitable among members of any truly participatory group of children; it should not and probably cannot be eliminated completely. The spontaneous and inevitable social problems that arise when children work and play together put the teacher in an ideal position to advance children's social development. (p. 59)

In other words, prosocial guidance does not become meaningful for young children until a real social problem arises.

When to Intervene

When possession conflicts or group access conflicts occur as mentioned, the teacher's first response should be one of waiting. You have given children many opportunities to develop their independence and self-direction. Now let them try to resolve these conflicts on their own. Be alert to what is happening, but give the children time to work out a resolution of their own. Most conflicts, in fact, can be settled by the children themselves without adult intervention.

It is important that they try to settle conflicts by themselves. If you intervene every time you see a dispute going on, the children will become dependent on you for managing their behavior—just the opposite of what you are trying to teach them. To develop self-control and independence, children need your support and patience in allowing them to struggle through to their own resolution in their conflicts.

The disagreement is their problem, not yours. Give them time to resolve it, if at all possible. Children may look your way to see if you are coming to intervene. When they see you return their look but not make a move in their direction, it gives them added impetus to create their own solution.

You need to use your common sense about intervening in children's conflicts. At times it is important to make a move without delay. Someone may be hurt or someone's behavior becomes so violent that intervention is necessary immediately. The following guidelines can help you determine if and when to intervene:

1. When behavior becomes violent or out of control
2. When children hit, bite, pull hair, or throw things
3. When children cry or scream
4. When conflict reaches an impasse with neither child willing to give in

How to Intervene

First, be sure your own emotions are in control. Do not rush into a children's conflict with frowning looks or angry words. Your facial features and tone of voice must project a sense of calmness. Then you can go to two children in conflict and gently remove them from others around them to talk with them in private. If more than two children are involved, pick the two most highly involved. Direct any other children back to their own activities.

If the children in conflict are too upset to listen or talk, stay with them but give them time to calm down. Speak their names quietly and repeatedly until they become calmer. If there is a couch or corner you can retreat to, all the better. If one or both children are crying, give them a chance to get it out of their system. Adults often do not understand the reason for crying and thus do their best to stop it. Instead, psychologists have found crying to be a beneficial emotional release. Solter

Be sure your own emotions are in control when you intervene in a conflict. Your facial features and tone of voice should project a sense of calmness.

(1992) notes, "The purpose of emotional crying is to remove waste products from the body. Chemical toxins build up during stress and are then released in tears. . . . Crying not only removes toxins from the body but also reduces tension" (p. 65).

Children who are allowed to release their pent-up feelings through crying tend to feel more happy and secure afterward. To force children to stop crying is to distract them from feelings that need to be expressed and acknowledged. As Solter explains (1992), "Crying is not the hurt, but the process of becoming unhurt" (p. 66).

Whether or not they are crying, children in conflict need a few minutes to regain their composure as well as to realize you are not angry at them. Making eye contact with them is often enough to defuse their anger or allay their fears. When children see your calm look, they know you are not upset but are there to help them resolve their difficulties. After all, you should be a transformer of conflicts, not an angry teacher. Be sure to stay at eye level when you talk with the children, rather than looming over them in an intimidating fashion. Then you will be able to involve them in this new *conflict conversion technique*. It consists of four parts:

1. Ask each child to tell what happened.
2. Accept what each child says without blaming or shaming.
3. Ask each child to tell how the other child feels.
4. Assist each child in finding ways to help the other child feel better.

As you note, the technique involves helping each child recognize and respond to emotions—the other child's emotions. Preschoolers have often been asked how they feel, but this is something different. This conversion technique directs their attention to the other child and how she feels.

HELP EACH CHILD VERBALIZE WHAT HAPPENED DURING INTERPERSONAL CONFLICT

In a typical conflict over possessions, Justin, who has been building a block road, wants to use the truck Tony is playing with to run on his road. Tony won't let him, so Justin grabs the truck away from Tony. Tony immediately hits him and Justin cries. The crying alerts your attention to the situation, although you did not observe what brought it on. You approach both boys, calmly speaking their names, and directing them over to the couch in the book area where you all sit down.

As you give the boys a chance to calm down, you note the still-angry look on Tony's face and the tear-stained, innocent "he hit me" look on Justin's. Your face should display no emotion other than a matter-of-fact calmness. When the boys are ready, you will be asking them each to tell you what happened. Do it in a pleasant conversational tone, not in an accusing manner. Start with whichever boy appears to be ready to talk. If neither is ready, then wait for a while. Finally you can say, "What happened, Justin? You seemed to be upset over something." Justin tells how Tony hit him, that he was just playing with the block road he had built and Tony hit him. "Tony is always hitting," Justin declares angrily. "It's his fault." You listen without comment, or you may say, "I hear what you're saying, Justin. Now let's hear from Tony." Tony speaks up angrily, too, telling that it's Justin's fault. He started it all. He came over and grabbed the truck Tony was playing with. He grabbed it and ran over to his road with it, and he, Tony, wants it back. You listen to this explanation, too, commenting, "All right, Tony, now I know what happened."

What is obvious to you is that each boy responds to the same situation from his own perspective. Knowing preschool children as you do, their explanations are not at all surprising. Each one sees what happened in a completely different light. Each feels he was in the right and was victimized by the other, that it was the other's fault for what happened and not his.

ACCEPT WHAT EACH CHILD SAYS WITHOUT BLAMING OR SHAMING

You accept what each child says because you want to hear their points of view. You want them to have every opportunity to tell the story as they see it. It is important for each of them to have his say and for to you to listen. Venting anger like this helps release negative emotions. Whether one is right and one is wrong is not the point. The point of asking children what happened is to get them to express their own version of the incident. Each one needs not only to justify his actions but also for you to hear his justification.

Accept what each child says in an interpersonal conflict without blaming or shaming. In prosocial guidance the teacher is more concerned with feelings than with fault.

You note that both have left out important details in the conflict: Justin does not mention that he grabbed Tony's truck away from him. Tony does not mention that he hit Justin. You understand why these particular details are omitted: because neither boy wants to take the blame for the conflict. Your concern, however, is not about these details. In this conflict conversion technique, you are not going to blame either boy for what happened. Therefore, you do not need to know who started it or whose fault it was.

Blame is not the point. Fault finding is not the point. *In prosocial guidance the teacher is more concerned with feelings than with fault.* It is no one's fault; it is everyone's fault—as are most conflicts. But this conflict situation is an excellent opportunity for children to learn other-esteem, and it may even prevent another similar conflict from occurring later. Without hesitating the teacher takes the third step in the four-point technique, discussed in the next section.

 HELP CHILDREN IN CONFLICT TELL
HOW THE *OTHER* CHILD FEELS

"Thanks for telling me what happened, Justin," the teacher continues. "Now, see if you can tell how Tony feels about it all."

This step is where the actual conversion takes place. Switching the focus from fault to feelings, the teacher asks the child to step out of himself and try to feel what the other child is feeling. This is a big leap for a preschool child. It is a big leap for anyone. (Try it yourself!) But it works. Young children are usually so surprised at this change of focus that they actually forget about themselves for the moment and really do try to feel what the other child feels.

Some may resist, but only for a moment, saying as Justin does, "But it's Tony's fault! He hit me!" Your matter-of-fact reply lets him know where your sentiments lie. "Yes, Justin. You said that before. I heard what you said about Tony. But now we're talking about feelings. How do you think Tony feels? Look at his face. What does his face tell you?"

Children can "read" faces almost better than we can. These nonverbal cues are a large part of their vocabularies especially before they become fully verbal. Chapter 1 describes how infants learn to distinguish facial expressions and body postures between 12 and 18 months.

Justin may eventually tell you that Tony looks "mad," and you may agree. If he says nothing, switch to Tony and come back to Justin later. "Tony, how to you think Justin feels?"

Tony may also reply with surprise: "But he took my truck! He started it!" "Yes," you may counter, "you told us about that already. Now we're talking about feelings. Look at Justin's face. How do you think he feels?"

If you stay with the situation, accepting everything the children say but eventually bringing them back to the other's feelings, you can usually elicit a meaningful reply. Then reiterate their answers, giving both a chance to expand if they want: "Justin, you say that Tony feels mad. Is that how you feel, Tony? Okay. And Tony, you say that Justin feels bad. Do you feel bad, Justin? Well, that's what I thought, too. Tony feels mad and Justin feels bad. I wonder what each of you can do to make the other person feel better? Wouldn't you like to feel better?"

We as adults sometimes assume that children know how others feel, but this is not necessarily the case unless it is pointed out to them or unless they discover it for themselves through a conflict conversion method like this. As Wittmer and Honig (1994) observe, "Helping young children notice and respond to the feelings of others can be quite effective in teaching them to be considerate of others" (p. 7).

 ## ASSIST EACH CHILD IN FINDING WAYS TO HELP THE OTHER CONFLICTEE FEEL BETTER

The final step in other-esteem conflict conversion asks you to help each of the children express what they think will make the other feel better. Obviously, you could make this decision yourself, but in turning over the responsibility of settling the conflict to the children themselves, you are more likely to see an end to this particular disagreement. In addition, you give children another opportunity to become independent and self-directed. Justin may say that giving the truck back to Tony will make him feel better. You need to ask Tony whether he agrees to that. Yes. But then Tony may surprisingly say that he will let Justin play with the truck, too, to make him feel better if he can play with him on his new road. Will Justin agree to this? Yes.

Children's own solutions to their conflicts are often much more to the point than those of adults. Wittmer and Honig (1994, p. 7) describe a situation in which one child socked another child during a struggle for a bike. When the teacher pointed out the hurt feelings of the other child and asked the hitter what he could do to make the crying child feel better, he offered him the bike. Had this been the teacher's solution ("He needs to have a turn on the bike now"), the hitting child might very well object and try to take the bike back at the next opportunity.

Recognizing feelings of the other person—this is the lesson children learn through other-esteem conflict conversion. A teacher in a Washington State preschool program told me that she liked using this technique with her children in conflict, because when she asked how they could help the other child feel better, they often hugged one another.

Using Other-Esteem Conflict Conversion

Children's extreme behavior, such as hitting, throwing things, and crying that is often difficult to control, seems to respond well to other-esteem conflict conversion. Teachers who have used it find an additional unexpected benefit: the other children in the class also learn to behave more prosocially from witnessing what happens with their peers during such outbursts. When the children in a classroom see that the teacher is more concerned with the feelings of those involved rather than whose fault it is, their behavior changes as well. And when they realized that conflictees are not punished but asked to help the other child feel better, their entire outlook may change.

Some teachers may resist using this type of conflict resolution because they feel it takes too long. It seems easier to send disruptive children to "time-out" than to talk with them. Perhaps they visualize much of their day being taken up by talking to children who create disturbances. This has not been the case for programs that practice other-esteem conflict conversion. Head Start teachers in Columbia, Missouri, for example, found that once children were familiar with their teachers' conflict conversion strategies, serious conflicts decreased:

> For the general group we use it once or twice a week. At the moment we have an extremely hostile child and we are using it every day, sometimes two or three times. It appears to be helping. He has not hit someone since we introduced it. (Worstell, 1993)

They noted that this was the only strategy that really worked for certain out-of-control children. The director made sure that one teacher was always free during the work/play periods to step in when needed if disruptions occurred in any of the learning centers. But she encouraged all the teachers to practice using other-esteem conflict conversion because of the prosocial behavior it taught everyone:

> We are practicing the conversion technique so that the children will have a background for use when the occasion arises. With practice we hope that empathy will become a part of our children's method of dealing with daily conflicts. (Worstell, 1993)

When children begin to see things from another child's point of view, when they begin to *feel* what another child feels, their own self-centered actions often change. Many children have not been encouraged to consider the feelings of others like this. To discover that the other child hurts just as badly as they do is a totally new experience for many. Then to find out that the other child is willing to help them feel better by giving up a toy or giving them a hug takes a lot of the pain away.

Can this strategy work as well for conflicts other than possession disputes? The following two cases present classroom incidents involving a group-entry dispute and an overly aggressive superhero play conflict. Remember that the three questions a teacher should ask each child at the appropriate times are as follows:

Other-Esteem Conflict Conversion Questions

1. What's happening here, _____ (child's name)?
2. How does _____ (other child) feel?
3. What will make _____ (other child) feel better?

Case 1: Maura and Larue in the Housekeeping Area

Maura and two other girls are playing house in the dramatic play center. Maura is the mother and gives orders to the other girls. Larue enters the area and picks up a baby doll. Maura rushes over and grabs it away from her.

Maura:	This is our house, Larue. You can't play with us. (Tries to push Larue out of the area.)
Larue:	I can, too! These toys are for everyone, Maura, not just for you! (Gets into pushing match with Maura, who gives her a big shove. Larue falls down and cries.)
Teacher:	(Comes over and helps Larue get up.) Are you all right, Larue? (Larue stops crying and nods yes.) What's happening here, Larue?
Larue:	Maura pushed me down and made me cry. She won't let me play in the housekeeping area.
Maura:	She just barged her way in here and took one of our babies. I had to get her out of here. She was waking up our children.
Teacher:	Well, it sounds like there is lots going on here in this house of yours today, girls.
Larue:	It's her fault. She thinks she owns the whole place!
Teacher:	I hear what you're saying, Larue. You wanted to play in the housekeeping area and Maura didn't want you to.
Maura:	She could've knocked on the door. You don't just barge into people's houses!
Teacher:	I hear what you're saying. too, Maura. You were playing in the area and Larue came in to play, too, without knocking on your door. How do you think Larue feels about it, Maura?

Maura:	(With surprise) Larue? Larue? Why should she feel anything? We're the ones. It's our house. She just barged in!
Teacher:	Yes, you said that before, Maura. Now let's talk about how people feel about it. How do you think Larue feels? Look at her face, Maura. How does it look to you? Can you tell how she feels?
Maura:	(Grumbling) I guess she feels bad, because she fell down.
Larue:	I did not! You pushed me!
Teacher:	So, Maura, you think Larue feels bad. Yes, I think you're right. She has tears on her face. And what about you, Larue? How do you think Maura feels?
Larue:	(With surprise) Maura? But it's her fault! She shouldn't feel anything!
Teacher:	Well, look at her, Larue. Look at her face. Do you think she is feeling something?
Larue:	(Mumbling) She looks mad.
Teacher:	Yes, she certainly looks mad to me, too. So now we know how you both feel about the affair. Larue feels bad because she couldn't play in Maura's house, and Maura feels bad because Larue came in without knocking. So, Larue, what do you think would make Maura feel better?
Larue:	If I knock on the door . . . and ask if I can come in?
Teacher:	Would that make you feel better, Maura? (Maura nods yes.) And how about you, Maura? What do you think would make Larue feel better?
Maura:	(Long silence.) Well, we could let her play, if she knocks on our door. But she can't be the mother. I'm the mother. She can be a sister.
Teacher:	Is that okay with you, Larue? Maura will let you play with them and be a sister if you knock on their door. Okay? (Larue nods yes.) Good. I'm glad you found a way to settle this without pushing one another. I'll come back later to see how your babies are getting along.

Teacher's Actions

In this case the teacher noticed the struggle in the dramatic play center and came over just as Larue fell down and started crying. She asks what's happening and then listens noncommittally to what each girl has to say, knowing that each will be telling her own side of the story. Because she only witnessed the end of the incident, the teacher needs to figure out what happened to cause the pushing. But she does not ask this question specifically because she knows that the answers will involve whose fault it is. She is not interested in this and does not want the girls to focus on blame. Thus, she always asks in a matter-of-fact and not angry tone of voice, "What's happening here?" to each girl.

After listening carefully to what each girl answers, she decides the focus of the conflict is Larue's wanting to play in the center and Maura's trying to keep her out. By repeating only the statements about gaining access, she acknowledges that she heard what each girl said. The pushing and falling down did not seem to be the focus, so the teacher ignores remarks about it.

She also is careful not to repeat fault-finding statements the girls make. By stressing only *what happened* in its briefest form, she still allows each child to justify her actions without getting involved in *whose fault it was*. The focus in conflict conversion is always on feelings and empathy, not blame and shame. But it is important to allow each child to justify her actions, whether or not what she says is accurate. This justification ("I did what I did because she did what she did") is often more significant to a child than anything else, and she wants to be sure the teacher hears it.

When the teacher asks question 2 (How does the other child feel?) children are often caught off guard. They expect to be asked how *they* feel. Once again the focus is on empathy—that is, feeling the way the other person feels. This question shifts the conflict away from the self and over to the other. It gives children something new and different to consider and takes their minds off what happened to them. Most children do not think about the feelings of another child during conflict because no one has ever asked them to. Most are surprised to learn that the other child feels just as badly as they do.

At this point after empathy has clicked in, the teacher asks question 3: what would make the other child feel better? Once again children may be surprised at the direction this conversation is taking. They expect to be asked what would make *them* feel better, not the *other child*. But by asking this third question, the teacher accomplishes three things: (a) she diffuses the children's negative feelings toward one another; (b) she allows each upset child to determine the final action to be taken—if the other agrees; (c) she does not impose her own solution on the children but allows them to settle their own disagreements, making it more likely the settlement will stick.

Had the teacher told the children what they should do, the results would not have been the same. She would have taken the conflict out of the children's hands and made it hers. Whatever solution she imposed would be disliked by at least one of the conflictees—the one who considered herself the loser—and the disagreement would probably continue after the teacher left. As DeVries and Zan (1994) remind us, "The child who is given opportunities for regulating his or her behavior has the possibility of constructing a confident self that values self and others positively" (p. 50).

The fact that both Maura and Larue agreed to their own solution so readily indicates how brief children's disagreements really are and how easily two adversaries can come together again in play. All it takes is a teacher willing to help them work through to converting a conflict to other-esteem. Everyone will then learn the powerful lesson that we all have feelings that can be hurt by others but that these feelings can also be healed by someone who takes time to show other-esteem. Even children who are onlookers, such as the other two girls in the housekeeping corner, learn this lesson.

Practicing other-esteem conflict conversion is like a pebble dropped in a pond whose ripples spread out affecting everyone in the program—including parents who learn from their children how the program handles conflict.

Case 2: Superalien Rinaldo Clashes with Andrew

Rinaldo is pretending to be an alien from another planet as Andrew and Tomas play with trucks in the block center. He zooms in and round the boys, moving his right arm up and down when he gets near their trucks. Andrew tries to protect his truck from being "karate chopped" by Rinaldo's flashing arm and gets a hard chop on his own arm instead. He cries.

Teacher:	(Comes over and sits on floor by Andrew in block center. Motions Tomas away and motions Rinaldo to come join them.) Andrew, Rinaldo, what's happening here, boys? (Andrew continues to cry.) What's going on, Rinaldo?
Rinaldo:	(With great excitement) I'm a superalien from Mars! Nobody can hurt me! I got superpowers over everybody. Even trucks and cars!
Teacher:	So I see, but sometimes superpowers can get out of control and hurt people, don't you think?
Rinaldo:	Not if they're superaliens like me. Nothing can hurt me!
Andrew:	(Who has stopped crying to listen) He just thinks no one can hurt him! My truck can run right over his alien!
Teacher:	(Who now realizes Rinaldo is holding a small toy figure of a spaceman in his right hand) Oh, are you boys playing "outer space" together, Andrew?
Andrew:	No, Tomas and me are playing with our trucks, and Rinaldo is trying to get his superalien to dive-bomb us.
Teacher:	Is that right, Rinaldo? Are you dive-bombing Andrew and Tomas with your spaceman?
Rinaldo:	(Who has settled down and is less excited) It's just pretend. It's not a weapon. (The class had made a rule about no toy weapons in the classroom.)
Teacher:	So it sounds like Andrew and Tomas were playing with their trucks and you, Rinaldo, have been playing with your spaceman. Is that right? (Rinaldo nods yes.) And then you dive-bombed Andrew's truck but hit his arm. How do you think Andrew feels, Rinaldo?
Rinaldo:	It's not my fault. My superalien just likes to zoom around.
Teacher:	So I see. But now look at Andrew's face. How do you think he feels?
Rinaldo:	It was an accident.
Teacher:	Maybe it was. But let's think a minute about how Andrew feels. Can you tell how he's feeling?
Rinaldo:	He looks sad.
Teacher:	Yes, he looks sort of sad to me, too. Do you feel sad, Andrew? (Andrew nods yes.) Show us your arm. (It has a red mark.) Let me feel it. (Teacher rubs it lightly.) Does that feel better? (Andrew nods.) How do you think Rinaldo feels about it all, Andrew?
Andrew:	He doesn't feel nothing! It was his fault!
Rinaldo:	It was not! My alien was dive-bombing, not me!
Teacher:	(Quickly) Okay, I hear you, but we're not talking about whose fault it was now. You already said that. We're talking about feelings. Look at Rinaldo's face, Andrew. Look close. Can you tell how he feels?
Andrew:	(Who has calmed down) He feels sorry.

Teacher: (Somewhat surprised at this answer) He feels sorry, you think, Andrew? Do you feel sorry, Rinaldo? (Rinaldo nods yes.) Well, I guess it was an accident, all right, and Rinaldo is sorry it happened. What do you think will make Andrew feel better, Rinaldo?

Rinaldo: (Long silence while he thinks) Maybe if I give him my superalien. He can give him a ride in his truck. That's why he was coming to Earth, anyway, to get a ride in a truck. They don't have trucks on Mars.

Teacher: (Again surprised) Hey, Rinaldo, that's a great idea. Would you feel better, Andrew, if Rinaldo gave you his spaceman and you could give him a ride in your truck? (Andrew nods yes.) And what do you think would make Rinaldo feel better, Andrew?

Andrew: (Who has gotten caught up in the story) He could get another alien out of the toy box and let Tomas give him a ride in his truck. Or (working up excitement) he could get another truck and another alien and we could have a truck race with our aliens!

Teacher: That sounds great! Would that make you feel better, Rinaldo? (He nods yes.) But you won't let those aliens drive the trucks too fast, will you? We know how they get out of control sometimes. Tell you what—when you're ready, come and get me and I'll take a photo of your race. Okay?

Teacher's Actions

This teacher is alerted to the conflict by a child crying. He had seen Rinaldo zooming around the other two boys in the block area, coming close with his moving arm, but he would not have interfered with their play until Andrew was hit and started crying. He believes that children should resolve their own play problems as much as possible. But when someone is hurt, it is time for him to step in.

We can tell by his questions to the boys that it is not really clear to the teacher whether the boys were playing together or Rinaldo was an outsider, trying to "crash the party," so to speak, with his "alien." It is important for children to tell their stories and verbalize their justifications for their actions, as previously mentioned. The teacher notes that Rinaldo is really into his role as superalien, perhaps not even realizing that something has gone wrong. But when he does, Rinaldo quickly switches and becomes himself again, distancing himself from the spaceman in his hand who, after all, is the one who did the damage!

The tone of the teacher's questioning is not accusatory but fact finding. It takes the boys' minds off the hitting and crying aspects of the conflict and helps them both relax and think about feelings.

The way they resolve the conflict is typical of many children's creative solutions if they are given the opportunity to express themselves freely and become aware of the other's feelings. Had the teacher tried to impose such a solution on them, they both may have rejected it. The teacher's decision to take a photo of the truck race certainly validated their solution but also provided the teacher with a centerpiece for later discussions with the boys or others about how they can learn to play together even when things get out of hand. They may even want to dictate a story for the class scrapbook about "the day Rinaldo's superalien came to Earth for a ride in Andrew's truck."

Superhero Play

Superhero play like this has invaded almost every preschool classroom whose children have television in their homes. Youngsters are intrigued with these powerful figures they see on TV: Ninja Turtles, Power Rangers, Superman. Everywhere you look these heroes are featured: on television, movies, videocassettes, video games, and comic books. This media barrage then supports a merchandising blitz of toys, dolls, weapons, games, costumes, T-shirts, cereal boxes, and on and on. How can anyone escape?

Here are superpeople that no one can harm. They fight evil with powerful karate chops, kicks, and blasts. Preschoolers, especially boys, are drawn to such exciting characters and may burst into the classroom shouting their latest hero's challenge, scattering other children right and left. They get so caught up in the play that it seems almost real to them. Then someone gets hurt and cries—and voices suddenly hush. Now the teacher must deal with the consequences of superhero play. What will you do?

Superhero play is nothing new for children. Although the superheroes themselves may be new every season, certain action-oriented children have always gravitated to pretend play featuring power roles: cops and robbers, monsters, space invaders, or war play. Because young children are nearly powerless themselves and must depend on the adults around them for everything, such powerful roles are alluring indeed. For a few minutes in their lives they can be in charge, and nobody can stop them.

Yet is this what we want? Do we want our children to learn that violence can resolve conflicts? That people can be controlled by force? Should such superhero role-play be banned? Gronlund (1992) has this to say about it:

> Superhero play can be bewildering and frustrating to teachers. We see its necessity for children as a way for them to feel powerful in a scary world, yet we also try to maintain a safe, caring environment. Sometimes, meeting both of these needs seems impossible. (p. 25)

Many teachers answer this dilemma simply by banning superhero play. They feel that children already have enough violence in their lives and that no matter what its positive side may be, violence begets more violence. This is perfectly logical adult reasoning. It does not, however, take into consideration the underlying reasons for children's attraction to superhero play.

In pretend play, young children try out the roles and situations they see around them to make sense of their world. They pretend to be someone in charge such as a mother, father, or doctor. In playing this last role they are often dealing with a strong emotion: fear. Children are afraid of going to the doctor's and getting a shot. But they act out this fear therapeutically when they pretend to be a doctor giving the baby doll a shot. In like manner children subconsciously play out their fears about the violence

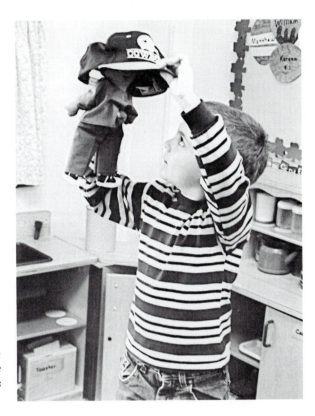

Superhero play in the classroom can often be managed if the superheroes are miniature figures or dolls.

they see in the world around them through superhero play. Some teachers recognize this play as a safety valve allowing them to work through and blow off strong emotions of all kinds.

For them the problem is not about banning superhero play but controlling it. These teachers often sit down with the children for a discussion of the pros and cons of their favorite superheroes. What are the good things these superheroes do? What bad things sometimes happen? How can we have pretend superheroes in our classroom without the bad things happening? Often special limits have to be made: superheroes can play outside on the playground only, or superheroes can play in the classroom only on special "superhero days," or superheroes can play in the classroom only with miniature figures. Even with such rules things can easily get out of hand, as we noted with Rinaldo and his superalien.

Preschool teachers have the right to ban superhero play from the classroom and playground if it cannot be controlled. However, they need to realize what they are doing: refusing to allow children to act out a therapeutic drama that may help them deal with fear and control issues. Some educators such as Boyd (1997) feel that teachers who ban superhero play are overreacting and confusing superhero play with aggression. Instead it is more like "rough-and-tumble play" with its chasing, mock battles, and feigned attacks. According to Boyd, "When we ban superhero play (or any behavior children find interesting), we ignore a powerful opportunity for helping children learn valuable lessons in a familiar and appealing context" (p. 27).

If superhero play is indeed an opportunity for children to learn valuable lessons, then perhaps instead of banning it, we should treat it as we do children's conflict, another opportunity for children to learn how to behave. When it gets out of control, we can also use other-esteem conflict conversion to help superheroes learn to empathize with others' feelings.

MODEL OTHER-ESTEEM BY DEMONSTRATING HOW TO RESPOND TO FEELINGS WITH PUPPETS, BOOK CHARACTERS, AND YOUR OWN ACTIONS

Children look to the adults around them to see how they should respond to other's emotions. Do the teachers show empathy when they notice a child feeling bad? Do they thank other children for also noticing and sympathizing? Teachers need to take every opportunity to demonstrate other-esteem themselves, and not just about the down side of others' feelings. When they see someone smiling, they can comment on how nice it is to see Rhonda's happy face or Jamie's grin. When children show excitement about a coming event, teachers can remark about how good it is to see everyone in such a happy mood. Teachers need to take and acknowledge the feeling pulse of the children on a daily basis. How else can children learn other-esteem if we do not practice it ourselves? Hyson (1994) reminds us:

> Emotion regulation is supported in a climate where children focus on other people. Coordinating one's own desires with those of others is impossible unless one is aware of others' feelings and unless one genuinely cares about the effects one's behavior has on others. (p. 152)

Puppets

Children can also learn to recognize other's feelings through role-play with puppets. Do you have any "feelings puppets" in your room? Keep several puppets apart from others the children play with to be used exclusively for expressing feelings. When children are involved in possession conflicts, bring out a pair of feelings puppets and have them act out a possession conflict drama on your two hands in front of a small group of children.

Give the puppets names and have the first one try to grab a toy away from the second puppet on your other hand. Have one argue and the other hit. Then ask the children how they can resolve their dilemma. If nobody suggests asking how the other puppet feels, you can replay the conflict, playing the role of the teacher/mediator yourself and asking the three conflict conversion questions to each puppet.

Children can make their own feelings puppets with a pair of mittens and a sheet of colored pull-off circles for eyes, nose, and mouth. Let them name their own puppets and tell what feelings they represent. Have them draw smiling or frowning mouths with markers. Then they can reenact their own feelings drama as you did, or two children can act out a drama together with a puppet on each hand.

Book Characters

Rinaldo's teacher decided to look for an outer space story about feelings to read to his children, a small group at a time. He noted that several of Rinaldo's friends also played with the spaceman figures in the block center and thus might be interested in learning more about feelings from such a story. The story he chose, *Dogs in Space* by Nancy Coffelt (1993), turned out to be just the thing, even though it did not focus on feelings.

In colorful chalk-like illustrations against glistening black pages the story unfolds as four dogs (one purple, one yellow, one brown, and one white with black spots) take the Great Solar System Tour to each of the planets. Simple text in white typeface at the bottom of each black double page tells the story about what they find on each planet. The teacher had to fill in the "feelings" part himself by asking his listeners how they thought the dogs felt when they landed on each planet. To make it even more dramatic and meaningful, he brought in four stuffed dog toys and had each child in the small group hold one and respond for it.

Children had to sit close to the teacher to see illustrations of the dog's reactions. On Mercury it was too hot and bright, and they had to wear sunglasses. Venus was even hotter and stuffier. The red dust of Mars made them sneeze. Then they had to pass through the dangerous Asteroid Belt on their way to Jupiter where the wind was so strong they could fly their kites. They played hide-and-seek with Saturn's 18 moons, but no one else was at home so off they flew to Uranus where they spun sideways. On Neptune they had to wear sweaters it was so cold, and Pluto had little light at all.

Children had each of their dogs talk about feeling hot and cold at first, but then scared, brave, hungry, happy, lost, and lonely. Everyone wanted a turn at being a dog in space and going on a "feelings tour" of the solar system. Rinaldo, of course, took his superalien along.

Think of other books your children enjoy that could also feature feelings in the same way if the children empathize with the characters. You might choose one of these:

Abuela, A. Dorros (New York: Dutton, 1991) (Hispanic Rosalba and her grandmother fly around New York City.)

Amazing Grace, M. Hoffman (New York: Dial, 1991) (African-American Grace pretends to be storybook characters until her classmates say she can't play the role of Peter Pan because she's a girl and black.)

At the Crossroads, R. Isadora (New York: Greenwillow, 1991) (African children wait all night for their fathers to come home from the mines.)

Carlos and the Squash Plant, J. R. Stevens (Flagstaff, AZ: Northland, 1993) (Hispanic Carlos won't wash his ears, and a squash plant grows out of one.)

Cleversticks, B. Ashley (New York: Crown, 1991) (Ling Sung can't seem to do anything right at his new preschool until he picks up cookie pieces with inverted paintbrushes as chopsticks.)

The Mud Family, B. James (New York: Putnam's, 1994) (A severe drought is disrupting life for Sosi's Pueblo Indian family, so she finds a mud hole and creates a whole new family of mud people who love her.)

To learn about others' feelings, children can role-play the feelings of book characters with dolls, puppets, or costume props.

Encourage children to role-play these characters in the dramatic play center. Put out props and clothing for the children to take on all the pretend roles Grace does in *Amazing Grace*. Have children pretend to be Rosalba in *Abuela* flying around New York City (the classroom). Bring in a sombrero for someone to play Carlos's role in *Carlos and the Squash Plant*. Perhaps chopsticks in the housekeeping area will motivate someone to be Ling Sung from *Cleversticks*. Ask the children about their feelings in these roles. Can they feel the same way the character did in the book?

As you see, learning about other people's feelings can be a happy and rewarding activity, not just one involving conflict or negativity. Other-esteem conflict conversion should be centered around converting negative feelings to positive ones. Follow-up activities with puppets, character dolls, and role-play helps children learn to recognize feelings in others, which in turn affects their behavior toward others. As Wittmer and Honig (1994) remind us, "A child's ability to identify accurately the emotional state of another, as well as the empathic ability to experience the feelings of another, contribute to prosocial behavior" (p. 7).

REFERENCES

Boyd, B. J. (1997). Teacher response to superhero play: To ban or not to ban? *Childhood Education, 74*(1), 23–28.

DeVries, R., & Zan, B. (1994). *Moral classrooms, moral children: Creating a constructivist atmosphere in early education.* New York: Teachers College Press.

Eisenberg, N., & Mussen, P. H. (1989). *The roots of prosocial behavior in children.* New York: Cambridge University Press.

Gilchrist, M. A. (1994). *Conflict and other-esteem: The counterpart of self-esteem?* Unpublished manuscript, Central Missouri Foster Grandparents Program.

Gronlund, G. (1992). Coping with ninja turtle play in my kindergarten classroom. *Young Children, 48*(1), 21–25.

Hyson, M. C. (1994). *The emotional development of young children: Building an emotion-centered curriculum.* New York: Teachers College Press.

Katz, L. G., & McClellan, D. E. (1997). *Fostering children's social competence: The teacher's role.* Washington, DC: National Association for the Education of Young Children.

Solter, A. (1992). Understanding tears and tantrums. *Young Children, 47*(4), 64–68.

Wittmer, D. S., & Honig, A. S. (1994). Encouraging positive social development in young children. *Young Children, 49*(5), 4–12.

Worstell, G. (1993). [Interview with author.]

SUGGESTED READINGS

Beaty, J. J. (1995). *Converting conflicts in preschool.* Fort Worth, TX: Harcourt Brace.

Beaty, J. J. (1998). *Observing development of the young child.* Upper Saddle River, NJ: Merrill/Prentice Hall.

Boyatzis, C. J. (1997). Of Power Rangers and V-chips. *Young Children, 52*(7), 74–79.

Buffin, L.-A. (1996). Hard joys: Managing behavior with a creative mind and a playful spirit. *Child Care Information Exchange, 111,* 58–60.

Freeman, N. K. (1997). Education for peace and caring go hand in hand. *Dimensions of Early Childhood, 25*(4), 3–8.

Greenberg, J. (1995). Making friends with Power Rangers. *Young Children, 50*(3), 60–61.

CHILDREN'S BOOKS

Ashley, B. (1991). *Cleversticks.* New York: Crown.

Coffelt, N. (1993). *Dogs in space.* San Diego: Harcourt Brace.

Dorros, A. (1991). *Abuela.* New York: Dutton.

Hoffman, M. (1991). *Amazing Grace.* New York: Dial.

Isadora, R. (1991). *At the Crossroads.* New York: Greenwillow.

James, B. (1994). *The mud family.* New York: Putnam's.

Stevens, J.R. (1993). *Carlos and the squash plant.* Flagstaff, AZ: Northland.

VIDEOTAPES

Educational Productions. (Producer). *Doing the groundwork* (no. 1). (Available from Educational Productions, 9000 S.W. Gemini Drive, Beaverton, OR 97008)

Educational Productions. (Producer). *Connecting with every child* (no. 2). (Available from Educational Productions, 9000 S.W. Gemini Drive, Beaverton, OR 97008)

Educational Productions. (Producer). *Understanding difficult behavior* (no. 3). (Available from Educational Productions, 9000 S.W. Gemini Drive, Beaverton, OR 97008)

LEARNING ACTIVITIES

1. How can children learn other-esteem? What can you do to help them? How will you know that they are beginning to learn other-esteem? Try it and see what happens.

2. When should you intervene in children's interpersonal conflicts? How should you do it? Try it and record results.

3. What if children in conflict try to blame one another instead of talking about feelings? How can you address this? Try it and record results.

4. How would you have handled case 1 or case 2? Describe your proposed actions, dialogue, and what you think the outcome would be.

5. Should superhero play in preschool be banned? Give reasons for or against it, and describe how you would cope with it if a conflict occurred.

CHAPTER 10

Promoting Positive Communication among Children and Adults

- Listen carefully to a child's communication, and respond with respect.
- Help each child engage in conversations every day.
- Help children learn what to say to avoid conflicts.
- Carry out small-group role-plays about feelings and behaviors.
- Model respectful speaking no matter what the situation.

For prosocial guidance to be successful, positive communication is the key. Speaking, listening, processing information, and acting on it—these are the necessary elements for young children's success. Preschool children, however, are still at the early stages of language development. How are they to communicate even their own feelings, let alone those of others? That is where you come in.

You understand that prosocial guidance depends on words: children verbalizing their feelings, making friends, making rules; teachers reflecting on children's behavior, modeling friendship, expressing congratulations. If the words we speak sound positive in nature, children are more likely to respond in a positive manner. You may also realize that communication between teachers and children and between children and children can be taught and practiced through modeling, coaching, role-playing, story reenactment, and classroom setup.

Positive communication thus entails respectful speaking, active listening, and helping children learn what words to use in specific situations. Learning to communicate like this is based, for both teachers and children, on listening. And for young children to learn listening skills, teachers must make it a point to model and teach active listening.

LISTEN CAREFULLY TO A CHILD'S COMMUNICATION, AND RESPOND WITH RESPECT

Most teachers generally agree that modeling good listening skills should not be too difficult for them. Jalongo (1995) is not so certain. According to recent studies, she finds:

> American adults listen at only 25% efficiency; most adult listeners are preoccupied, distracted and forgetful nearly 75% of the time. Research also suggests that adults expect much more from children than they do from themselves. (p. 13)

Is this true for you? Do you tell children to listen carefully, while you yourself rarely practice this same concentration? Good listening requires more from you than just stopping your own talking while the other person speaks. You must also follow these guidelines:

1. Quiet your mind's incessant "stream of consciousness."
2. Receive and process the incoming data.

3. Concentrate on the key points of what is being said.

4. Filter out unnecessary sensory input, and eliminate distractions.

5. Get involved emotionally with what you hear.

In other words, as Garman and Garman (1992) point out, "We hear with our ears, but we listen with our minds" (p. 5). How do you rate yourself as a listener? Do you use your mind to concentrate on what is being said, or do you daydream as someone talks, catching just a word now and then while you wait for your chance to reply? To find out, ask someone you know what their opinion is on a certain issue. Then, rather than replying, go back over their response in your mind to see if you caught it all. Now talk it over with them. How did you do? Most of us catch less than half of what we hear, even when we concentrate.

We can learn to do better. It is important that we become skilled listeners before we expect the same from the children, but we can also learn to do this together. Both teachers and children can become involved in specific listening activities that you set up for everyone, if you make good listening a priority in the program.

Becoming a Listening Model

First, to practice good listening you must face the person who is speaking and make eye contact. That may mean squatting down or sitting down next to a young child rather than leaning over her. Next, listen carefully to what is being said, allowing the speaker to finish without interrupting. Finally, reply by repeating something that was said. This lets the speaker know you have heard her. If your repeated words are incorrect, the speaker can correct you.

You need to remember that you are an important listening model for the children to follow. If you spend time and effort as well as emotional energy directed toward listening to the children in the manner described here, you can expect youngsters to pick up on your behavior and try it themselves. As one teacher notes:

> Adults can teach children to listen, first and foremost, by being good listeners themselves. Listening to our students is an essential skill for teachers to have, because when we listen, the kids feel valued. As the expression goes, "Kids don't care how much we know until they know how much we care." (Jalongo, 1995, p. 14)

Contributing to Children's Listening Ability

Children's listening ability is directly related to several factors:

- Auditory acuity (the ability to hear)
- Auditory perception (the ability to discriminate between sounds)
- Attention (the ability to focus attention on what is being said)
- Motivation (the reason for listening)

Children who do not seem to hear what you are saying or pay little attention to the speaking that goes on around them may need to be screened for hearing impairments or attention deficits. If such impairments are present, be sure the children are referred for appropriate professional assistance. Otherwise most youngsters can be motivated to listen if your listening activities include some of these elements:

- Listening walk
- Sound surprise table
- Headsets and book tapes
- Reading and telling of stories daily
- "Show-and-ask" group

Listening Walk

Take a small group of children at a time on a listening walk around the inside and then the outside of the building. Take a tape cassette recorder along and have the children listen for sounds that you will then record. When you return, ask the children what sounds they remember. Then play the tape and see how many sounds they can identify. Be sure to repeat this activity with small groups until everyone has had a turn. It may be so popular that the activity will become a weekly event. Then children can remember and compare the sounds from one week to another.

Sound Surprise Table

A sound surprise table can be anything you make it that involves sounds. Some teachers set up a table like this once a week with several small boxes sealed shut. Inside each is a different sound maker such as paper clips, marbles, sand, potato chips, nails, stones, or shells. The boxes are numbered, and each child must shake them one at a time and guess what is making the sound. Guesses can be recorded on paper by one of the teachers or on the tape recorder by the children themselves. When everyone has had a turn to guess, open the boxes to see how many guessed correctly. But be sure this is not a contest with winners or losers. Everyone is a winner every time they participate in such an interesting listening task.

Headsets and Book Tapes

Headsets and book tapes to go along with many of the books in your book center make excellent listening devices. Inexpensive jackboxes and headsets are available from educational supply houses to be plugged into a cassette player, allowing several children at a time to listen to the same book. This means you will want several copies of that book. To make the experience meaningful, be sure children are looking at the book at the same time that they listen to the tape. Go through the experience with each one to help them understand about turning a page when they hear the signal on the tape. Keep books and tapes stored together in plastic bags for children to use independently. Some books about feelings with cassettes available from Weston Woods Studios (1265 Post Rd. W., Westport, CT 06880; phone, [203] 226-3355) include these:

Noisy Nora, R. Wells (1997) (about a family too busy to listen)
Owen, K. Henkes (1993) (about giving up a fuzzy blanket)
The Very Worst Monster, P. Hutchins (1994) (about who is the monster in the family)
A Weekend with Wendell, K. Henkes (1986) (about pushy Wendell and shy Sophie)

Reading and Telling of Stories Daily

Children love to hear stories about characters they can identify with. If you purchase or make puppets to serve as main characters in favorite books, you or the children can have the puppet speak for the character in their own words when the time comes. Children will need to listen closely to the story for their cue and then listen to what the reader or other characters say. Animal book characters are special favorites, especially bunnies with their long ears for listening. Animal character dolls or puppets also can be purchased from educational supply houses to be used with several books about listening. (For example, contact Demco, P.O. Box 7488, Madison, WI 53707-7488.) A child can listen and speak for the animal character he is holding when the time is right.

The following titles are appropriate for these sorts of activities:

Guess How Much I Love You, S. McBratney (1995) (stuffed bunny)
Is Your Mama a Llama? D. Guarino (1989) (also in Spanish; llama puppet)
Little Beaver and the Echo, A. MacDonald (1990) (beaver puppet)
Polar Bear, Polar Bear, What Do You Hear? B. Martin (1993) (polar bear puppet)
What Have You Done, Davy? B. Weninger (1996) (stuffed bunny)

Whether or not you have character dolls or puppets, be sure to read or tell stories to the children on a daily basis. With more than one staff member in the program, someone is always available to read a book to an individual child who asks. In addition, teachers should plan small-group reading of stories in the book center. Although all book reading requires listening on the part of the audience, certain stories also feature listening.

In *Even That Moose Won't Listen to Me* by Martha Alexander (1988), Rebecca discovers a moose eating their vegetable garden, but nobody in her family will listen to her, leaving it up to her to scare off the stubborn animal. In *Listen Buddy* by Helen Lester (1995), little Buddy bunny may have beautiful ears, but he never puts them to use listening to what his family asks him to do, resulting in a hilarious mix-up of things. After reading such stories, play listening games like "Simon Says" to see whether the children can really listen and respond correctly.

Rhyming stories and predictable tales in which children try to guess what comes next by the sound of the word are excellent listening activities. In *Is Your Mama a*

Read stories to small groups fea-turing listening on the part of the book character as well as on the children's part.

Llama? by Deborah Guarino (1989), a little llama goes around asking each of his ani-mal friends whether his mama is a llama. The animal responds in verse telling what his mama is like, but readers must turn the page for the correct answer. Most young-sters can tell from picture cues what each animal's mama really is, but rhyming words also help. Dave's mother lives in a cave. That is not the way llamas behave. The little llama agrees about *that* and says Dave's mother sounds more like a *bat*. Have your listeners call out the name before you turn the page.

In *Louella Mae, She's Run Away!* by Karen Beaumont Alarcon (1997), an excited farm family runs out into the cornfield, in the hay, by the stream, in the barn, and finally back to the house looking for Louella Mae in rhyming verses that make the reader turn the page to see where they are. On the last page they finally find her and call Uncle Henry and Chub to tell them she's sleeping in the *tub*. Louella Mae turns out to be a plump, pink pig! Each time you read the story, though, why not make the sleeper a new and surprising stuffed animal that you produce after children have tried to guess who is in the tub? Such a switch should create a few more avid listeners.

"Show-and-Ask" Group

Jalongo (1995) suggests having small-group listening activities such as "show-and-ask," a variation of show-and-tell in which one child in a small group shows the others an object and then invites questions from the others. The teacher can model this activity with an object of her own—for example, a piece of bark from a sycamore tree. She could start off the session by holding up the bark and saying, "Here is something I found on the sidewalk on the way to school this morning. What do you think it is?" Pass it around for closer examination and give everyone a chance to guess. Then say, "Yes, Ron and Alicia were correct. It is a piece of bark. What else would you like to know about this piece of bark?" She should try to elicit questions such as, Where did it come from? (A sycamore tree.) How did it come off? (Sycamore trees shed their bark.) What could we do with it? (Make a collage; put it in our terrarium; make a bark rubbing, etc.) Then plan to have one child each day do her or his own show-and-ask with an item or toy from home.

Activities like this in which everyone gets a chance to participate quickly because the group is small and everyone must ask and answer questions keep children's attention focused and develop their active listening skills.

HELP EACH CHILD ENGAGE IN CONVERSATIONS EVERY DAY

Some children ages 3, 4, and 5 are skilled conversationalists, especially if they have been around other youngsters their same age or slightly older. Those who are new to the classroom or new to group play may not be as skilled. Yet learning to take part in conversations is essential to their success in getting along with the others. How will they learn it? Surprisingly, not primarily by listening to you or engaging in conversations with you. Although many teachers feel they are the principal contributors to children's language learning, that is not necessarily the case. Most children of this age learn conversation skills from one another. Talking with one another, listening to what others have to say, making themselves heard, and trying to get their own points across gives them exceptional practice in learning to converse. As Wolf (1996) points out:

> Many researchers and practitioners have found that child-to-child conversation is perhaps the most effective situation in which to help children make major language gains. Bilingual programs have gathered evidence that *peer tutoring* is probably the fastest and most motivating way to teach a young child a second language. (p. 42)

Motivating Children's Conversations

If this is the case, then what is your role in promoting children's conversation skills, you may wonder? First, you must provide the *time* and *motivation* for conversations among children to occur. Arrange your classroom physically for small-group activities to take place. Most of the learning centers should support four to six children if at all possible. Then set up activities requiring communication of participants. For example:

Art center: Cover a table with a large sheet of paper and ask several children to make a mural of their trip to the zoo.

Block building: Ask several children to build a house for the guinea pig.

Book center: Stand a big book on an easel, and ask several children to tell a group story about it into the tape recorder.

Dramatic play center: Can the children in the housekeeping area put on a "pizza party" for the children in the pretend store?

Music center: Have several children play rhythm instruments together. Can they become a band and record their music?

Playground: Mount tire swings in a horizontal position so that several children can use them at once.

Writing center: Spread out a large sheet of paper on the table or desk, and have everyone make a group greeting card to the class next door.

Although you may not set out group activities like this in each center every day, you remember the importance of children's peer conversations and thus give them frequent opportunities to practice. In addition to the activities, be sure to allow enough time during free-choice periods for children to become deeply involved in their chosen work, giving them time to talk together. Child-directed activities like this should dominate the schedule.

Set up tire swings horizontally so that several children can use them at once, thus promoting conversation.

Observing Children's Conversations

Next, you need to observe (and record if possible) children's conversations—especially those of children who do not seem to participate as fully or freely as others. Be aware of the elements of successful conversations to see whether these children use any of them. Such guidelines, however, are for your information only, not rules you should be teaching to the children. You may note or check off some of these points as you watch and listen to the children talking together:

Guidelines for Successful Conversations
____   Knows how and when to listen
____   Knows how and when to join in
____   Talks by taking turns with others
____   Keeps to the same topic
____   Knows how to add to the topic
____   Looks at the person he or she is talking to
____   Builds on what others say

Helping Children Become Involved in Conversations

It is at this point you yourself may be able help a child who is having difficulties in conversing with others. You can join a play group where a child is listening but not participating and become involved in a conversation yourself. Talk with various role-players who are putting on the pizza party in the dramatic play center, for instance, but be sure to include the listening child. "What kind of topping do you want on your pizza, Charlene?" "Cheese? That sounds good to me. Why don't you ask Rhonda to help you find the cheese and show you how to put it on the pizza."

For a child who is not engaged in any group play, invite him to join something interesting with you that will eventually lead him to interact with others. For example, pick up the class camera and invite the child to be a news photographer with you this morning. "C'mon, Raphael, I need help this morning. I'm taking pictures for the class newspaper. Want to help? Where should we start? You choose a center for our first picture." "The block center? What does it look like they're doing there?" "Okay. You hold the camera and see if you can get it all in. What do you see?" "Sounds good. Go ahead and take the picture."

If an observer like Raphael is not quite ready to join a group or converse with others, do not force the issue. Help him keep a conversation going with you instead. But if he gets caught up in the spirit of the activity, perhaps he will join one of the groups so that you can take a picture of him, too. As Trawick-Smith (1994) notes, "It is now believed that children learn language so that they may form relationships with other people" (p. 11).

These relationships are an important cornerstone for children's prosocial development in preschool. Teachers can and should intervene in children's play from time to time to help nonspeakers get started. They can also assist the other players in advancing their own conversation skills by making comments or asking questions about the play. But it is the peer conversations themselves that help children develop communication skills most effectively. When listeners begin to speak with others, it is time for the teacher to withdraw. According to Trawick-Smith (1994):

> Children not only acquire and apply linguistic rules through play with peers; they develop knowledge of how language can be used to influence others. Children have been found to learn, as they play, specific strategies for persuading their playmates. (p. 11)

HELP CHILDREN LEARN WHAT TO SAY TO AVOID CONFLICTS

Children who hang back or those who approach their peers aggressively may need your help in learning to communicate, especially in potential conflict situations. Much of Chapter 9 was devoted to discussing how to help children verbalize *after* interpersonal conflict had happened. They were asked to tell what had happened and how they thought the other conflictees felt. This item, on the other hand, from the Teacher Prosocial Guidance Checklist asks teachers to help children learn to avoid conflicts in the first place by learning what to say *before* they get out of hand.

A conflict that never happens can be just as much a learning opportunity for preschool children as those that do occur. Youngsters can learn how to use language to influence their peers in ways that avoid conflict. Some children already know what to say in such situations. Others may need your help. This calls for careful observation on your part to identify potential conflicts.

Possession Conflict

For example, you notice that Latasha, who has been playing with a toy electronic keyboard, is now struggling with Jackie, who is trying to take it away from her. You know both girls well enough to realize this conflict may well end in blows. But *before* this can happen you call Jackie over and ask why she is pulling the keyboard away from Latasha. Jackie explains that she has waited long enough for a turn and Latasha still won't give up the keyboard.

Because you want Jackie to learn how to resolve a possession conflict like this through communicating rather than fighting, you first ask what she has said to Latasha. Did she ask whether she could use the keyboard? Jackie replies no, she didn't ask because Latasha would never give it up. "Try it and see," you might suggest. "Maybe she will give you a turn if you ask her in a nice way. If it doesn't work, come back, and we'll think of another way."

Coaching a child like this by suggesting what she might do or say is often enough to resolve the problem on the spot. If this doesn't work, you might ask Jackie what she could do or say to "work out a deal" with Latasha. Given the chance to negotiate, children can often come up with an acceptable compromise. Jackie, who is wearing a computer center necklace, says she will ask Latasha if she would trade the keyboard for a turn at the computer. An excellent suggestion, you tell her.

If she can't think of anything, you might propose that both girls use the keyboard together. Could she ask Latasha to play while she sings or drums, and then she could record their music on a tape cassette? Or if it is a long keyboard, could both children play it at once? The idea is for one child (not you) to speak to another rather than fight with another for possession of toys or equipment. The other child sees you in the background and realizes you are encouraging this negotiation.

You may want to ask Jackie what words she will say to Latasha to convince her to give up her toy. Role-play the situation if necessary, saying you are Latasha, and have Jackie address you the way she would address Latasha. If she seems at a loss about what to say, you can suggest the actual words to use. If she sounds too demanding, you might suggest she make her voice sound more friendly and have her practice again. Little by little children come to learn the skills of negotiating and compromising if you support them in their efforts.

Group-Entry Conflict

Although possession conflicts are the most frequent kinds of interpersonal disagreements in preschool, gaining access to ongoing play is a close second. Once children begin their play in the block center, sand table, or dramatic play area, they are reluctant to admit newcomers. Ramsey (1991) tells why:

> Interactions in preschool classrooms are short, so children are constantly having to gain entry into new groups. This process is made more difficult because children who are already engaged with each other tend to protect their interactive space and reject newcomers. (p. 27)

Some newcomers try to "crash the party" by disrupting the play physically when they are rejected. Some may yell or even cry. Others come running to the teacher for her to force the players to accept them. In all cases you can help children keep this conflict from escalating through child-child communication.

Child development researchers who have observed the strategies preschoolers use to gain entry into group play note that certain approaches almost always work for the youngsters and others usually fail. Using their findings, you can help unsuccessful children find ways to gain access without resorting to physical or verbal assaults. Their conclusions show that often a child needs more than one strategy to gain access and that these strategies need to be tried in a particular order (Corsaro, 1979; Dodge, Schlundt, Schocken, & Delugach, 1983; Ramsey, 1991; Shantz, 1987):

1. Watch and listen to the group.
2. Play parallel to the group.
3. Make a play-oriented statement.

Talk with the child trying to gain entry, and suggest that she go over to the group and watch what they are doing. She doesn't have to say a word at first. Then once she understands the content of their play she can begin playing unobtrusively along-

Talk to a child who is trying unsuccessfully to gain group entry, suggesting that he might try to watch what the group is doing and then play parallel to them doing the same kind of play.

side them in the same way. Finally, she can talk about the play from her perspective, as if she is already included.

For instance, Josh tells you that the boys in the block center won't let him play with them. You might suggest that he first watch what Ramon and Nevis are doing and then try building a similar structure next to theirs—a kind of parallel play. When he hears that they are making a tower for spotting UFOs, he could say, "This is a landing pad for when the UFOs come down." If neither boy seems to object, he will have entered their play without conflict.

The same strategies work in the dramatic play center. You might suggest that the outsider first listen to what's happening in the play and then join in by carrying on the same play herself. Once she is involved she can tell the others what she is doing. On the other hand, asking directly whether she can play with the others almost always brings a rejection. Obviously, you could force the issue by making children accept outsiders into their play. Such a move, however, will surely defeat your goal of helping children develop their independence and ability to resolve their own problems.

Group-entry conflicts should seldom arise if children remember to use self-regulating devices such as the learning center necklaces or tags previously mentioned in Chapter 4. When these devices are in use, children have the independence to regulate their own access to the centers. You can then help outsiders negotiate for turns in the centers they want by trading necklaces. You may need to coach a youngster from time to time on what words to use if she seems at a loss. But in the long run you will have helped children learn an important skill: to avert or resolve their own group-entry conflicts through parallel play and communication.

CARRY OUT SMALL-GROUP ROLE-PLAYS ABOUT FEELINGS AND BEHAVIOR

Children can learn what words to use in conflict situations by listening to what you and their peers have to say, by your coaching, and also by being directly involved in the conflicts themselves. Another important method for children's learning of words to express their feelings is through role-plays that you carry on after conflicts have occurred.

Everyone learns from conflict, even those not directly involved. Children watch carefully what happens to others who cause disruptions. In other-esteem conflict conversion (as described in Chapter 9), they see that each of the children involved in an interpersonal disagreement has a chance to resolve the problem through words. You can give onlookers that same opportunity to try out words when you role-play conflicts in a small-group setting.

Some teachers like to read picture books about conflicts to a small group of children and then ask them how they think each of the book characters feels. In *Noisy Nora* by Rosemary Wells (1997), little Nora mouse causes several attention-getting conflicts in her family because she always has to wait while Mother takes care of baby Jack and Father plays with older sister Kate. Nora bangs the window, slams the door, dumps her sister's marbles on the kitchen floor, and later knocks down a lamp and some chairs. But she doesn't use words. Large action-filled illustrations with a rhyming sentence at the bottom make this an excellent book for riveting the attention of a small group of preschoolers.

Be sure each member of the group is sitting close enough to see the pictures as the story progresses. If they like it, they will want you to read it again. Repeat the story as many times as they request. It is short and to the point, and they will soon know it almost by heart. Then ask them what they think Nora feels like in each of the situations. Can they come up with words such as *sad, unhappy, tricky, impatient, fidgety, bored, naughty,* and *quiet*? You may need to help with a few new words. But even the youngest children love to roll big new words around their tongues. *Fidgety* sounds wonderful to them.

How do they think the other characters feel while Nora is fidgeting around? How would they feel if they were Nora? Would they like to be Nora and tell their parents and sister Kate how they feel in each situation? Have each child in the small group take turns being Nora as you read the story. They can speak for the silent Nora as the episodes unfold. Better still, bring in a mouse doll or puppet for them to hold and speak through, maybe in a squeaky voice. You can be the mother and father who listen and respond to what Nora has to say: "Oh, Nora, I didn't know I was neglecting you like that. I'm really sorry." Next time the children can take the roles of the mother, father, and Kate, following your lead.

Picture books showing children's conflicts like this are especially good teaching devices for helping children role-play how they would act and what they would say in the same situation. Then you can leave the book and a character doll or puppet on the book center table so children can role-play on their own. Repeat the story and role-play for a small group of children until everyone has a chance to be each of the characters. In a large group children have to wait so long for a turn they end up feeling (and perhaps acting) like Noisy Nora.

Plan to purchase certain books that speak to common conflicts that may arise among the children. For example:

Bootsie Barker Bites, B. Bottner (1992) (about an aggressive bully of a little girl, Bootsie Barker, who terrorizes the narrator of the story until she finds a way to stop her)

Don't Call Me Names! J. Cole (1990) (a longer story about shy little Nell, a frog, who is terrorized by two bullies Mike, a fox, and Joe, a pig, who tease her and call her names)

Just Not the Same, A. Lacoe (1992) (about three sisters—Celo, Mirabelle, and Gertrude—who refuse to share anything)

If you have no books, make up your own stories about children's conflicts based on disputes you have witnessed in the classroom. Change the names of the conflictees, of course, but have fun elaborating on the incident. If children enjoy such role-plays, make simple paper headbands for each character to wear when they play their role. Children can choose the color for the headband, and you can print the character's name on each. Or have children make simple paper-bag hand puppets to operate when they play a role. Peel-off stickers can serve as eyes, nose, and mouth at the bottom of the bag (which is the face of the puppet). Even children who choose to listen rather than play a role eventually come to learn the words a person uses to express feelings and may even join in when they feel comfortable.

MODEL RESPECTFUL SPEAKING NO MATTER WHAT THE SITUATION

Children deserve our respect just as the adults around us do. We can show this regard by speaking respectfully no matter how upsetting the circumstances. Respectful speaking involves the words we use, our tone of voice, its loudness or softness, and the body language that accompanies our speaking.

Respect involves the teacher-child relationship we have carefully developed by the way we treat the children and expect them to act toward us. In many classrooms respect is a one-way street: children are expected to respect the teacher. But for preschool youngsters to learn prosocial behavior, they must experience it themselves. We must treat them with respect as well. This mutual respect can be expressed in the language we use on a daily basis no matter how emotional the situation. Stone (1993), in her assessment of child care providers, calls such talk *responsive language,* which she defines as:

language that conveys a positive regard for children and a respect for and acceptance of their individual ideas and feelings. Responsive language encourages verbal give-and-take and independent thought, implies alternatives and choices, and includes other-oriented induction, in which reasons and explanations are provided. (p. 13)

Stone (1993) contrasts this way of speaking to young children with *restrictive language* in which teachers use words to control youngsters by issuing "unnecessary or disrespectful commands, threats, punishments, and criticisms" (p. 13). A teacher using restrictive language in a conflict situation might say, "Sondra, if I see you taking Maria's crayon one more time, I'm sending you to time-out!" In the same situation a teacher using responsive language might say, "Sondra, look at Maria. How do you think she feels when you take her crayon like that? Could you ask to borrow her crayon?"

In all cases of conflict we need to remember that this is a learning situation for the children. If we intervene, it should be to help children resolve the problem themselves. If we intervene with threatening words or an irritated tone of voice, we are taking over the situation ourselves. It may take self-control on our part for our voices and faces to show concern instead of anger when tempers flare, but it is essential if we want to set the stage for children's own respectful speaking. Stone (1993) reminds us:

Let us hope that [children] will find responsive caregivers who provide a warm and nurturant environment and who, through responsive language let children know that they are valued and respected, that they matter in this world. (p. 17)

REFERENCES

Corsaro, W. A. (1979). "We're friends, right?" Children's use of access rituals in a nursery school. *Language in Society, 8,* 315–336.

Dodge, K. A., Schlundt, D. C., Schocken, I., & Delugach, J. D. (1983). Social competence and children's sociometric status: The role of peer group entry strategies. *Merrill-Palmer Quarterly, 29*(3), 309–336.

Garman, C. B., & Garman, J. F. (1992). *Teaching young children effective listening skills.* York, PA: William Gladden Foundation.

Jalongo, M. R. (1995). Promoting active listening in the classroom. *Childhood Education, 72*(1), 13–18.

Ramsey, R. G. (1991). *Making friends in school: Promoting peer relationships in early childhood.* New York: Teachers College Press.

Shantz, C. U. (1987). Conflicts between children. *Child Development, 58,* 238–305.

Stone, J. (1993). Caregiver and teacher language—Responsive or restrictive? *Young Children, 48*(4), 12–18.

Trawick-Smith, J. (1994). Authentic dialogue with children: A sociolinguistic perspective on language learning. *Dimensions of Early Childhood, 22*(4), 9–16.

Wolf, D. P. (1996). Children's conversations: Why are they important? *Child Care Information Exchange, 110,* 40–42.

SUGGESTED READINGS

Beaty, J. J. (1995). *Converting conflicts in preschool.* Fort Worth, TX: Harcourt Brace.

DeVries, R., & Zan, B. (1995). Creating a constructivist classroom atmosphere. *Young Children, 51*(1), 4–13.

Gartrell, D. (1994). *A guidance approach to discipline.* Albany, NY: Delmar.

Jalongo, M. R. (1996). Teaching young children to become better listeners. *Young Children, 51*(2), 21–26.

Miller, D. F. (1996). *Positive child guidance.* Albany, NY: Delmar.

CHILDREN'S BOOKS

Alarcon, K. B. (1997). *Louella Mae, she's run away!* New York: Holt.

Alexander, M. (1988). *Even that moose won't listen to me.* New York: Dial.

Bottner, B. (1992). *Bootsie Barker bites.* New York: Putnam's.

Cole, J. (1990). *Don't call me names!* New York: Random House.

Guarino, D. (1989). *Is your mama a llama?* New York: Scholastic.

Henkes, K. (1986). *A Weekend with Wendell.* New York: Greenwillow.

Henkes, K. (1993). *Owen.* New York: Greenwillow.

Hutchins, P. (1994). *The very worst monster.* New York: Morrow.

Lacoe, S. (1992). *Just not the same.* Boston: Houghton Mifflin.

Lester, H. (1995). *Listen Buddy.* Boston: Houghton Mifflin.

MacDonald, A. (1990). *Little Beaver and the echo.* New York: Putnam.

Martin, B. (1993). *Polar bear, polar bear, what do you hear?* New York: Holt.

McBratney, S. (1995). *Guess how much I love you.* Cambridge, MA: Candlewick.

Wells, R. (1997). *Noisy Nora.* New York: Dial.

Weninger, B. (1996). *What have you done, Davy?* New York: North South.

VIDEOTAPES

Educational Productions. (Producer). *Let's talk* (Good Talking with You series no. 2) and *Now you're talking* (Good Talking with You series no. 3). (Available from Educational Productions, 9000 S.W. Gemini Drive, Beaverton, OR 97008)

Educational Productions. *Connecting with every child* (Reframing Discipline series no. 2). (Available from

Educational Productions, 9000 S.W. Gemini Drive, Beaverton, OR 97008)

Goldman, B. D., Roberts, J. E., & Nychka, H. *SMALLTALK: Creating conversations with young children.* (Available from Child Development Media, 5632 Van Nuys Blvd., Suite 286, Van Nuys, CA 91401-4602)

LEARNING ACTIVITIES

1. What are some steps you can take to become a good listening model? How will you know whether you have succeeded? Try it and see. Record the results.

2. How can children be taught to listen? Try one of the book activities suggested and record the results.

3. Observe a child who rarely participates in conversations with others. Which of the guidelines for

successful conversations apply to this child? Try helping the child converse by using one of the suggested activities. Record the results.

4. Help a child who has difficulty gaining entry into group play learn what to do and say to gain access without a conflict. Record the results.

5. Carry out a small-group role-play about feelings by reading one of the books mentioned and inviting children to take character roles. Record the results.

CHAPTER 11

Promoting Family Involvement in Prosocial Guidance

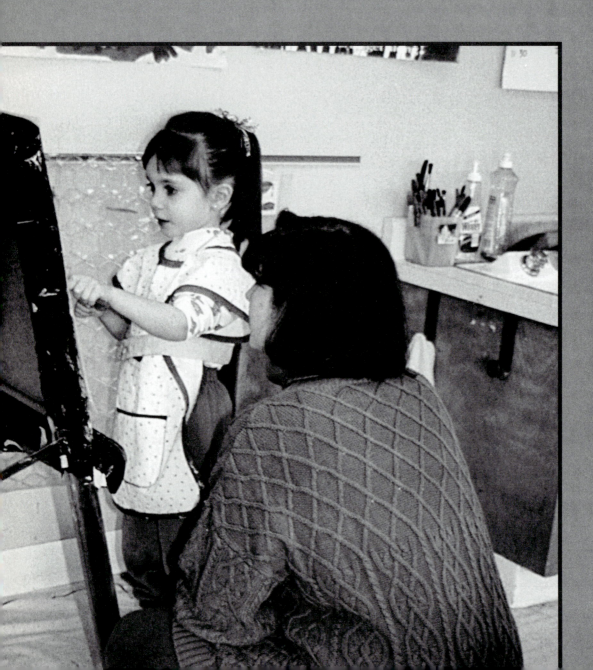

Involve families in prosocial guidance through ongoing, two-way communication.

□ Encourage family members to observe children's prosocial behavior.

□ Lend picture books with prosocial themes to families for reading to children.

□ Hold parent conferences for children based on prosocial behavior.

□ Model other-esteem by accepting differences in the culture, lifestyle, and language of children's families.

Families know their children best. As most people agree, parents are their children's first and most important teachers. Yet preschool teachers also know these same children. They too have similar goals of helping the children grow and develop to the best of their ability. Working together, families and teachers should be able to make a significant difference in the lives of preschool children.

"Working together," however, is sometimes a stumbling block for busy teachers and harassed parents. Both sides may have uneasy feelings about face-to-face encounters with the other. Parents may remember uncomfortable meetings when things were going wrong with their children. Teachers may recall tense parent conferences in which their work came under criticism. Even parents who would like to work together with their children's teachers may have little time to get together since they work all day.

The time has come to change previous perceptions and feelings. There are meaningful ways to work together without necessarily getting together. For prosocial guidance to be effective, to take hold in the lives of young children, family understanding and support are essential ingredients. Two-way communication between teachers and parents is the key. Teachers and families can promote this understanding through positive, ongoing communication with one another. Once started, families usually not only are eager to talk face-to-face with teachers but somehow find time to do so, too.

INVOLVE FAMILIES IN PROSOCIAL GUIDANCE THROUGH ONGOING, TWO-WAY COMMUNICATION

How do teachers go about communicating this new guidance technique to busy parents so they not only understand how it works but also buy into supporting it? The first step, as in any initial approach to someone new, is to establish rapport with them. Parents need to learn who you are and how you work with their children before they can feel comfortable about communicating with you. Duffy (1997) lists parents' three basic concerns very simply:

Do you know and like my child?

Can I trust you?

Is my child normal? (p. 40)

In the Beginning

How can you communicate to parents that you do know and like their child and can be trusted? Many programs have special days at the beginning of school or at the end of the previous year for parents to visit the program with their children and meet the teachers. Or you may have met a family member during the enrollment process. Make it a point to take part in intake interviews whenever possible. This may be your first contact with the family. Help them feel at ease in your presence and at home in the program. Show them around the classroom and point out some of the features children like best. Ask them what things their children like to do. Let them know how much you look forward to meeting their child if he is not already present.

Some teachers have the opportunity to see parents daily when they bring in or pick up their children. Informal face-to-face meetings, no matter how brief, help parents learn what teachers look like, talk like, how they interact with children, and how children respond to them.

Your focus should always be on the children, not the program. Take time during initial face-to-face meetings to say specific, positive things about a child. "Latasha's helping everyone learn to play the keyboard in the music center. I've never seen anything like it in a 4-year-old. She's really talented." Or "Brad put a puzzle together from start to finish this morning without any help. He was so proud of it." Always use the child's name when speaking about her: "We're so happy to have Charlene with us this year. It is so satisfying to see her open up to the others as she gets used to the program."

If you have not met the parents in person at the beginning of the year, it is important to give them a phone call and introduce yourself. This introduction should be the start of an ongoing and fruitful series of communications between you and a child's family. For Workman and Gage (1997), ongoing communication like this serves as the basis for parent involvement in their child's program:

> [E]ach child should have a primary caregiver or teacher who knows the child well and is responsible for sharing day-to-day happenings with the family. This communication should occur on a regular basis and be positive in nature. (p. 11)

Families want to know what's happening with their child in your program from the very start. How is he getting along with the others? Is he able to do what is expected of him? What kinds of things is he involved in doing? Does he seem to like them? Is he giving you a hard time? How do you like him? Put yourself in the shoes of a parent with a new child in preschool. What you would like to find out about your child?

It is not up to the child to answer these questions, even if he could. You must design a means for regular two-way communication between home and school. Your coworkers must be involved to keep up with individual children and their accomplishments in a timely fashion. Workman and Gage (1997) believe that:

> trust between family members and staff is the single most important factor in promoting individual growth, involvement, and the development of self-sufficiency. . . . Establishing relationships and developing trust involve entering into a dialogue to explore issues together and offer information, resources, and personal assistance. (p. 11)

Two-Way Communication

Begin brainstorming with the staff about the design of your two-way parent involvement communications at the beginning of school. Make it both exciting and meaningful—but also doable. Staff members will keep up their end of the communication link if it is not too time-consuming. Parents will respond if they find the information to be meaningful and useful. Think of ways you can entice them into a worthwhile dialogue with you about their children.

Phoning can be helpful at the start for introductions to you and the program but too time-consuming for contacting every family on a daily or weekly basis. Some programs fill out "accomplishment cards" every few days, stating one thing the child did and leaving a space for parents to respond under "Parent Comments." These can be put in an envelope and clipped to a child's clothing or books. Other programs use a weekly newsletter featuring class projects and activities that mention children's names—and always with space at the bottom for "What's happening in your child's life?" What other ways can you think of to make communication a two-way activity?

When the focus is on their children, most parents respond readily. Many programs survey parents during the initial enrollment process, asking them about their goals for their children, what activities their children like to do, and how they (the parents) can contribute to the program. Another question should be added: what is the best way for you and the teachers to communicate with one another about your child? Parents themselves need input into how they can carry on two-way communication if it is to be successful. If the survey uses a checklist format, you might list several methods for families to consider:

___ Phone
___ Notes carried by child
___ Mailed letters
___ In person when child is picked up
___ Photos and videotapes
___ Conferences
___ Parent nights
___ Parent workshops
___ Other (please describe)_____

Be prepared to have the "other" category filled in with one of the new forms of communication: "E-mail," "voice mail," "car phone," or "fax," for instance. Are you prepared to send E-mail messages?

Newsletters

Brand (1996) discovered from teachers in a workshop she taught that "many were surprised to learn from their parent surveys that parents felt uninformed about the daily experiences in the classroom." This inspired one teacher to start something new:

I started a weekly class newsletter with children's quotes about what they liked best and least about school that week. Writing it while the children dictate allows me to get it out and, although it's not a perfect-looking product, the positive feedback I have gotten from parents makes it well worth doing. (p. 77)

Some programs have staff members who put together weekly newsletters for families containing information the teachers provide about what's going on in their classroom each week. Every week such a newsletter might contain items like the words of a new song or fingerplay the children have learned, a recipe for a new snack they made together, the name of a favorite book that can be borrowed from the library, and especially *news about individual children demonstrating one of the prosocial behaviors the class is working on.*

Some programs send a special *Prosocial Behavior Newsletter* once a month with notes about how each child performed one of the prosocial behaviors listed on the Child Prosocial Behavior Checklist (see Figure 11-1). To make such newsletters part of two-way communication, a second sheet is always included entitled *Let's Hear from You,* with space for family members to fill in headlined "What Prosocial Behaviors Did Your Child Display at Home This Month?" (self-esteem, self-control, other-esteem, friendliness, generosity, cooperation, helpfulness, or respect) and "Tell Us What Your Child Did to Display This Behavior."

Videotapes and Photos

Other teachers show parents what's going on in preschool through videotapes they make with a camcorder. Staff members take turns videotaping activities children are involved in day by day, making sure to include every child. They especially look for scenes of interaction showing children playing roles in dramatic play, helping one another build a block structure, helping the teacher make a snack, picking up blocks, displaying friendliness toward a newcomer, treating materials with respect, or resolving a conflict over toys.

At the end of the week they play the tape for the children to see and comment on. Then it is put in the book-lending library for children to sign out for an overnight viewing at home. Families without VCRs can rent one from a video store for overnight use. Included in the package containing the videotape is a comment sheet for families to respond on. It also asks what else family members would like to see their child engaged in on the next video they make.

Such tapes often turn out to be the most popular part of parent involvement as family members gather to see live action of their children actually engaged in classroom activities and interactions with others. Be prepared for such videos to be the focus of parent-teacher conferences. Showing videos of their children is also a great motivator for bringing parents into the program for a family night get-together.

Another successful approach to two-way communication is by sending home a photo of their child involved in classroom activities along with a brief explanation of the photo and a space for parents to write "How my child likes to play at home." No matter what type of communication you send home with the children, be sure to

Name_____ Age_____

1. *Self-Esteem: Feeling Good about Self*

_____Smiles, seems happy much of time

_____Is not afraid of people or things

_____Stands up for own rights

2. *Self-Control: Developing Control over Own Behavior*

_____Abides by established limits most of the time

_____Uses classroom self-regulating devices

_____Expresses strong feelings in words rather than actions

3. *Other-Esteem: Feeling Good about Other Children*

_____Gets along with other children

_____Shows concern for another child in distress

_____Can tell how another child feels

4. *Friendliness: Making Friends among Other Children*

_____Seeks other children to play with

_____Makes friends with other children

_____Plays with others in congenial manner

5. *Generosity: Giving and Sharing Things with Others*

_____Shares toys and materials with other children

_____Takes turns without a fuss

_____Gives something (a toy, a turn) to another child

6. *Cooperation: Doing Things with Others*

_____Engages in cooperative play in group activity

_____Allows others to enter ongoing play without a struggle

_____Complies with adult requests

7. *Helpfulness: Doing Things for the Common Good*

_____Picks up and puts away toys and materials

_____Helps another do a task

_____Takes on chores willingly

8. *Respect: Treating People and Materials Considerately*

_____Uses toys, materials in constructive manner

_____Treats other people's materials with respect

_____Listens and responds to adults with consideration

Figure 11-1   Child Prosocial Behavior Checklist

Note: The publisher grants permission to reproduce this checklist for evaluation and record keeping.

include a place for parents to respond—making it real two-way communication. After all, you also want to know what's going on with the child at home and what the parents think about the videos or photos of their children in the program.

ENCOURAGE FAMILY MEMBERS TO OBSERVE CHILDREN'S PROSOCIAL BEHAVIOR

Once you have established rapport with family members, you can begin talking with them about child behavior and your new approach in helping youngsters develop internal self-control by focusing on their positive behavior. When the time seems right share with parents a blank copy of the Child Prosocial Behavior Checklist (Figure 11-1). Talk to them about how the teaching staff and children are working together this year to establish friendly, cooperative relationships with one another. Mention one or two of the prosocial behaviors, and tell how their own child displays them.

Are any of these behaviors encouraged at home? If family members are interested and comfortable talking about child behavior, they may want to become involved in promoting prosocial behavior in their own child by actually observing their youngster at home, using the Child Prosocial Behavior Checklist. Such observations would be for their eyes only unless they feel comfortable about sharing the results with you—something you would welcome but not expect from everyone.

This focus on their child is welcomed by most parents, so long as it is not negative in nature. Most parents are delighted to learn all they can about their children's behavior, especially if they are doing well in school. When they note that the checklist features positive items only, they may readily agree to participate in home observations.

Parent Meetings

As your two-way communication progresses week by week, ask how their home observations are coming along. Let parents know that you and the staff also are doing similar observations of their child and all the other children in school. Would they like to compare notes on what they have observed with what you have observed about their child? If so, set up a time for the two of you to get together. Whether parents bring their checklist to the meeting is immaterial. What counts is their knowledge about the prosocial behavior items you are helping children develop.

Let parents know you do not expect a child to exhibit all, or even many, of these behaviors at first. It takes time for young children to learn what is expected of them and a much longer time for them to adopt certain behaviors as their own. They must first become comfortable with the classroom environment, the teachers, and their peers. Then they must feel good about themselves as worthy people before they start feeling good about others.

You need their family's support in your endeavor of focusing on positive and downplaying negative behavior. As you and the parents compare their child's home behavior with your observations of his school behavior, you may both decide to focus on one prosocial skill at a time. How can the child learn generosity and sharing in

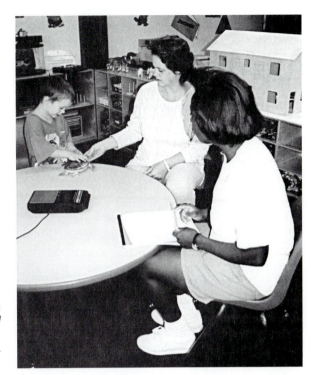

If parents show an interest in observing and recording prosocial behavior of their child at home, invite them to observe in the classroom also.

school, for instance? Tell parents what has worked for you in helping other children share toys and take turns. Ask them what they could try at home. Tell them you will let them know how their child is coming along in his ability to share when you send home the next newsletter. Ask them to write you a note about his home behavior as well.

Parents Observing in the Classroom

If parents show a real interest in observing and recording prosocial behaviors, invite them to the classroom to observe and record their child in this environment. Some employers give parents flextime to use with their children. Or you can suggest they come in during the lunch period, an excellent time to observe children's interactions with others at the lunch table. Parents should be aware, however, that children sometimes act out when their parents are present. Having the parent sit behind their child in an unobtrusive manner sometimes helps.

Observing their child for prosocial behaviors on one of the classroom videotapes is still another possibility. A private session gives both teacher and parents a chance to discuss freely the child's behavior when the child is not present. Talking about her in front of the child is not only disrespectful but harmful to a child's self-esteem.

Using a checklist is not the only way to observe children's prosocial behavior. It especially helps nonspecialist observers get started, as well as letting them know what you expect of child behavior. Checklist items also help parents learn what is normal for a child of this age, something that concerns every parent.

Once parents know what to look for, they will be noticing these behaviors informally as they interact with their children or watch them interact with others. Ask parents for their suggestions about how you can support their youngsters in developing this positive way of acting. You are all in this together, remind them, and you can benefit as much from their knowledge of their child as they do from yours.

 ## LEND PICTURE BOOKS WITH PROSOCIAL THEMES TO FAMILIES FOR READING TO CHILDREN

Many programs have a library of children's books for lending to children to take home overnight. If your program cannot afford many hardcover books, consider purchasing paperback copies of the books in the classroom library. These can be given away to the families at the end of the year and repurchased new for use with the next year's class.

Children enjoy hearing their favorite stories read over and over. When the same picture books are read to them both in school and at home, they begin to get a sense of continuity about the kind of behavior that is expected of them and the book characters they come to know both at home and in school.

Figure 11-2 presents an inexpensive library of paperback books you might consider ordering. Be sure to obtain two copies of each book, one for the classroom and one for overnight lending to be read at home. Children can choose and check out the books themselves.

Paste a pocket on the inside cover of each book for holding the two-way communication cards you will be sending home with the book, and the family members will be returning. You might use a 3-by-5 card with one side for your communication about "What Happened at School Today." It takes only a few seconds to write a sentence such as "Ask Josh how big he built his block building today," or "Monika played with others in the dramatic play area for the first time." On the reverse side parents can respond under "What Happened at Home Today."

Family Reading in the Classroom

If family members like the idea of reading these books to their children at home, ask for volunteers to come into the classroom and read the same ones to another child or small group of children. Sometimes family members are intimidated about reading to a total group of children. You can assure them that you prefer to have books read to individuals or small groups. They may also want to share a book of their own that their child enjoys.

Do the readers talk to their children about the stories? Ask them personally or by note card. Preschool children may be too young to answer questions like "What do you think this story means?" But they enjoy responding to "What would you have done if you were Jamaica or Horace or Gah-Ning?" Children get a great deal more

Self-Esteem

Famous Seaweed Soup by A. T. Martin

> Sara and her family go to the beach, but no one will help her gather the ingredients for her famous seaweed soup, so she does it all herself.

I Like Me by N. Carlson

> Miss Piggy tells about the many things she can do and why she likes herself.

I'll Do It Myself by J. Marton

> Michelle brushes her hair by herself for the first time, but doesn't get it quite right.

Self-Control

It Wasn't My Fault by H. Lester

> A bird lays an egg on Murdley Gurdson's head, but it isn't his fault, starting a chain of hilarious happenings about being responsible for what you do.

Mean Soup by B. Everitt

> Horace has an unbelievably bad day in school, so his mother puts on a pot of water to make mean soup. For the ingredients they both scream and growl their troubles away until they end up smiling.

Where Is Gah-Ning? by R. Munsch

> Gah-Ning tries desperately to go shopping, but when she finally follows her father's directions, she ends up there in spite of herself.

Other-Esteem

Feelings by Aliki

> In one little episode a boy comforts a girl whose pet mouse has died.

Island Baby by H. Keller

> Simon, a Caribbean boy, helps his grandfather care for injured birds. He finds a baby flamingo with a broken leg and helps nurse it back to health.

When You Were Little and I Was Big by P. Galloway

> A little girl tells her mother a story about how she would treat the mother if she were little and the girl big.

Friendliness

My Friends by T. Gomi

> A little girl tells on each page what she learns from each of her animal friends and finally at the end from her friends in school.

Space Case by E. Marshall

> Buddy befriends a creature from outer space who comes to Earth on Halloween night, and he takes it trick-or-treating and to school the next day.

Figure 11-2 Paperback books with prosocial themes for home lending

Will I Have a Friend? by M. Cohen

In this classic story Pa takes Jim to preschool and Jim spends the day looking for a friend, finally finding one.

Generosity

Jamaica's Find by J. Havill

Jamaica finds a red hat and stuffed toy dog on the playground but turns in only the hat to the lost and found. Her mother talks to her about it, and Jamaica finally returns the dog the next day. Then she finds the girl who lost it and shows her where it is.

Maebelle's Suitcase by T. Tusa

Maebelle lives in a treehouse and makes hats for a living. She is making one for the town's annual hat contest when Binkle Bird drops in to borrow a suitcase for his trip south. He loads it with too many priceless possessions and can't budge it. But one by one he gives them each to Maebelle for her contest hat. She doesn't win, but a special category is created for "most original hat."

Sharing by T. Gomi

Two little girls show how they share every item they have even when they're not equal. Then they share their love for their cat.

Cooperation

Dad's Car Wash by H. A. Sutherland

John plays with his cars all day long out in the dirt and gets really covered with it. But at the end of the day he cooperates with his dad and lets his dad give him a bath in "dad's car wash."

Jamaica Tag-Along by J. Havill

Jamaica's older brother won't let her play basketball with him at the park, so she plays in the sand. At first she won't let little Berto join her, but when she realizes she is doing the same thing as her brother, she asks Berto to help build a sand castle.

Will You Come Back for Me? by R. Kramer

Four-year-old Suki reluctantly goes to the child care center when her mother goes to work. Her mother shows Suki with a cutout paper heart how she will leave part of her heart at the center but always come back for it/her. Suki then joins the others in play.

Helpfulness

I Love My Baby Sister (Most of the Time) by E. Edelman

A little girl tells the story of how she plays with her baby sister and helps her mother take care of her.

Figure 11-2   *continued*

Not Yet, Yvette by H. Ketteman

Yvette helps her father clean and decorate their house, bake a cake, shop for flowers, and wrap a present for her mother's birthday—but she can hardly wait.

Sam Is My Half Brother by L. Boyd

Hessie visits her father's and stepmother's home in the summer where they have a new baby, Hessie's stepbrother, Sam. She has some trouble adjusting to the baby's needs but finally helps take care of him.

Respect

For Sale: One Sister—Cheap! by K. Alder & R. McBride

Little Sarah makes her brother mad by squirting toothpaste on his painting, pouring soup on his sandwich, and tearing up his homework, so he decides to sell her. No one wants her but a policeman, who eventually brings her home. Meanwhile, the brother begins to miss Sarah and when she rushes in the door they both hug.

The Meaning of Respect by D. Bouchard

A Canadian Indian boy shows no respect for his teacher, so his mother sends him off to the reservation to visit his grandfather for "spiritual guidance." He puts the boy to work trapping, hunting, and fishing in the brutal winter weather. But his grandfather also teaches him to respect every living thing: people, animals, fish, even plants if they want to survive.

Wilfrid Gordon McDonald Partridge by M. Fox

Wilfrid lives next door to an old folks home and gets to know all the people who live there. He listens to their stories, he runs errands for them, and he respects their differences. When he finds out that Miss Nancy has lost her memory, he finds out what a memory is from half a dozen different people and sets out to gather these items and return them to 96-year-old Miss Nancy, who then begins to remember.

from a story when the reader discusses it with them. Many of these are problem-solving stories that the children can try to resolve themselves if encouraged to compare themselves with the characters.

Bilingual Readers

Who does the most reading to the children at home? Often it is a grandparent or big brother or sister. Be sure they know that they are welcome to visit the class and read to other children. Can anyone in the family read in another language? Books in Spanish are also available. Have some in your lending library and invite Spanish readers to visit the classroom to read to the children, whether or not the children understand Spanish. It is important that they hear familiar storybooks in another language. Be sure to have some of these same books available in English, too. Some books in Spanish featuring prosocial topics are cited in Figure 11-3.

Figure 11-3　Picture books in Spanish with prosocial themes

Blaming

The Gorilla Did It (*Fue el gorila*)

Chores, Helping

A Chair for My Mother (*Un sillon para mi mama*)

You and Me, Little Bear (*Tu y yo, Osito*)

Feelings

A Cool Kid Like Me (*Un chico valiente como yo*)

Contrary Mary (*Ines del reves*)

The Grouchy Ladybug (*La mariquita malhumorada*)

Guess How Much I Love You (*Adivina cuanto te quiero*)

I'm Angry (*Tengo rabia*)

I'm Jealous (*Tengo celos*)

I'm Sad (*Estoy triste*)

I'm Scared (*Tengo miedo*)

Giving, Sharing

I Had a Hippopotomus (*Yo tenia un hipopotamo*)

Jamaica's Find (*El hallazgo de Jamaica*)

The Rainbow Fish (*El pez arco iris*)

Respect

Now One Foot, Now the Other (*Un pasito . . . y otro pasito*)

Self-Esteem

I Like Me (*¡Me gusto como soy!*)

Family Resource Library

In addition to the paperback picture books you have on hand to lend to families, be sure to keep paperback books and pamphlets on child development, parenting skills, and guidance available for lending. Some of the articles listed at the ends of each chapter that you have found particularly helpful can be photocopied for lending to parents. Videotapes such as *I Am Your Child: The First Years Last Forever* can be made available also. See "Family Resource Materials" at the end of this chapter for ideas.

HOLD PARENT CONFERENCES ABOUT CHILDREN BASED ON PROSOCIAL GUIDANCE

Most programs hold parent conferences only when their children are experiencing some sort of difficulty. Programs promoting children's prosocial behavior, on the other hand, have a different reason for scheduling meetings with parents. It is important for

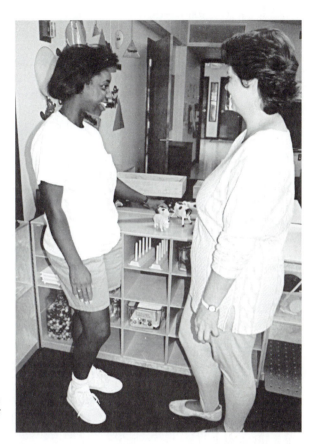

Hold conferences with parents based on the prosocial behavior of their children.

everyone involved to learn about the child's progress in developing prosocial behavior skills both in the classroom and at home. How is he getting along with other children? Can he express anger in words rather than striking out? Does she seek other children to play with or stay by herself? Can she resolve conflicts through the conversion technique? What about sharing and taking turns?

If your ongoing, two-way communication with families has been successful, you will already know a great deal about the child's behavior at home and the parents' goals for him at school. As Manning and Schindler (1997) point out, "The groundwork for close communication needs to be established long before the first face-to-face conference" (p. 27).

When you invite parents to a conference, be sure they understand the purpose: to discuss their child's development of prosocial behaviors. You may want to concentrate on certain behaviors for a particular child—for example, helpfulness and sharing for Greg. He has come a long way since the beginning of the year when he refused to help pick up the toys he had scattered. Now he not only picks up all the blocks without being asked but also takes on classroom chores eagerly. On the other hand, Greg still needs help learning to share. He often refuses to give up a toy when it is someone else's turn.

Focusing on positive behaviors should help put both you and the parent at ease. Greg's mother already knows about his prosocial behaviors at home since she has been observing him using the Child Prosocial Behavior Checklist. She has exchanged communications with the teaching staff through "Accomplishment Cards" in the pockets of the books Greg brings home for overnight reading. Now she will meet the teacher face-to-face for the first time to discuss Greg's progress.

Structure of Parent Conferences

Meeting face-to-face with a child's parent needs to be a happy experience for both of you. You will be talking about a child you both hold dear. You will be describing his progress in learning how to get along with others. You will be sharing anecdotes, looking at examples of Greg's work, and consulting together on what your future roles should be in helping Greg progress even further. How will you handle it?

1. *Set the stage by establishing rapport.*   Welcome the parent to the center, and express your delight in meeting her at last. Exchange pleasantries. Tell her how glad you are she came because of the importance of Greg's home life on his school success.

2. *Listen to what the parent has to say.*   Ask how Greg is getting along at home. Listen attentively to what the parent has to say. Then ask how the parent feels about his school activities. Allow all the time necessary for the parent to express feelings and opinions without interruptions.

3. *Share something the child has done or produced.*   Show the parent a photo of the child engaged in an activity, one of his art products such as a painting or collage, a prewriting sample, a page from his daily journal (if the child has given permission), or a tape recording of a child's story.

4. *Discuss prosocial behaviors the child displays.*   Talk about the child's progress in accomplishing a particular prosocial behavior—in Greg's case, helpfulness. Tell how you and your coworkers continue to support his development in this area by making positive comments and giving him tasks to be in charge of.

5. *Discuss prosocial behaviors the child needs to work on.*   Ask the parent what other behaviors she thinks the child needs to work on. Try to focus on only one behavior. In Greg's case you would hope the parent would mention sharing. But if this is not a problem at home, accept whatever she says and discuss with her how he displays this behavior at school. You can still work on sharing with Greg in addition to helping him develop the behavior the parent mentions.

6. *Make plans for helping Greg at home and in school.*   If the parent wants Greg to develop *respect*, for instance, and not talk back when he is corrected by his family members, you might offer suggestions about talking with Greg about feelings: how the other person feels when Greg talks back and how Greg feels that makes him talk like that. Is there some other way he can express his feelings? Is there some other way family members can talk to him?

You can ask the parent for ideas about helping Greg show respect in the classroom, if this is a problem. In other words, you are showing the parent that it takes both home and school working together to help children develop prosocial behaviors. You are grateful for the parent sharing her ideas with you, and you hope that your ideas will help her.

You will be communicating with her from time to time in the future, telling how Greg is doing in school and asking her to tell you the same about Greg at home. Does she want to get together again to compare notes? Jot down whatever the two of you decide to do in specific terms and give her a copy. Then give her sincere thanks for coming, and invite her to drop in on the class anytime. As Duffy (1997) explains:

> Parent conferences provide a way to enter into the richness of their child's school world. To each parent everywhere, her child is special. This is one mother's summation: "My child is my most precious jewel." Conferences provide a setting for both parents and teachers to display those jewels, even the rough cut ones. (p. 43)

MODEL OTHER-ESTEEM BY ACCEPTING DIFFERENCES IN THE CULTURE, LIFESTYLE, AND LANGUAGE OF CHILDREN'S FAMILIES

Just as you have accepted all the children in the program as worthy human beings deserving of your help and attention, so must you accept their families. After all, children are an extension of their families. For you to understand fully how and why children function as they do means that you must also get to know their families. If their families are of a different culture, ethnic group, or lifestyle than your own, you may need to spend extra time establishing a comfortable relationship. If their families are bilingual or non-English-speaking, you may need to ask for help from a translator.

Comfortable two-way communication works just as well for families of other cultures as it does for mainstream families. But you must "tune up your sensitivity," as Gonzalez-Mena (1997, p. 56) points out, to communicate successfully. Try to be your relaxed, friendly self when you meet with a parent from another culture just as you are with every parent. Following the parent conference guidelines described in the previous section, your first aim will be to establish rapport and put the parent at ease. Welcome her to the center and tell her how glad you are to meet her. Make a positive comment about her child. Remember that your principal focus will be on the child, not the program or even the family.

Next you will want to listen to what the parent has to say about her child. Set aside your own cultural values and beliefs, and listen with sensitivity. Your attitude should be one of acceptance for whatever she has to say and of genuine interest in learning all you can from the parent. Give the parent as much control over the conversation as possible. As Gonzalez-Mena (1997) suggests:

> Give up your concern with your agenda and really listen to the parent—not only the words, but the feelings behind them. Listen until the person stops talking. Don't interrupt. When it's your turn, instead of arguing, educating, or responding from your own perspective, try to state the perspective of the other person. (p. 56)

When the time is right, you can share something the child has produced in class: a photo of his giant block building or the printed words in her first emergent writing. Once again allow time for the parent to comment. Then ask what else the parent might like to see.

When the topic shifts to prosocial behavior, continue to keep the conversation on a personal level. Don't talk jargon. Parents understand terms like *sharing, cooperating,* and *helping* but perhaps not *prosocial behavior.* You can give examples by sharing personal stories of behavior dilemmas from your own childhood. Telling a humorous story or brief anecdote about yourself as a child is an excellent method for putting a parent from another culture at ease. She should soon come to realize that you are just as human as she is.

What about the parent's own experiences in growing up? What were her parents' approaches to discipline, for example, and how did she feel about them? You can relate what she has to say to your own experiences. Even though your approach to behavior management today may be different from that of your own parents or from the parent you are talking with, all of you have the best interests of children at heart.

You also need to point out that child behavior in the classroom is often different from child behavior at home. Because of the number of children involved from totally different backgrounds, your behavior rules or limits and your methods for enforcing them may be different from a parent's. This does not mean that your way is better than her way, or vice versa. There can be different ways of teaching children how to behave under different circumstances. But both of you should be able to agree on the eight aspects of prosocial behavior that you want children to develop (see Figure 11-1, the Child Prosocial Behavior Checklist).

Talk about her child's accomplishments in developing some of these behaviors. As you conclude your conference, jot down what the parent feels might be most helpful for her child's development of these behaviors and any strategies or activities both of you might use to help.

Non-English-Speaking Parents

Because some parents may be bilingual or non-English-speaking does not mean two-way conversations are impossible. All parents want to know how their children are doing in school. It is up to you to find a comfortable way to make this happen. Greet the parent just as you would any guest to your program. Try to learn a greeting in the parent's language if you can. If you show a sincere interest in meeting such parents and finding a way to communicate, they will do their part. Smiles help. Sign language in which you point to yourself and say, "My name is Beth Stoddard," and then point to the parent, and ask, "And your name is . . . ?" can get you started. As Lee (1997) tells us:

> When a parent speaks another language, it is important to establish a relationship which is one of equality and respect from the start, setting the tone for the future. If parents feel embarrassed about their English skills, it is sometimes helpful for providers to share how frustrated they feel at not being able to communicate in the parents' language. (p. 58)

Often children may speak English as a second language more fluently than their parents. Invite a child from the family to help translate if necessary. Written communications to and from the family also need to be translated. Perhaps an older sibling can stop by to help. You may prefer to use photos and videotapes of their child to show parents how he is coming along in school.

Using Prosocial Photos of Children

One program with several non-English-speaking parents decided to take eight photos of each family's child, with the child demonstrating each of the eight prosocial behaviors the class was working on. The children themselves decided how they would pose for each photo. Here is one example:

Self-esteem: Child smiling
Self-control: Child putting on learning center necklace
Other-esteem: Child offering hand to fallen child
Friendliness: Child shaking hands with another
Generosity: Child giving toy to another
Cooperation: Two children building block structure
Helpfulness: Two children picking up blocks
Respect: Child looking up at teacher

Each photo was mounted under the word representing the prosocial behavior along with the child's name. Parents who spoke little English liked the idea so well that teachers photocopied the two pages of photos and gave each parent a copy. The other children liked the idea so much that they too wanted their pictures taken for their parents, even though they spoke English and could understand what the words meant without picture cues.

The two photocopied pages of children's pictures became the centerpiece for one of the best parent communication experiences the program had known. Parents loved seeing their children showing off good behavior. They understood that the photos were only poses and not necessarily the actual behavior of their children, but it could be true. Their children could learn to behave that way. And everyone, including the children, knew it.

For the first time questions and comments about behavior flooded communication channels. "How do I get Jorge to share his toys like it shows in the picture, without punishing him?" and "Juanita finally understands what other-esteem means. She told me she felt how her sister felt when she pushed her down!" were some of the comments teachers received.

Teachers invited parents to watch videos of their children as a stimulus to a roundtable discussion on behavior. Everyone at the meeting exchanged ideas on how to support the new prosocial behavior shown in their children's photos, so it would continue. Tonya said her mother gave her a hug every time she performed one of the behaviors in her photos that were mounted on their refrigerator. She said she liked hugs better than the stars that her big brother got on his homework.

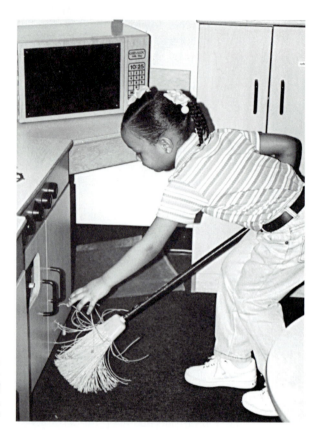

For non-English-speaking parents, take photos of their child performing the eight prosocial skills and label each like this: "Helpfulness— Malinda."

Teachers learned from parents, parents from teachers, and everyone learned from the children themselves.

The original pictures were made into a class photo album for everyone to look at. Afterward when children sometimes forgot to act in a prosocial manner, others quickly reminded them of their good actions in the photo album! The teachers knew they had stumbled onto a method worth repeating.

CONLUSION

Teachers who have set up a prosocial physical environment, who have learned to use positive intervention methods to help manage children's inappropriate behavior, who have helped children learn to behave prosocially, who have involved parents in their children's learning, know an important secret they would like to share with everyone: prosocial guidance works! Preschool children can learn how other children in conflict feel. They can learn to express their own feelings in words. They can develop inner control over their own behavior and feel so good about it that it shows in everything they do. Then little by little most of the inappropriate classroom behavior fades away.

These teachers also found that teaching and learning prosocial behavior takes time, effort, and patience on the part of the early childhood staff, the children, and their families. But it is time well spent. This kind of learning—to behave in a prosocial manner toward others—brings instant rewards to anyone who adopts its Golden Rule: if I treat you well, you will treat me well. It is behavior that needs to be learned by everyone. And the rewards can last a lifetime.

REFERENCES

Brand, S. (1996). Making parent involvement a reality: Helping teachers develop partnerships with parents. *Young Children, 51*(2), 76–81.

Duffy, R. (1997). Parents' perspectives on conferencing. *Child Care Information Exchange, 116,* 40–43.

Gonzalez-Mena, J. (1997). Cross-cultural conferences. *Child Care Information Exchange, 116,* 55–57.

Lee, L. (1997). Working with non-English-speaking families. *Child Care Information Exchange, 116,* 57–58.

Manning, D., & Schindler, P. J. (1997). Communicating with parents when their children have difficulties. *Young Children, 52*(5), 27–33.

Workman, S. H., & Gage, J. A. (1997). Family-school partnerships: A family strengths approach. *Young Children, 52*(4), 10–14.

SUGGESTED READINGS

Beaty, J. J. (1998). *Observing development of the young child.* Upper Saddle River, NJ: Merrill/Prentice Hall.

Coleman, M., & Churchill, S. (1997). Challenges to family involvement. *Childhood Education, 73*(3), 144–148.

Gonzalez-Mena, J. (1997). Lessons from my mother-in-law: A story about discipline. *Child Care Information Exchange, 113,* 44–46.

Gonzales-Mena, J. (1997). *Multicultural issues in child care.* Mountain View, CA: Mayfield.

Heath, H. E. (1994). Dealing with difficult behaviors: Teachers plan with parents. *Young Children, 49*(5), 20–24.

Hildebrand, V., Phenice, L. A., Gray, M. M., & Hines, R. P. (1996). *Knowing and serving diverse families.* Upper Saddle River, NJ: Merrill/Prentice Hall.

Sturm, C. (1997). Creating parent-teacher dialogue: Intercultural communication in child care. *Young Children, 52*(5), 34–38.

CHILDREN'S BOOKS

Alder, K. (1986). *For sale: One sister—Cheap!* Chicago: Children's.

Aliki. (1984). *Feelings.* New York: Mulberry.

Bouchard, D. (1994). *The meaning of respect.* Winnipeg: Pemmican.

Boyd, L. (1990). *Sam is my half brother.* New York: Puffin.

Carlson, N. (1990). *I like me!* New York: Puffin.

Cohen, M. (1967). *Will I have a friend?* New York: Collier.

De Paola, T. (1981). *Now one foot, now the other.* New York: Putnam's.

Edelman, E. (1986). *I love my baby sister (most of the time).* New York: Puffin.

Everitt, B. (1992). *Mean soup.* San Diego: Voyager (Harcourt).

Fox, M. (1985). *Wilfrid Gordon McDonald Partridge.* Brooklyn: Kane/Miller.

Galloway, P. (1984). *When you were little and I was big.* Toronto: Annick.

Gomi, T. (1990). *My friends.* San Francisco: Chronicle.

Gomi, T. (1981). *Sharing.* South San Francisco: Heian International.

Havill, J. (1986). *Jamaica's find.* Boston: Houghton Mifflin.

Havill, J. (1989). *Jamaica tag-along.* Boston: Houghton Mifflin.

Ketteman, H. (1992). *Not yet, Yvette.* Morton Grove, IL: Whitman.

Keller, H. (1992). *Island baby.* New York: Mulberry.

Lester, H. (1985). *It wasn't my fault.* Boston: Houghton Mifflin.

Marshall, E. (1980). *Space case.* New York: Puffin.

Martin, A. T. (1993). *Famous seaweed soup.* Morton Grove: IL: Whitman.

Marton, J. (1989). *I'll do it myself.* Toronto: Annick.

Munsch, R. (1994). *Where is Gah-Ning?* Toronto: Annick.

Sutherland, H. A. (1988). *Dad's car wash.* New York: Aladdin.

Tompert, A. (1988). *Will you come back for me?* Morton Grove, IL: Whitman.

Tusa, T. (1991). *Maebelle's suitcase.* New York: Aladdin.

CHILDREN'S BOOKS IN SPANISH

Available from Lectorum Publications, 111 Eighth Ave., New York, NY 10011.

Carle, E. *The grouchy ladybug (La mariquita malhumorada).*

Carlson, N. *I like me (¡Me gusto como soy!)*

De Paola, T. *Now one foot, now the other (Un pasito . . . y otro pasito).*

Havill, J. *Jamaica's find (El hallazgo de Jamaica).*

Hazen, B. S. *The gorilla did it (Fue el gorila).*

Jerman, A. *Contrary Mary (Ines del reves).*

Lee, H. V. *I had a hippopotamus (Yo tenia un hipopotamo).*

McBratney, S. *Guess how much I love you (Adivina cuanto te quiro).*

Moses, B. *I'm angry (Tengo rabia).*

Moses, B. *I'm jealous (Tengo celos).*

Moses, B. *I'm scared (Tengo miedo).*

Moses, B. *I'm sad (Estoy triste).*

Pfister, M. *The rainbow fish (El pez arco iris).*

Waddlell, M. *You and me, Little Bear (Tu y yo, Osito).*

Wilhelm, H. *A cool kid like me (Un chico valiente como yo).*

Williams, V. B. *A chair for my mother (Un sillon para mi mama).*

FAMILY RESOURCE MATERIALS

Books

Dewsnap, L. (1995). *Common sense discipline: Building self-esteem in young children.* Glen Burnie, MD: Telshare.

Dreikurs, R. (1990). *Children the challenge.* New York: Plume/Penguin.

Eyere, L., & Eyere, R. (1993). *Teaching children your values.* New York: Fireside/Simon & Schuster.

Joslin, K. R. (1994). *Positive parenting from A to Z.* New York: Fawcett Columbine.

Brochures

Honig, A. S. *Love & learn: discipline for young children.* No. 528. Washington, DC: National Association for the Education of Young Children.

National Association for the Education of Young Children. *Helping children learn self-control.* No. 572. Washington, DC: Author.

Videotapes

GMMB&A. (Producer). (1997). *I am your child: The first years last forever.* (Available from GMMB&A, 1010 Wisconsin Ave. N.W., Suite 800, Washington, DC 20007)

VIDEOTAPES

National Association for the Education of Young Children. (Producer). *Partnerships with parents.* (Available from NAEYC, 1509 16th St. N.W., Washington, DC 20036-1426)

LEARNING ACTIVITIES

1. How can you involve the parents of one of your children in two-way communication with you? Try it and record the results.

2. Talk to a set of parents about observing their child demonstrating prosocial behaviors. Will they try it at home, in the classroom, or on a videotape?

3. Begin lending picture books with prosocial themes to parents for home reading to their children. Would any of them volunteer to read in the classroom? What is their response to this reading?

4. Invite one set of parents to a conference focused on their child's prosocial behavior. Follow the guidelines described, and record what happens.

5. Establish rapport with a family from a different culture or ethnic background than yours. Try to get them involved in helping their children learn or improve their prosocial behaviors.

Topical Children's Book Index

Name-Calling

Bootsie Barker Bites, 96
Don't Call Me Names, 96
Fighting Words, 96
Emily Umily, 96
Move Over, Twerp, 96
My Name Is Not Dummy, 96
Oliver Button Is a Sissy, 96
A Porcupine Named Fluffy, 36
Willy the Wimp, 96

Other-Esteem

Feelings, 191
Island Baby, 191
When You Were Little and I Was Big, 191

Respect

For Sale: One Sister—Cheap! 193
The Meaning of Respect, 193
Wilfrid Gordon McDonald Partridge, 193

Self-Control

It Wasn't My Fault, 191
Mean Soup, 191
Where Is Gah-Ning? 191

Self-Esteem

The Balancing Girl, 135
Cleversticks, 138
Famous Seaweed Soup, 191
Harry and Willy and Carrothead, 135
I Like Me, 191
I'll Do It Myself, 191
Kelly in the Mirror, 129

Index

About the Author

Janice J. Beaty, Professor Emerita, Elmira College in Elmira, New York, is presently a fulltime writer of early childhood college textbooks from her home in Pensacola, Florida. Dr. Beaty continues her long career of preparing teachers and caregivers to work with young children. Her writing includes children's books *Nofu and the Turkeyfish, Plants in His Pack,* and *Seeker of Seaways.* College textbooks she has written include *Observing Development of the Young Child,* fourth edition, *Skills for Preschool Teachers,* fifth edition, *Building Bridges with Multicultural Picture Books* (all published by Merrill/Prentice Hall); *Preschool Appropriate Practices, Picture Book Storytelling;* and *Converting Conflicts in Preschool.* Dr. Beaty also participates in the Early Childhood Professional Development Network, a distance-learning television project, and has helped to develop a video series *Take a Closer Look: A Field Guide to Child Observation.* She is presently involved in doing workshops for Native American Head Start programs and working in the new field of transcultural children's literature.

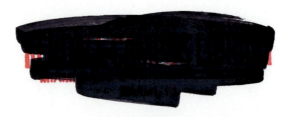